Lecture Notes in Economics and Mathematical Systems 478

Springer-Verlag Berlin Heidelberg GmbH

Sönke Hartmann

Project Scheduling under Limited Resources

Models, Methods, and Applications

Springer

Author

Dr. Sönke Hartmann
University of Kiel
Institut für Betriebswirtschaftslehre
Olshausenstr. 40
24118 Kiel, Germany

Library of Congress Cataloging-in-Publication Data

Hartmann, Sönke.
Project scheduling under limited resources : models, methods, and applications / Sönke Hartmann.
p. cm. -- (Lecture notes in economics and mathematical systems ; 478)
Includes bibliographical references (p.).
ISBN 978-3-540-66392-8 ISBN 978-3-642-58627-9 (eBook)
DOI 10.1007/978-3-642-58627-9
1. Production scheduling--Mathematical models. I. Title.
II. Series.
TS157.5.H37 1999
658.5'3--dc21 99-41942
CIP

ISSN 0075-8442
ISBN 978-3-540-66392-8

Originally published by Springer-Verlag Berlin Heidelberg New York in 1999

"Gedruckt mit Unterstützung der Deutschen Forschungsgemeinschaft D8"

Typesetting: Camera ready by author

Printed on acid-free paper SPIN: 10699796 42/3143-543210

To my parents
Jutta and Gerd Hartmann

Acknowledgements

This book is the result of my research on project scheduling at the University of Kiel which started in the summer of 1995. Since 1996, I have been supported by the *Studienstiftung des deutschen Volkes.* The publication of this book was sponsored by the *Deutsche Forschungsgemeinschaft.*

The challenging research topic as well as many people made these years enjoyable and pleasant. In what follows, I would like to thank those people who supported me during this time.

First of all, I wish to express my gratitude to my thesis advisor, Professor Dr. Andreas Drexl. He has created a very stimulating and motivating research environment, and he always had the time for helpful and inspiring discussions. Besides, he refereed this work.

Professor Dr. Sönke Albers co-refereed this thesis. I am indebted to him for his assessment.

Moreover, I would like to thank my colleagues at the *Institut für Betriebswirtschaftslehre* for many helpful comments and suggestions. I am especially grateful to Dr. habil. Rainer Kolisch. The joint research with Rainer led to the results of Chapters 4 and 6. He also proof-read the entire manuscript.

For the technical support at the computer laboratory, I am indebted to Stefan Wende. Ethel Fritz, Ina Kantowski, and Claudia Jürgensen of our department's office were also always helpful.

Dr. med. Thies Fitting provided the information and data for the case study of Section 8.1. Susie Schättiger of IVE Research International supported me with the case description of Section 8.2. I would like to thank both for their help.

Last but not least, Adriane deserves special thanks — for proof-reading the manuscript and, of course, for being there all these years.

Kiel, June 1999 Sönke Hartmann

Contents

1 Introduction **1**

2 Project Scheduling Models **5**

2.1 Basic Model: The RCPSP . . . 5
2.1.1 Problem Setting . . . 5
2.1.2 Deriving Time Windows . . . 7
2.1.3 Mathematical Programming Formulation . . . 9
2.2 Variants and Extensions . . . 11
2.2.1 Multiple Execution Modes . . . 11
2.2.2 Generalized Temporal Constraints . . . 15
2.2.3 Generalized Resource Constraints . . . 17
2.2.4 Alternative Objectives . . . 20
2.2.5 Multiple Projects . . . 22
2.3 Relations to Packing and Cutting Problems . . . 22
2.3.1 Motivation . . . 23
2.3.2 Different Dimensions . . . 25
2.3.3 Different Types . . . 28
2.3.4 Additional Features . . . 30

3 Exact Multi-Mode Algorithms **33**

3.1 Enumeration Schemes . . . 34
3.1.1 The Precedence Tree . . . 35
3.1.2 Mode and Delay Alternatives . . . 37
3.1.3 Mode and Extension Alternatives . . . 39
3.2 Bounding Rules . . . 41
3.2.1 Time Window Based Rules . . . 41
3.2.2 Preprocessing . . . 42
3.2.3 Dominating Sets of Schedules . . . 43
3.2.4 The Cutset Rule . . . 45
3.2.5 Immediate Selection . . . 46
3.2.6 A Precedence Tree Specific Rule . . . 47

3.3 Theoretical Comparison of Schedule Enumeration 48
3.3.1 Complete Enumeration 48
3.3.2 Enumeration with Bounding Rules 51
3.4 Computational Results 55
3.4.1 Effects of the Bounding Rules 55
3.4.2 Comparison of the Algorithms 57

4 Classification of Single-Mode Heuristics 61
4.1 Schedule Generation Schemes 62
4.1.1 Serial Schedule Generation Scheme 62
4.1.2 Parallel Schedule Generation Scheme 64
4.2 Priority Rule Based Heuristics 65
4.2.1 Priority Rules 66
4.2.2 Proposed Methods 67
4.3 Metaheuristic Approaches 70
4.3.1 General Metaheuristic Strategies 70
4.3.2 Representations 73
4.3.3 Proposed Methods 78
4.4 Other Heuristics 80
4.4.1 Truncated Branch-and-Bound Methods 80
4.4.2 Disjunctive Arc Based Methods 80
4.4.3 Further Approaches 81

5 Single-Mode Genetic Algorithms 83
5.1 Evolution and Optimization 83
5.1.1 The Theory of Evolution 84
5.1.2 Basic Genetic Algorithm Scheme 85
5.2 Activity List Based Genetic Algorithm 86
5.2.1 Individuals and Fitness 86
5.2.2 Crossover and Mutation 87
5.2.3 Selection 90
5.3 Random Key Based Genetic Algorithm 91
5.3.1 Individuals and Fitness 91
5.3.2 Crossover and Mutation 92
5.4 Priority Rule Based Genetic Algorithm 93
5.4.1 Individuals and Fitness 93
5.4.2 Crossover and Mutation 94
5.5 Computational Results 94
5.5.1 Configuration of the Genetic Algorithms 95
5.5.2 Comparison of the Genetic Algorithms 97
5.5.3 Impact of Genetic Operators 99
5.6 Extending the Genetic Algorithm 100
5.6.1 Generalized Genetic Algorithm Paradigm 100

5.6.2 Extended Representation . . . 101
5.6.3 Improved Initial Population . . . 103
5.6.4 Adapting the Genetic Operators . . . 105
5.6.5 Adding a Local Search Phase . . . 105
5.6.6 Configuration of the Extended Genetic Algorithm . . 112

6 Evaluation of Single-Mode Heuristics 115
6.1 Test Design . . . 115
6.2 Computational Results . . . 117
6.2.1 Best Heuristics . . . 118
6.2.2 Performance of Metaheuristics . . . 122
6.2.3 Performance of Priority Rule Based Heuristics . . . 122
6.2.4 Impact of Schedule Generation Scheme . . . 123
6.2.5 Impact of Resource Parameters . . . 124
6.2.6 Computation Times . . . 126

7 Multi-Mode Genetic Algorithm 129
7.1 Components of the Genetic Algorithm . . . 130
7.1.1 Individuals and Fitness . . . 131
7.1.2 Initial Population . . . 132
7.1.3 Crossover and Mutation . . . 133
7.2 Improving Schedules by Local Search . . . 135
7.2.1 Single Pass Improvement . . . 136
7.2.2 Multi Pass Improvement . . . 137
7.2.3 Inheritance Beyond the Genetic Metaphor . . . 138
7.3 Computational Results . . . 138
7.3.1 Configuration of the Algorithm . . . 139
7.3.2 Population Analysis . . . 141
7.3.3 Comparison with other Heuristics . . . 144

8 Case Studies 149
8.1 Scheduling Medical Research Experiments . . . 149
8.1.1 Problem Description . . . 150
8.1.2 Modeling Approach . . . 152
8.1.3 Computational Results for Original Data . . . 156
8.1.4 Optimality Issues . . . 157
8.1.5 Impact of Data Variations . . . 159
8.1.6 Concluding Remarks . . . 162
8.2 Selecting Market Research Interviewers . . . 163
8.2.1 Problem Description . . . 164
8.2.2 Modeling Approach . . . 168
8.2.3 Dynamic Planning Environment . . . 173

9 Conclusions **177**

A Test Instances **181**
A.1 Patterson Instance Set 181
A.2 Instance Sets Generated by ProGen 182
A.2.1 Single-Mode Instance Sets 183
A.2.2 Multi-Mode Instance Sets 184

B Solving the MRCPSP using AMPL **187**
B.1 AMPL-Formulation of the MRCPSP 187
B.2 AMPL-Data File for the MRCPSP 190

Bibliography **193**

List of Abbreviations **209**

List of Basic Notation **211**

List of Tables **215**

List of Figures **217**

Index **219**

Chapter 1

Introduction

A project consists of activities which must be carried out to achieve a predefined goal. One of the main tasks in project management is the scheduling of the project, that is, the temporal arrangement of the activities. Within a project schedule, certain requirements must be observed, especially limited availabilities of resources that are needed to perform the activities.

Projects can be found in various areas (cf., e.g., Badiru [11], Cleland and King [33], and Hax and Candea [97]). Typical examples include construction projects such as building skyscrapers, bridges, and highways. Many production planning problems involve projects, especially in make-to-order and small batch production of, e.g., ships and planes. Furthermore, research and development projects should be mentioned. Also mass meetings such as large-scale international political conferences or sports events such as olympic games or soccer world cups can be viewed as projects.

The first approaches to project scheduling were developed in the 1950's. The critical path method (CPM, cf. Kelley [110]) assumes deterministic activity durations and precedence relations between the activities. It basically allows a temporal analysis of the project. The program evaluation and review technique (PERT, cf. Malcolm et al. [139]) considers probabilistic activity durations. In the graphical evaluation and review technique (GERT, cf. Pritsker and Happ [168]), also the precedence relations are probabilistic.

In the following years, these early models have been continuously extended and improved to meet the diverse requirements occuring in practice. Considering the deterministic approaches which will be discussed in this work, the most noteworthy extension was the integration of resources. Resources are required to perform the activities and are available with limited capacities, allowing to capture manpower, machines, or a budget for the project. The consideration of resources established the field of resource-constrained project scheduling. Here, the activities are to be scheduled subject to precedence and resource constraints while considering a management objective. One of the most common objectives is an early project completion, that is, the minimization of the project's makespan. An early project end is important in many practical applications: It leads to free resource capacities for future projects. It also reduces the risk of violating a deadline (in many cases, high penalty costs occur if a project is not completed by the deadline). Moreover, considering especially construction and building projects, an early project end is desirable because a large portion of the payment is typically made when the project is completed.

Recent years have witnessed a tremendous increase in research on resource-constrained project scheduling. This led to the development of many new modeling concepts as well as scheduling algorithms. We refer to the literature surveys of Brucker et al. [26], Herroelen et al. [102, 101], Icmeli et al. [106], Kolisch and Padman [128], and Özdamar and Ulusoy [156].

Moreover, a large number of software systems for project management have been developed (cf. Kolisch [123] and Kolisch and Hempel [127]). They support the project manager in planning and scheduling the project as well as in controlling it during its realization. A key feature of many of these systems is a component for constructing a project schedule. In particular, accurate planning and scheduling helps to reduce risks such as time and budget overruns (cf. Williams [211]). A specific type of project management software called Leitstand system has been developed for make-to-order manufacturing and assembly management (cf. Drexl et al. [60] and Drexl and Kolisch [63]).

In this work, we discuss modeling concepts, solution methods, and applications for deterministic project scheduling under resource constraints. The main focus will be on the development and evaluation of project scheduling algorithms which can be applied within project management software. The outline is as follows:

In Chapter 2, we introduce the models we will be dealing with. We consider the standard model, the so-called resource-constrained project scheduling problem (RCPSP) which consists of activities interrelated by simple precedence relations, renewable resources, and makespan minimization as objective. Then we give an overview of some of its generalizations which make the model more suitable for practical applications. Of special interest will be the definition of multiple modes for an activity which reflect alternative ways to accomplish it (e.g., by using different resources), leading to the so-called multi-mode RCPSP (MRCPSP). We will also deal with the relationships between project scheduling models and other combinatorial optimization problems from the field of operations research.

Chapter 3 discusses methodologies to compute optimal solutions for the MRCPSP. These exact algorithms play an important role as they allow to compute optimal solutions for benchmark problems, which are then used to evaluate the performance of practically relevant heuristics. We introduce a new branch-and-bound approach and compare it with two other procedures from the literature in order to point out the most efficient exact method.

Chapter 4 gives an overview of heuristic algorithms that have been suggested for the standard RCPSP in the literature. The heuristics are classified with respect to their components such as schedule generation scheme, priority rules, or metaheuristic strategies. This classification provides the basis for the introduction and evaluation of new heuristic procedures in the following chapters.

In Chapter 5, we propose several genetic algorithm approaches for the RCPSP. We proceed in two steps: First, we define three genetic algorithms based on different problem representations and determine the best one in computational tests. Second, we extend the best approach in order to further improve its performance. The most important extensions are a generalized representation which decides on the algorithmic concept to be used as well as a local search phase.

Chapter 6 provides an evaluation of the new genetic agorithms of Chapter 5 and several state-of-the-art heuristics reviewed in Chapter 4. In an experimental study based on standard test instances, we point out the most promising heuristic algorithm for the RCPSP. Moreover, we analyze which of the underlying concepts are responsible for the success of the heuristics.

With Chapter 7, we return to the multi-mode case. Using the best genetic algorithm for the single-mode case as a starting point, we delevop a genetic algorithm for the MRCPSP. Our approach is enhanced by multi-mode-specific local search components. Subsequently, we compare the multi-mode genetic algorithm with some heuristics for the MRCPSP that have been proposed in the literature.

Chapter 8 examines real-world applications of project scheduling. We provide two case studies which demonstrate the applicability of the modeling concepts and scheduling algorithms discussed in this work. We consider a scientific research project which consists of medical experiments which has been performed at the medical faculty of the University of Kiel (Germany). Furthermore, we deal with market research projects which consist of personal interviews as conducted at the market research company IVE Research International in Hamburg (Germany).

Finally, Chapter 9 draws some conclusions. It provides a summary of the main results obtained in this work and outlines opportunities for future research on resource-constrained project scheduling.

Chapter 2

Project Scheduling Models

Until today, many different project scheduling models have been proposed, covering a broad variety of real-world requirements. This chapter introduces the basic components of these models such as activities, precedence relations, and resources. The models discussed here provide the basis for developing project scheduling algorithms and analyzing applications in the remainder of this work.

In Section 2.1, we begin with the classical resource-constrained project scheduling problem (RCPSP). Then, in Section 2.2, we discuss some variants and extensions of the basic RCPSP which allow to model various real-world project scheduling situations. Finally, Section 2.3 examines the mathematical relationships between project scheduling problems and other classes of important combinatorial optimization problems, namely packing and cutting problems.

2.1 Basic Model: The RCPSP

This section deals with the RCPSP which has evolved as some kind of standard model for resource-constrained project scheduling in the literature. Although rather simple, it allows to cover many aspects that are relevant in real-world project scheduling. After a description of this problem, we perform an analysis of the temporal constraints within a project. The latter is then used to set up a mathematical programming formulation of the project scheduling problem.

2.1.1 Problem Setting

A project consists of activities (or jobs) that are linked by two kinds of restrictions, namely precedence and resource constraints. For each activity, the duration, the resource requests, and the precedence relations with other activities are given. For each resource, the availability is given. All information on durations, precedence relations, and resource requests and availabilities are assumed to be deterministic and known in advance.

We consider a project with J activities which are labeled $j = 1, \dots, J$. For notational convenience, we will refer to the set of activities as $\mathcal{J} = \{1, \dots, J\}$. The processing time (or duration) of an activity j is denoted as p_j. We assume that the planning horizon is divided into time intervals of equal length called periods (e.g., days), and that the processing times p_j are given as discrete multiples of one period. Once started, an activity may not be interrupted, i.e., preemption is not allowed.

Due to technological requirements, there are precedence relations between some of the jobs. Consider, e.g., a building project. Clearly, an activity "roof tiling" may only be started if another activity "erecting walls" has been finished. The precedence relations are given by sets of immediate predecessors $\mathcal{P}_j$ indicating that an activity j may not be started before each of its predecessors $i \in \mathcal{P}_j$ is completed. Analogously, $\mathcal{S}_j$ is the set of the immediate successors of activity j. The transitive closure of the precedence relations is given by sets of (not necessarily immediate) successors $\overline{\mathcal{S}}_j$. The precedence relations can be represented by an activity-on-node network which is assumed to be acyclic.

We consider two additional activities $j = 0$ and $j = J + 1$ representing the start and end of the project, respectively. Activity 0 is assumed to be the unique source of the network while activity $J + 1$ is the unique sink. Both activities are "dummy" jobs; their processing time is $p_0 = p_{J+1} = 0$. The set of all activities including the dummy jobs is denoted as $\mathcal{J}^+ = \{0, \dots, J+1\}$.

With the exception of the source and sink activities, each activity requires certain amounts of resources to be performed. The resources are called renewable because their full capacity is available in every period. Examples for such resources are manpower and machines. The set of renewable resources is referred to as $\mathcal{K}^\rho$. For each resource $k \in \mathcal{K}^\rho$ the per-period-availability is assumed to be constant and given by R_k^ρ. Activity j requires r_{jk} units of resource k in each period it is in process. W.l.o.g., we assume that the dummy source and the dummy sink activity do not request any resource, i.e., $r_{0k} = r_{J+1,k} = 0$ for all $k \in \mathcal{K}^\rho$.

The parameters are assumed to be nonnegative and integer valued. The objective is to find a schedule which allows for the earliest possible end of the project, i.e., the minimal makespan. Clearly, the precedence and resource constraints may not be violated. A schedule assigns a start time s_j to each activity j. Alternatively, a schedule may be given by finish times f_j.

Throughout this work, we will refer to both time instants and periods. We say that a period t starts at time instant $t - 1$ and ends at time instant

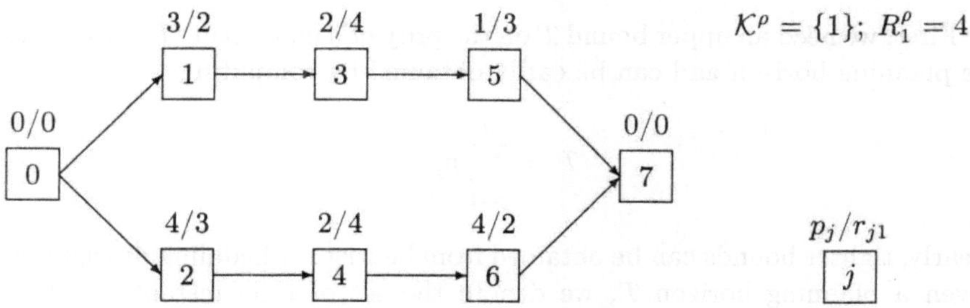

Figure 2.1: Project instance

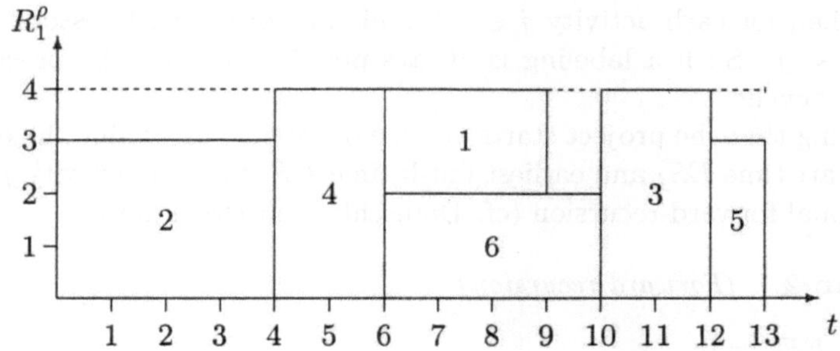

Figure 2.2: Example schedule

t. Consequently, an activity j which starts at time s_j and finishes at time $f_j = s_j + p_j$ is in process (and requires resources) in periods $t = s_j + 1, \ldots, f_j$.

Figure 2.1 depicts an example project instance with $J = 6$ non-dummy activities and one renewable resource with a capacity of $R_1^\rho = 4$ units in each period. It will be used to illustrate many definitions and algorithmic approaches throughout this work. A feasible schedule for this instance is displayed in Figure 2.2. There, the start and finish times as well as the resulting resource usages in each period are visualized.

2.1.2 Deriving Time Windows

An important step in the analysis of a project instance is to compute so-called time windows for the activities. These time windows essentially provide information about those start and finish times of an activity that allow to complete the whole project within some planning horizon. As will be explained later on, this information can be used in solution approaches.

First, we need an upper bound T on the project's makespan. T constitutes the planning horizon and can be easily obtained by computing

$$T := \sum_{j=1}^{J} p_j.$$

Clearly, tighter bounds can be obtained from heuristic scheduling procedures. Given a planning horizon T, we denote the set of time instants as $\mathcal{T} = \{0, \ldots, T\}$ and the set of periods as $\mathcal{T}' = \{1, \ldots, T\}$.

For simplifying the description of the following time window calculation, we assume that the activities are numerically labeled w.r.t. the precedence relations, i.e., for each activity $j \in \mathcal{J}^+$ and each of its predecessors $i \in \mathcal{P}_j$ we have $i < j$. Such a labeling is always possible because the precedence network is acyclic.

Assuming that the project starts at time 0, we now determine the earliest possible start time ES_j and earliest finish time EF_j for each activity $j \in \mathcal{J}^+$ by traditional forward recursion (cf. Domschke and Drexl [55]):

Algorithm 2.1 *(Forward recursion)*

$ES_0 := 0;\ EF_0 := 0;$
FOR $g := 1$ TO $J + 1$ DO
BEGIN
    $ES_j := \max\{EF_i \mid i \in \mathcal{P}_j\};$
    $EF_j := ES_j + p_j;$
END.

Analogously, we perform traditional backward recursion to compute the latest possible start time LS_j and latest finish time LF_j for each activity $j \in \mathcal{J}^+$ as follows:

Algorithm 2.2 *(Backward recursion)*

$LF_{J+1} := T;\ LS_{J+1} := T;$
FOR $g := J$ DOWNTO 0 DO
BEGIN
    $LF_j := \min\{LS_i \mid i \in \mathcal{S}_j\};$
    $LS_j := LF_j - p_j;$
END.

Clearly, activity j must start within the time window $\{ES_j, \ldots, LS_j\}$ and finish within the time window $\{EF_j, \ldots, LF_j\}$. Otherwise, the precedence relations would be violated. Note, however, that resource constraints are not considered by the time windows. Starting each activity at its earliest start time (by setting $s_j := ES_j$ for all $j \in \mathcal{J}^+$) thus leads to a precedence-feasible, but not necessarily resource-feasible schedule (which is of course optimal if no resource constraints exist).

Time windows can be exploited in two ways: First, as we will see in the following subsection, the number of variables in the mathematical programming formulation can be reduced. Second, the time windows allow to evaluate partial schedules within tailored scheduling procedures. As we will see in Chapter 3, this leads to a substantial acceleration of the algorithms.

Considering again our example of Figure 2.1, we compute $T = 16$ and obtain the earliest and latest start and finish times given in Table 2.1.

j	*0*	*1*	*2*	*3*	*4*	*5*	*6*	*7*
ES_j	0	0	0	3	4	5	6	10
EF_j	0	3	4	5	6	6	10	10
LS_j	6	10	6	13	10	15	12	16
LF_j	6	13	10	15	12	16	16	16

Table 2.1: Time windows for example instance

2.1.3 Mathematical Programming Formulation

We now develop a mathematical programming formulation for the RCPSP. The purpose of such a problem formalization is twofold: First, it serves as an accurate problem definition. Second, it can be implemented in mathematical standard software to yield an optimal solution without requiring algorithmic knowledge.[1] Such an approach (for an extension of the RCPSP) is discussed in Appendix B.

So far, we have established the problem parameters in Subsection 2.1.1 and the time windows in Subsection 2.1.2. In order to set up an integer programming formulation of the RCPSP, we now introduce decision variables to reflect the finish time of the activities. We define a binary variable x_{jt} for each activity $j \in \mathcal{J}^+$ and each time instant $t \in \mathcal{T}$ by

$$x_{jt} = \begin{cases} 1, & \text{if activity } j \text{ is finished at time } t \\ 0, & \text{otherwise.} \end{cases}$$

[1] Whereas the following mathematical model can indeed be used within standard solvers, this does not hold for so-called conceptual model formulations. The latter serve merely as a problem definition, but their—often simpler—structure does not allow an application within mathematical software. For the RCPSP, a conceptual model has been given by, e.g., Demeulemeester and Herroelen [48].

Following the approach of Pritsker et al. [169], we now obtain the following model of the RCPSP:

$$\text{Minimize} \quad \sum_{t=EF_{J+1}}^{LF_{J+1}} t \cdot x_{J+1,t} \tag{2.1}$$

subject to

$$\sum_{t=EF_j}^{LF_j} x_{jt} = 1 \qquad j \in \mathcal{J}^+ \tag{2.2}$$

$$\sum_{t=EF_h}^{LF_h} t \cdot x_{ht} \leq \sum_{t=EF_j}^{LF_j} (t - p_j) \cdot x_{jt} \qquad j \in \mathcal{J}^+, \ h \in \mathcal{P}_j \tag{2.3}$$

$$\sum_{j=1}^{J} r_{jk} \sum_{b=t}^{t+p_j-1} x_{jb} \leq R_k^\rho \qquad k \in \mathcal{K}^\rho, \ t \in \mathcal{T} \tag{2.4}$$

$$x_{jt} \in \{0, 1\} \qquad j \in \mathcal{J}^+, \ t \in \mathcal{T} \tag{2.5}$$

Objective (2.1) minimizes the finish time of the dummy sink activity and, therefore, the project's makespan. Constraints (2.2) secure that each activity is executed exactly once. The precedence and resource restrictions are observed by Constraints (2.3) and (2.4), respectively. Finally, Constraints (2.5) define the binary decision variables.

As already mentioned, we can use the time windows to reduce the number of necessary variables. To do so, we replace Constraints (2.4) with

$$\sum_{j=1}^{J} r_{jk} \sum_{b=\max\{t,EF_j\}}^{\min\{t+p_j-1,LF_j\}} x_{jb} \leq R_k^\rho \qquad k \in \mathcal{K}^\rho, \ t \in \mathcal{T}. \tag{2.6}$$

Now we only need variables x_{jt} with $j \in \mathcal{J}^+$ and $t \in \{EF_j, \ldots, LF_j\}$ (instead of $t \in \mathcal{T}$). As the original Constraints (2.4) are slightly easier to survey, however, we will use that formulation when extending the model in the next section.

Having set up the model of the RCPSP, we want to know how difficult it is to solve, that is, we want to examine its complexity. In fact, it has been shown by Blazewicz et al. [19] that the RCPSP belongs to the class of the NP-hard problems. In other words, there is no algorithm known that would find an optimal schedule for any instance of the RCPSP in polynomial time (to be accurate, it has not been proven yet that no such algorithm exists, but it seems unlikely that there is one, cf. Garey and Johnson [84]). Note, however, that this is a worst case result. There are instances for which a polynomial time algorithm exists: Actually, the earliest start schedule computed by (polynomial time) Algorithm 2.1 is feasible and, consequently, also optimal for the resource-unconstrained case. Nevertheless, most instances occuring in practice are highly resource-constrained and difficult to solve.

2.2 Variants and Extensions

While the RCPSP as introduced in the previous section is already a powerful model, it does not cover all situations that occur in practice. Therefore, many researchers have developed more general project scheduling models, often using the standard RCPSP as a starting point. This section summarizes some of the most important model extensions proposed in the literature. While an exhaustive overview is beyond the scope of this work, we sketch out some important recent developments. The focus is on modeling concepts that will be used in the following chapters.

We proceed as follows: Subsection 2.2.1 generalizes the activity concept by introducing multiple modes of accomplishment for each activity. Alternative precedence constraints and network characteristics are summarized in Subsection 2.2.2. Subsection 2.2.3 gives some extensions of the resource concept. Different objectives are outlined in Subsection 2.2.4 and, finally, Subsection 2.2.5 deals with the simultaneous consideration of different projects.

2.2.1 Multiple Execution Modes

The basic RCPSP assumes that an activity can only be executed in a single way which is determined by a fixed duration and fixed resource requirements. Starting with the work of Elmaghraby [72], many researchers extended the activity concept as given in the standard RCPSP by allowing several alternatives or *modes* in which an activity can be performed. Each mode reflects a feasible way to combine a duration and resource requests that allow to accomplish the underlying activity. Once started in one of its modes, an activity must be completed in that mode; mode changes and preemption are not permitted. The objective is to determine a start time and a mode for each activity, such that the project's makespan is minimal.

The concept of multiple execution modes results in a powerful model which is capable of mapping many important real-world situations occuring within a project. Consider, e.g., an activity which requires a duration of four periods and two workers. Possibly, this activity can also be carried out by only one worker in eight periods, or by four workers in two periods. This case is called time-resource tradeoff. A similar case, the so-called resource-resource tradeoff, occurs if, e.g., an activity can be performed in four periods by two experienced workers or, alternatively, by one experienced worker and two apprentices within the same duration.

In project scheduling models with multiple modes, often three different kinds of resources are considered, namely renewable, nonrenewable, and doubly constrained resources. This resource categorization has been developed by Slowinski [184, 185] and Weglarz [205]. Renewable resources are limited on a per-period basis. Examples include manpower and machines. In contrast, nonrenewable resources are limited for the entire project. An example for this resource category is money; hence, nonrenewable resources allow to model a budget for the project. While renewable resources are already part of the basic (single-mode) RCPSP, nonrenewable ones need only be considered in a multi-mode environment. Finally, doubly constrained resources are limited both for each period and for the whole project. Again, money is an example if both the budget and the per-period cashflow of the project are limited. As a doubly constrained resource can be incorporated by a renewable and a nonrenewable resource, doubly constrained resources do not enhance the expressive power of the model. Hence, they need not be treated explicitly.

Standard Multi-Mode Model: The MRCPSP

For formally modeling the multiple mode extension of the RCPSP, we denote the number of modes in which activity j can be performed as M_j. $\mathcal{M}_j = \{1, \dots, M_j\}$ then is the set of modes of activity j. The processing time of activity j being executed in mode m is referred to as p_{jm}.

The sets of the renewable and nonrenewable resources are denoted as $\mathcal{K}^\rho$ and $\mathcal{K}^\nu$, respectively. Resources $k \in \mathcal{K}^\rho \cap \mathcal{K}^\nu$ are doubly constrained. As mentioned above, we need not consider them explicitly. Thus, w.l.o.g., we can assume $k \in \mathcal{K}^\rho \cap \mathcal{K}^\nu = \emptyset$ which eases the description in the following chapters. Renewable resource $k \in \mathcal{K}^\rho$ has a constant per-period availability of R_k^ρ units, while the capacity of nonrenewable resource $k \in \mathcal{K}^\nu$ is R_k^ν units for the entire project. The request of activity j being executed in mode m for resource $k \in \mathcal{K}^\rho \cup \mathcal{K}^\nu$ is r_{jmk}.

For modeling purposes, we assume that the (dummy) source and sink activities have only a single mode with a duration of zero periods and no request for any resource. Again, all parameters are assumed to be nonnegative integers.[2]

Analogously to the RCPSP, we derive time windows before formally stating the model. The proceeding of Subsection 2.1.2, however, has to be

[2]This assumption is realistic for most applications and, moreover, useful when designing solution methods. The algorithms presented in the following chapters assume that only nonnegative resource parameters are given. For dealing with negative resource parameters, modifications of the procedures would be necessary. There are, however, situations in which negative resource parameters are useful to capture real-world requirements. An example is the travel route scheduling problem introduced in Hartmann et al. [94] which borrows the concept of nonrenewable resources and explicitly allows negative resource requests and capacities.

adapted for the multi-mode case. Here, the upper bound on the makespan is given by the sum of the maximal durations of the activities. We then use the shortest duration of each activity in Algorithms 2.1 and 2.2 and obtain earliest and latest start and finish times for the multi-mode case.

As already mentioned, we need to determine not only the start time of each activity as in the RCPSP but also the mode when computing a schedule. In the following integer programming formulation, this is expressed by a decision variable for each activity $j \in \mathcal{J}^+$, mode $m \in \mathcal{M}_j$, and time instant $t \in \mathcal{T}$ with

$$x_{jmt} = \begin{cases} 1, & \text{if activity } j \text{ is performed in mode } m \text{ and finished at time } t \\ 0, & \text{otherwise.} \end{cases}$$

Now we are ready to set up the binary model of the multi-mode resource-constrained project scheduling problem (MRCPSP) which has been introduced by Talbot [197]:

$$\text{Minimize} \quad \sum_{t=EF_{J+1}}^{LF_{J+1}} t \cdot x_{J+1,1,t} \tag{2.7}$$

subject to

$$\sum_{m=1}^{M_j} \sum_{t=EF_j}^{LF_j} x_{jmt} = 1 \qquad j \in \mathcal{J}^+ \tag{2.8}$$

$$\sum_{m=1}^{M_h} \sum_{t=EF_h}^{LF_h} t \cdot x_{hmt} \leq \sum_{m=1}^{M_j} \sum_{t=EF_j}^{LF_j} (t - p_{jm}) \cdot x_{jmt} \qquad j \in \mathcal{J}^+,\ h \in \mathcal{P}_j \tag{2.9}$$

$$\sum_{j=1}^{J} \sum_{m=1}^{M_j} r_{jmk} \sum_{b=t}^{t+p_{jm}-1} x_{jmb} \leq R_k^\rho \qquad k \in \mathcal{K}^\rho,\ t \in \mathcal{T} \tag{2.10}$$

$$\sum_{j=1}^{J} \sum_{m=1}^{M_j} r_{jmk} \sum_{t=EF_j}^{LF_j} x_{jmt} \leq R_k^\nu \qquad k \in \mathcal{K}^\nu \tag{2.11}$$

$$x_{jmt} \in \{0, 1\} \qquad j \in \mathcal{J}^+,\ m \in \mathcal{M}_j,\ t \in \mathcal{T} \tag{2.12}$$

Similarly to the single-mode RCPSP, Objective (2.7) minimizes the makespan of the project. Constraints (2.8) secure that each activity is assigned exactly one mode and one finish time. Precedence feasibility is maintained by Constraints (2.9). Constraints (2.10) and (2.11) take care of the renewable and nonrenewable resource limitations, respectively. Finally, Constraints (2.12) define the binary status of the decision variables.

Clearly, if only one mode per activity and no nonrenewable resources are given, we obtain the standard RCPSP. Consequently, also the MRCPSP is NP-hard. Moreover, already the feasibility problem of the MRCPSP, i.e., the assignment of modes such that the nonrenewable resource capacities are not exceeded, is NP-complete if at least two nonrenewable resources are given (cf. Kolisch and Drexl [125]).

Mode Identity

The MRCPSP has been extended by Salewski et al. [172] who introced so-called mode identity constraints. The motivation for this model is that there may be several activities that should be performed in the same way, e.g., by allocating the same resources to them. Salewski et al. [172] mention that such a requirement occurs in audit staff scheduling. However, in the MRCPSP as stated above, the modes of different activities are selected independently. Therefore, the model can be extended as follows: The set of activities $\mathcal{J}$ is partitioned into U sets of activities $\mathcal{H}_u$, $u = 1, \ldots, U$. The activities of each set $\mathcal{H}_u$ must be performed in the same mode. That is, $i, j \in \mathcal{H}_u$ implies that activities i and j are performed in modes $m_i \in \mathcal{M}_i$ and $m_j \in \mathcal{M}_j$, respectively, with $m_i = m_j$. This requires, of course, $M_i = M_j$ and thus $\mathcal{M}_i = \mathcal{M}_j$ for all activities $i, j \in \mathcal{H}_u$. Formally, the mode identity constraints are given by

$$\sum_{m=1}^{M_h} m \cdot \sum_{t=EF_h}^{LF_h} x_{jmt} = \sum_{m=1}^{M_j} m \cdot \sum_{t=EF_j}^{LF_j} x_{jmt} \qquad \begin{array}{l} u = 1, \ldots, U, \\ h, j \in \mathcal{H}_u. \end{array} \tag{2.13}$$

Adding constraints (2.13) to the MRCPSP of (2.7)–(2.12) yields the mode identity resource-constrained project scheduling problem (MIRCPSP). The above formulation of the MRCPSP with mode identity (2.7)–(2.13) is slightly shorter than the original one given by Salewski et al. [172]. Note that the MIRCPSP contains the MRCPSP as a special case; we obtain the latter by fixing $U = J$ and $\mathcal{H}_j = \{j\}$ for all $j = 1, \ldots, J(= U)$.

Special Cases

Several researchers considered special cases of the MRCPSP and proposed solution methods that make use of the special problem structures. In the discrete time-resource tradeoff problem, there is one renewable resource, but no nonrenewable one. Moreover, the workload ω_j for each activity j is given. Each mode m of activity j represents a possible efficient combination of duration and resource request that results in the required workload. That is, we have $r_{jm1} \cdot p_{jm} \geq \omega_j$ as well as, considering the efficiency assumption, $(r_{jm1} - 1) \cdot p_{jm} < \omega_j$ and $r_{jm1} \cdot (p_{jm} - 1) < \omega_j$. As in all previous models, the parameters r_{jm1} and p_{jm} are assumed to be non-negative and integer-valued. For this problem setting, a branch-and-bound algorithm is given in Demeulemeester et al. [46]. A tabu search heuristic has been developed by de Reyck et al. [41].

Analogously, the discrete time-cost tradeoff problem considers one non-renewable resource (which is interpreted as representing the costs of the activities). There is no renewable resource. An exact algorithm is provided by Demeulemeester et al. [52] while heuristics can be found in Akkan [4]. Although only one nonrenewable and no renewable resource is given, the problem is NP-hard, as proven by De et al. [40].

Recently, Ahn and Erenguc [2] presented a variant of the MRCPSP by introducing so-called crashable modes. In their model, the duration of a mode can be shortened at the expense of additional costs. While they consider a different, cost based objective function, the crashable modes can be transformed into the standard mode concept of the MRCPSP. Ahn and Erenguc [2, 3] devolop exact and heuristic methods to deal with this problem.

2.2.2 Generalized Temporal Constraints

Many different kinds of temporal contraints have been considered in the project scheduling literature, for overviews see, e.g., Bartusch et al. [12] and Franck and Neumann [79]. In the classical RCPSP, an activity must have finished before any of its successors can be started. We now summarize several extensions of these basic precedence relations.

Minimal Time Lags

The basic precedence concept can be extended by so-called minimal time lags d_{ij}^{FS} between the finish time f_i of an activity i and the start time s_j of successor activity $j \in \mathcal{S}_i$, implying $f_i + d_{ij}^{FS} \leq s_j$ (cf., e.g., Klein and Scholl [116]). Clearly, in the standard RCPSP, we always have $d_{ij}^{FS} = 0$ for $i \in \mathcal{J}^+$ and $j \in \mathcal{S}_i$. Allowing negative minimal time lags implies that the corresponding precedence related activities may overlap. In addition, we may also consider minimal time lags d_{ij}^{SS} between the start time of activity i and the start time of activity j, minimal time lags d_{ij}^{SF} between the start time of activity i and the finish time of activity j, and minimal time lags d_{ij}^{FF} between the finish time of activity i and the finish time of activity j. These four minimal time-lag types have been considered by, e.g., Elmaghraby [72], Moder et al. [146], and Demeulemeester and Herroelen [50]. Note, however, that they can all be transformed into each other such that one type is enough to obtain the full expressive power of minimal time lags. As an example, $d_{ij}^{FS} = d_{ij}^{SS} - p_i$ obviously holds (cf. also Figure 8.2 in Chapter 8). We omit further details here and refer to the transformation rules provided in Bartusch et al. [12]. It should be mentioned, however, that these transformations are not possible if a multi-mode model (cf. Subsection 2.2.1) is considered. Restricting ourselves to the minimal finish-start time lags d_{ij}^{FS}, we can extend the basic RCPSP model by replacing Constraints (2.3) with

$$\sum_{t=EF_h}^{LF_h} t \cdot x_{ht} + d_{ij}^{FS} \leq \sum_{t=EF_j}^{LF_j} (t - p_j) \cdot x_{jt} \qquad j \in \mathcal{J}^+, \;\; h \in \mathcal{P}_j. \tag{2.14}$$

Maximal Time Lags

Similarly to minimal time lags, maximal time lags can be defined (cf., e.g., Bartusch et al. [12], de Reyck and Herroelen [43], Dorndorf et al. [58], Franck and Schwindt [80], Möhring et al. [147], Schwindt [181], and Zimmermann [213]). We denote a maximal time lag between the finish time of activity i and the start time of activity j as $\bar{d}_{ij}^{FS}$, which means that $f_i + \bar{d}_{ij}^{FS} \geq s_j$ must hold. Analogously, maximal start-start, start-finish, and finish-finish time lags are given by $\bar{d}_{ij}^{SS}$, $\bar{d}_{ij}^{SF}$, and $\bar{d}_{ij}^{FF}$, respectively. Clearly, the concepts of minimal and maximal time lags can also be considered within multi-mode models such as the MRCPSP (see Heilmann [98]). It should be noted that maximal time lags typically lead to cyclic network structures, which have an impact on scheduling algorithms. This will not be considered here in more detail; we refer to Franck and Neumann [79] for a discussion of this issue.

Release Dates and Deadlines

Two special cases of the time lags discussed above should be mentioned (cf., e.g., Demeulemeester and Herroelen [50] and Klein and Scholl [116]). First, a release date (or ready time) $\underline{\delta}_j$ gives the earliest time instant at which activity j may be started (assuming that time instant 0 corresponds to the start of the project). Mathematically, that is

$$\sum_{t=EF_j}^{LF_j} t \cdot x_{jt} - p_j \geq \underline{\delta}_j \qquad j \in \mathcal{J}^+. \tag{2.15}$$

Second, a deadline $\overline{\delta}_j$ denotes the latest time instant at which activity j must be finished.

$$\sum_{t=EF_j}^{LF_j} t \cdot x_{jt} \leq \overline{\delta}_j \qquad j \in \mathcal{J}^+. \tag{2.16}$$

Note that a release date $\underline{\delta}_j$ is equivalent to a minimal finish-start time lag between the dummy source activity and activity j, i.e., $\underline{\delta}_j = d_{0j}^{FS}$. Analogously, a deadline $\overline{\delta}_j$ can be imposed by a maximal finish-finish time lag between the dummy source activity and activity j, i.e., $\overline{\delta}_j = \bar{d}_{0j}^{FF}$. Both release dates and deadlines play an important role when simultaneously planning multiple projects (see Subsection 2.2.5). We remark here that the notion of a deadline is also used with a different meaning in the literature. Whereas a deadline as defined above may not be violated, Kapuscinska et al. [109] consider deadlines which can be exceeded at some penalty cost. To avoid confusion, we call the latter case a due date.

Networks with Logical Nodes

Several researchers, e.g., Elmaghraby [71] and Belhe and Kusiak [14], have extended the precedence network concept by adding logical nodes. In the RCPSP model, an activity node which has several successor nodes implies that this activity must be finished before any of the successors may be started. This controls the temporal arrangement of the activities. As *all* successor activities must be executed, the activity nodes can be viewed as logical "AND" nodes. Extending this concept, some activity nodes might be declared as logical "OR" nodes, implying that at least one successor activity of an "OR" node has to be performed. Analogously, "XOR" (exclusive-or) nodes induce that exactly one successor activity must be executed. These network extensions are, for example, useful to model research and development projects: After an "XOR"-activity "test prototype" has been performed, either activity "modify prototype" or activity "start production" is executed, depending on the outcome of the test. In the project management literature, networks with logical nodes are mostly treated in connection with stochastic concepts, see Neumann [151].

Activity-on-Arc Networks

Finally, we briefly address an issue concerning the way the activities are represented within the network. Throughout this work, we use the so-called activity-on-node representation, that is, each activity corresponds to a node in the network, while the precedence relations are given by arcs between the activity nodes. In the literature (cf., e.g., Babu and Suresh [9], Elmaghraby [72, 73], Padman et al. [159], and Phillips [164]), also an alternative representation can be found, namely the actvity-on-arc network. There, each activity corresponds to an arc, while the nodes represent events. For a summarizing discussion of the similarities and differences between both representations, we refer to Kolisch and Padman [128].

2.2.3 Generalized Resource Constraints

The basic RCPSP features only renewable resources. Two more resource categories, nonrenewable and doubly constrained resources, have already been described in connection with the the multi-mode extension of the RCPSP, the MRCPSP.[3] There are a few more resource types that have been proposed in the literature. Here, we consider partially renewable, continuously divisible, and dedicated resources. After their description, we turn to a generalization of the renewable resource concept which permits time-dependency of the resource parameters.

Partially Renewable Resources

Partially renewable resources have been introduced by Böttcher et al. [24]; see also Drexl et al. [62] and Schirmer and Drexl [175]. Consider, e.g., an employee who may work on every day from Monday through Friday and either on Saturday or on Sunday but not both. However, it is not specified on which of the latter he may work. This cannot be reflected using renewable resources. The gap is closed by partially renewable resources as they allow to model resource availability restrictions on subsets of periods. In our example, we would have separate capacities for weekdays and weekends.

We denote the set of partially renewable resources as $\mathcal{K}^\pi$. For each partially renewable resource $k \in \mathcal{K}^\pi$, we have a set Π_k of so-called period subsets. Each period subset $P_{ki} \in \Pi_k$ is a set of periods, i.e., $P_{ki} \subseteq \mathcal{T}'$. Moreover, each P_{ki} is associated with a capacity $R_k^\pi(P_{ki})$, denoting that the availability of resource k is $R_k^\pi(P_{ki})$ for the period subset P_{ki}. The request of activity j for partially renewable resource k is again denoted as r_{jk}.

In our example, the employee corresponds to a partially renewable resource. Each day (Monday through Sunday) would be one period, and each day from Monday through Friday makes up one separate period subset with an associated availability of 1. The weekend restriction is imposed by defining another period subset containing both Saturday and Sunday with a capacity of 1.

The resource-constrained project scheduling problem with partially renewable resources (RCPSP/π) is obtained from replacing constraints (2.4) in the standard RCPSP with

$$\sum_{j=1}^{J} r_{jk} \sum_{t \in P_{ki}} \sum_{b=t}^{t+p_j-1} x_{jb} \leq R_k^\pi(P_{ki}) \qquad k \in \mathcal{K}^\pi,\ P_{ki} \in \Pi_k. \tag{2.17}$$

Clearly, partially renewable resources can be incorporated in multi-mode models as well. Note that partially renewable resources generalize both renewable and nonrenewable (and henceforth also doubly constrained) resources. A renewable resource is a partially renewable one for which each

[3] As these two resource categories would not make sense in a single-mode environment, they are mostly considered together with multi-mode models. Therefore, their description is provided in Subsection 2.2.1.

period within the planning horizon constitutes a separate period subset. On the other hand, a nonrenewable resource is modeled as a partially renewable one by using only one period subset which contains all periods of the planning horizon. The availability of the renewable (or nonrenewable) resource defines the availability for the respective period subsets.

Continuously Divisible Resources

In the models discussed up to now, the considered resources were available in discrete quantities only, as in the cases of, e.g., manpower and machines. Weglarz et al. [208] generalized the concept of renewable resources by allowing continuously divisible resources. This is useful if the resources correspond to, e.g., energy or raw material like chemical liquids. Given the planning horizon T, the (constant) resource availability in each (real-valued) time instant t with $0 \leq t \leq T$ may not be exceeded. Additionally, the model allows preemption of the activities. An extension of this model is presented in Weglarz [206]. There, a continuously divisible variant of the doubly constrained resources is introduced. That is, both the resource availability in each (again real-valued) time instant $t \in [0, T]$ and the capacity for the entire project are limited.

Dedicated Resources

We now have a brief look at so-called dedicated resources. These are resources that can be assigned to only one activity at a time. Dedicated resources can be expressed by a renewable resources with an availability of one unit per period. Consequently, they are included in the RCPSP as a special case. Problems with dedicated resources are studied in, e.g., Bianco et al. [17].

Resource Parameters Varying with Time

So far, we have described several resource types. There is yet another possibility to generalize the resource constraints of the RCPSP, namely by time-dependent resource parameters. Up to this point, the availability of the renewable resources has been assumed to be constant over time, i.e., the capacity is the same in each period. This assumption, however, may not be useful in some cases. Consider, e.g., a changing availability of workers due to holidays. In order to cover time-dependent resource capacities (cf., e.g., Sprecher [190] and Klein and Scholl [116]), we denote the availability of renewable resource k at time t as $R_k^\rho(t)$ and obtain

$$\sum_{j=1}^{J} r_{jk} \sum_{b=t}^{t+p_j-1} x_{jb} \leq R_k^\rho(t) \qquad k \in \mathcal{K}^\rho,\ t \in \mathcal{T}. \tag{2.18}$$

This case can be further extended by resource requests varying with time. Consider, e.g., an activity that requires two workers in its first period and only one in the remaining periods of its processing time. Formally, this modeling approach is captured by using resource request parameters with an additional time index. $r_{jk}(t)$ denotes the request of activity j for renewable resource k in the t-th period of its processing time. This leads to the following constraints:

$$\sum_{j=1}^{J} \sum_{b=t}^{t+p_j-1} r_{jk}(t + p_j - b) \cdot x_{jt} \leq R_k^\rho(t) \qquad k \in \mathcal{K}^\rho,\ t \in \mathcal{T}. \tag{2.19}$$

If the basic RCPSP is extended by both time-varying resource availability and time-varying resource request by replacing Constraints (2.4) with (2.19), we will call the resulting model the resource-constrained project scheduling problem with time-dependent resource parameters (RCPSP/τ). A practical application of the RCPSP/τ will be discussed in Section 8.1.

2.2.4 Alternative Objectives

Motivated by real-world situations, a broad variety of objective functions for project scheduling models have been proposed. Due to the arguments summarized in Chapter 1, the objective to minimize the makespan is among the most popular ones. There are, however, more time-based objectives such as, e.g., the minimization of the weighted tardiness w.r.t. given due dates which generalizes the makespan objective (cf. Kapuscinska et al. [109]) or just-in-time objectives (cf. Anthonisse et al. [7]).

Resource-Based Objectives

In many real-world cases, the assignment of start times alone is less crucial than the resulting resource requests. Then time-oriented objectives are replaced with a resource-based objective such as resource investment or resource leveling (cf., e.g., Demeulemeester [45], Franck and Schwindt [80], Kimms [113], and Zimmermann [213]). In such a case, the project duration is usually controlled by imposing a deadline $\overline{\delta}_{J+1}$ on the dummy sink activity according to Constraints (2.16). As an example for resource-based objectives, we consider the resource investment problem, where the capacities of the (typically expensive) renewable resources are to be determined such that the given deadline is met and the resource investment costs are to be minimized. Assuming that providing a capacity of one unit of renewable resource $k \in \mathcal{K}^\rho$ for the entire planning horizon is associated with costs c_k^ρ, we treat the capacity of resource k as an additional variable and state the following objective:

$$\text{Minimize} \quad \sum_{k \in \mathcal{K}^\rho} c_k^\rho \cdot R_k^\rho. \tag{2.20}$$

Similarly, when dealing with multi-mode problems (see Subsection 2.2.1), we can minimize the amount of nonrenewable resources needed to complete the project on time. Interpreting a nonrenewable resource as money, this leads to a minimization of the mode-dependent costs. Imposing again a deadline and introducing a weight factor c_k^ν for $k \in \mathcal{K}^\nu$, we treat the nonrenewable resource availabilities as variables and obtain

$$\text{Minimize} \quad \sum_{k \in \mathcal{K}^\nu} c_k^\nu \cdot R_k^\nu. \tag{2.21}$$

Financial Objectives

Another important type of objective emerges if cash flows occur while the project is performed. Cash outflows are induced by the execution of activities and the usage of resources. On the other hand, cash inflows result from payments due to the completion of specified parts of the project. Typically, discount rates are also included. These considerations result in models with the objective to maximize the net present value (NPV) of the project, see Bey et al. [16], Doersch and Patterson [54], and Icmeli and Erenguc [105]. A comparison of models with cash flow based objectives is provided by Dayanand and Padman [39].

Quality Oriented Objectives

Icmeli-Tukel and Rom [107] developed two RCPSP-related models with the objective of maximizing quality. They are based on the assumption that incorrectly completing an activity leads to the need to rework this activity, which causes delays and costs. It is not known in the planning phase of the project which activities need to be partially or completely reworked. Quality is maximized by minimizing both estimated rework times and costs. The objective thereby leads to a schedule which is flexible in the sense that eventually required reworking induces the lowest possible additional times and costs.

Multiple Objectives

The models discussed above have a single objective function (e.g., makespan minimization) while all other features of a schedule are controlled by means of constraints (e.g., resource usages and costs). Hapke et al. [89] propose a multicriteria approach which allows to simultaneously consider several objectives, namely time based, resource based, and financial ones. Seeking for a "good compromise" between the different criteria, their heuristic computes a set of Pareto-optimal schedules. They incorporate an interactive system which allows the decision maker to enter his preferences to evaluate the Pareto-optimal solutions.

2.2.5 Multiple Projects

In practice, often not only one but several dependent projects have to be scheduled simultaneously. This is important if two or more projects share at least one resource and if they may be processed in parallel.

Pritsker et al. [169] introduce a model which simultaneously considers the activities of multiple projects, along with due dates and deadlines for the single projects. Clearly, with the network definition used here, we can comprise the activities of all project networks in a "super-network" by adding a "super-source" and a "super-sink". Due dates or deadlines for the single projects can then be imposed on the sink activities of the respective single projects.

Speranza and Vercellis [188] propose a hierarchical approach which consists of two steps. In the first step, each project is represented by an activity within a network. On this aggregated level, start times and resulting resource requirements are determined for each project. The second step consists of scheduling each single project on the basis of the decisions made in the first step.

Shtub et al. [183] develop multi-project models which assume that some project is repeated several times, as it may occur in small batch production. Their models consider learning effects that can be exploited if a team of workers (i.e., a resource) performs several identical projects. In this case, the time needed for one project may decrease with an increasing number of projects performed by the same team.

2.3 Relations to Packing and Cutting Problems

Packing and cutting problems are important classes of combinatorial optimization problems with many practical applications. Roughly speaking, a packing problem consists of packing small objects (e.g., boxes) into one or more large objects (e.g., containers) with respect to a given objective. A cutting problem consists of cutting large objects (raw material such as, e.g., tubes or wood) into small pieces. Note that there is some kind of duality between packing and cutting problems. For an overview of cutting and packing problems, we refer to Dyckhoff [68], Dyckhoff and Finke [69], and Wottawa [212].

In this section, we examine the relationships between project scheduling problems on the one hand and packing and cutting problems on the other hand. Although these two problem categories do not have much in common from an application-oriented point of view, they share some mathematical characteristics. Our goal is to show that many important cutting and packing problems are special cases of project scheduling models.

Before we start, we make some general assumptions on the packing and cutting problems considered here. First, we restrict ourselves to objects of rectangular shape. Second, we consider only orthogonal packing and cutting patterns, that is, the edges of the small objects (e.g., boxes to be packed) must be either parallel or orthogonal to the edges of the large objects (e.g., the containers). These first two restrictions are common in the literature. Third, we do not consider cutting problems in which only so-called guillotine cuts are allowed. A restriction to guillotine cuts occurs if the material can only be completely cut from one side to the other due to technical requirements (e.g., of a specific saw). As mentioned by Exeler [75], the main difference between packing and cutting problems is the restriction to guillotine cuts in many cutting problems; there is no equivalent of guillotine cuts in packing problems. To keep the description simple, we will only speak of packing problems from now on; due to the duality mentioned above, this includes the non-guillotine cutting problems as well.

This section is organized as follows: Subsection 2.3.1 takes a closer look at the motivation for this investigation. Subsection 2.3.2 examines a standard type of packing problems, namely the bin packing problem, in one, two, and three spatial dimensions. Subsection 2.3.3 considers two further problem types, namely the knapsack packing problem and the strip packing problem. Finally, Subsection 2.3.4 deals with some additional features and restrictions occuring within packing problems.

2.3.1 Motivation

Indentifying an optimization problem as a special case of another problem is an important issue in research on combinatorial optimization. The benefit of dealing with this is twofold: First, this allows to transfer solution approaches from one problem to the other: If a promising algorithm for the special case exists, the underlying concepts can probably be extended to the more general problem. On the other hand, a procedure for the general problem can be applied to the special case as well, eventually by additionally exploiting the special problem structure of the latter. Second, knowledge about relations between different problems is useful when establishing complexity proofs for specific problems because the core of a complexity proof is the polynomial-time transformation of one problem into another. Loosely speaking, if we know that some problem is NP-hard (and a few more technical assumptions are fulfilled), then a more general problem is NP-hard as well (cf. Garey and Johnson [84]).

With these points in mind, it is no surprise that the analysis of relationships between different problems plays an important role in the literature. The following list of references shows that a broad variety of combinatorial optimization problems have been shown to be special cases of project scheduling models.

Based on the ideas given in Schrage [178], Sprecher [190] formally describes how the job shop scheduling problem is included in the RCPSP as a special case. Moreover, Sprecher [190] shows that the flow shop problem and the open shop problem are special cases of the RCPSP. Schrage [178] additionally states that the RCPSP includes a variant of the two-dimensional cutting stock problem.

Sprecher [189] as well as de Reyck and Herroelen [42] consider the assembly line balancing problem. Sprecher [189] transforms it into an RCPSP with time-varying resource capacity while de Reyck and Herroelen [42] model it as an RCPSP with start-start precedence constraints (but with constant resource capacity).

Garey et al. [83] mention that their "resource-constrained scheduling problem" (which is an RCPSP where the durations of the non-dummy activities are equal to one) subsumes the bin packing problem.

Drexl and Salewski [65] express a school timetabling problem using project scheduling concepts including multiple modes, mode identity, partially renewable resources, minimal time lags, and a cost based objective.

Demeulemeester and Herroelen [49] show how concepts from production planning problems such as setup times and batches (cf., e.g., Jordan [108]) can be modeled using the RCPSP generalized by minimal time lags, release dates, deadlines, and resource availability varying with time.

The motivation to deal with the relationships between project scheduling and packing problems in this work is to point out the possibility to apply the project scheduling algorithms to be developed in the upcoming chapters to packing problems as well. The details given in the following subsections serve not only as proofs that the respective packing problems are special cases of project scheduling problems; they also provide a guideline how to formally capture some packing problem in order to employ a project scheduling method to solve it. Note, however, that this formalization alone does not necessarily lead to efficient packing procedures. Using the project scheduling methods as starting points, further exploitation of the special structures of the packing problems is still advisable.

2.3.2 Different Dimensions

We start our investigation with a look at the bin packing problem in one, two, and three dimensions. Generally, the bin packing problem is to pack a given number of boxes into a minimum number of identical containers (cf. Wottawa [212]). In order to allow a formal transformation into project scheduling models, we assume that the size of the boxes and containers is given in terms of discrete multiples of a basic length unit.

One Dimension

First, we consider the one-dimensional bin packing problem which can be stated as follows: We have B boxes with length l_b, $b = 1, \ldots, B$, which have to be packed into containers all of which are L units long. The objective is to use the minimum number of containers to pack all boxes, such that for each container the length limit is observed.

We remark here that also many other interpretations (and thus applications) are possible. An example is to view L as the limited weight capacity of the containers and l_b as the weight of box b, given that space is not scarce. We could also think of wooden planks which have to be cut into pieces of given lengths, and the objective would be to minimize the number of planks we'd have to buy. For the sake of simplicity, however, we will continue to use the notions "container" for the large objects and "box" for the small ones.

As outlined by Garey et al. [83], this problem can be transformed into the RCPSP as follows: For each box b, we define an activity j with processing time $p_j = 1$ and a request for the only renewable resource of $r_{j1} = l_b$ units. We have $J = B$ and $\mathcal{K}^\rho = \{1\}$. The constant capacity of the resource is given by $R_1^\rho = L$. There are no precedence relations between the activities (nevertheless, a dummy source and a dummy sink activity can be introduced). Performing an activity in the t-th period corresponds to packing the related box into the t-th container. Consequently, the minimal makespan corresponds to the minimal number of containers needed to pack all boxes.

Two Dimensions

Now we turn to the two-dimensional bin packing problem. Here, we have B boxes with length l_b and width w_b, $b = 1, \ldots, B$. They have to be packed into identical containers with length L and width W. Again, the objective is to use the minimum number of containers to pack all boxes, respecting the size of the containers.

In a rather simple approach for a similar problem, Schrage [178] proposed to reflect the two spatial dimensions with the resource dimension and the time dimension of an RCPSP with one renewable resource. Each box would correspond to a non-dummy activity, with a processing time equal to the width and a resource request equal to the length of the box. The problem of this idea is that a resulting schedule only contains start times (which correspond to the x-coordinates of the boxes), whereas the second dimension (the y-coordinates) needed for the packing (or cutting) pattern would not be considered. The reason for this is that the resource constraints of the RCPSP do not treat activities as geometric rectangles, that is, activities are not necessarily assigned to the same resource units over their processing times.

In order to obtain both x and y-coordinates as a result of our model-based approach, we have to adapt the above idea as follows: In addition to the time axis corresponding to the x-coordinates, we reflect the y-coordinates by L renewable resources $k = 1, \ldots, L$ (and hence $\mathcal{K}^\rho = \{1, \ldots, L\}$) with time-varying availability

$$R_k^\rho(t) = \begin{cases} 0, & \text{if } t = n \cdot (W+1) \text{ for some integer } n \geq 1 \\ 1, & \text{otherwise.} \end{cases}$$

Each "block" of consecutive nonzero resource capacity is related to a container.

Now we introduce an activity j for each box b. Each possible y-coordinate of some box b is reflected by a mode of the related activity j for which we obtain $M_j = L - l_b + 1$ different modes. The duration of any mode $m \in \mathcal{M}_j$ is given by $p_{jm} = w_b$. The (constant) request of mode m for resource $k \in \{1, \ldots, L\}$ is

$$r_{jmk} = \begin{cases} 1, & \text{if } k \in \{m, \ldots, m + l_b - 1\} \\ 0, & \text{otherwise.} \end{cases}$$

Having obtained a schedule containing start times and modes, the x-coordinate of the left bottom corner of a box is given by the start time s while the y-coordinate is given by the mode number m reduced by 1. From the makespan Z of the schedule, we compute the number of used containers as $\left\lceil \frac{Z}{W+1} \right\rceil$. Hence we have used the MRCPSP with time-varying resource capacity to comprise the two-dimensional bin packing problem.

The transformation idea is sketched out in Figure 2.3, where we have some box b with $l_b = w_b = 2$ and a container size of $L = 4$ and $W = 8$, resulting in three modes for the activity related to box b. Observe that this picture differs from the Gantt chart of Figure 2.2 because the y-axis now depicts 4 resources with a time-dependent capacity of 1 or 0 (and not one resource with capacity 4 or 0). Considering the example position of mode $m = 2$, we see that it starts at time $s = 3$ and requires only resources $k = 2$ and $k = 3$. This translates to box coordinates $x = 3$ $(= s)$ and $y = 1$ $(= m - 1)$.

So far, we assumed a fixed orientation for the boxes when they are packed. This assumption may be useful, especially when considering cutting problems

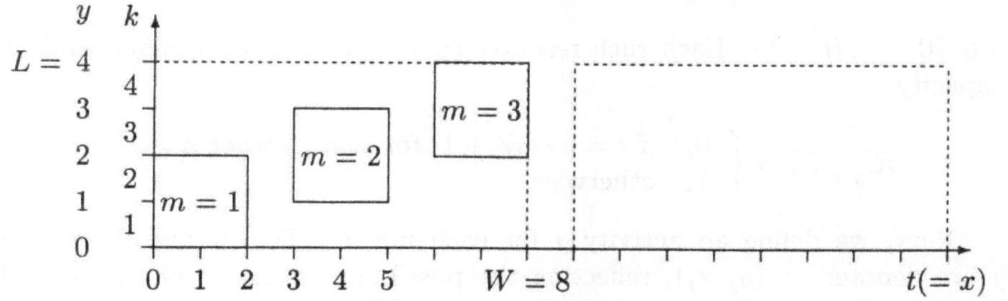

Figure 2.3: Transforming the two-dimensional bin packing problem

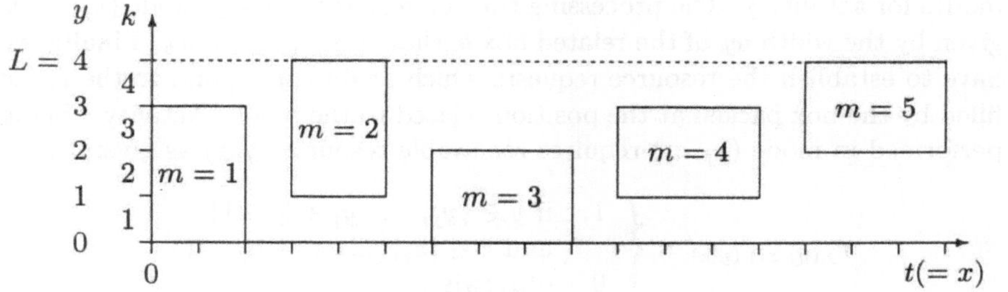

Figure 2.4: Two-dimensional bin packing problem — rotating boxes

with patterned raw material. In many cases, however, it is natural to allow the boxes to be rotated. We reflect rotation as follows: Technically, a rotated box b is obtained by swapping length l_b and width w_b. Following the mode construction above, this simply leads to additional modes that have to be considered. This idea is displayed in Figure 2.4.

Three Dimensions

Finally, we examine the three-dimensional bin packing problem. We have B boxes with length l_b, width w_b, and height h_b, $b = 1, \ldots, B$. They have to be packed into identical containers with length L, width W, and height H. The objective is to find the minimum number of containers to pack all boxes, observing the size of the containers.

Extending the approach for the two-dimensional case, we reflect the x-coordinate with the time-axis while both the y and z-coordinates are expressed using renewable resources. The project scheduling model under consideration is again the MRCPSP with renewable resource capacity varying with time.

We define $L \cdot H$ renewable resources. For the sake of comprehensibility, a resource will be referred to as a pair (y, z) with $y \in \{0, \ldots, L-1\}$ and

$z \in \{0, \ldots, H-1\}$. Each such resource (y, z) is assigned a time-dependent capacity

$$R^{\rho}_{(y,z)}(t) = \begin{cases} 0, & \text{if } t = n \cdot (W+1) \text{ for some integer } n \geq 1 \\ 1, & \text{otherwise.} \end{cases}$$

Next, we define an activity j for each box b. The modes of activity j are denoted as (y_j, z_j), reflecting the possible coordinates of the related box b in the length- and height-dimensions (the width-dimension is again captured by the activity's start time). Hence, we have $y_j \in \{0, \ldots, L - l_b\}$ and $z_j \in \{0, \ldots, H - h_b\}$, and we obtain $M_j = (L - l_b + 1) \cdot (H - h_b + 1)$ different modes for activity j. The processing time of activity j in any mode (y_j, z_j) is given by the width w_b of the related box b, that is, $p_{j,(y_j,z_j)} = w_b$. Finally, we have to establish the resource requests which again correspond to the space filled by the box packed at the position related to the mode. Activity j being performed in mode (y_j, z_j) requires renewable resource (y, z) as given by

$$r_{j,(y_j,z_j),(y,z)} = \begin{cases} 1, & \text{if } y \in \{y_j, \ldots, y_j + l_b - 1\} \\ & \text{and } z \in \{z_j, \ldots, z_j + h_b - 1\} \\ 0, & \text{otherwise.} \end{cases}$$

Clearly, if we want to allow the box to be rotated in some or all planes, we introduce additional modes in analogy to the two-dimensional case.

Given a schedule containing a start time and a mode for each activity j, the x-coordinate of the left bottom front corner of the related box is given by the start time s_j while the y and z-coordinates are given by the mode (y_j, z_j). The number of containers needed is again given as in the two-dimensional case.

2.3.3 Different Types

Up to now, we have considered only the bin packing problem which consists of packing a number of boxes into a minimum number of identical containers. This subsection discusses two other basic problem settings that are important with respect to real-world applications, namely the knapsack packing problem and the strip packing problem. Another problem class, the pallet loading problem, is not treated here in more detail because it is, according the general characterization of Wottawa [212], merely a knapsack packing problem with identical boxes. Further variants of the pallet loading problem can be found in Liu and Hsiao [136] as well as Morabito and Morales [148].

Knapsack Packing Problem

The knapsack packing problem (cf. Wottawa [212]) considers only one container. We have B boxes, and each box $b = 1, \ldots, B$ is associated with a value γ_b. The objective is to select boxes to be packed into the container such that the sum of the values of the packed boxes is maximal. Again, of course, the size of the container must be observed. Two special cases should be briefly mentioned: First, the objective to pack as many boxes as possible is obtained from defining $\gamma_b = 1$ for all boxes $b = 1, \ldots, B$. Second, the objective to use as much space of the container as possible is achieved by letting the value of each box be equal to its volume. For the three-dimensional case, e.g., we would set $\gamma_b = l_b \cdot w_b \cdot h_b$ for all boxes $b = 1, \ldots, B$.

We express the knapsack packing problem in terms of project scheduling concepts analogously to the bin packing problem (of the same dimension). We only need a few modifications: In addition to the modes of an activity defined for the bin packing problem, we need one more mode reflecting that the related box is not packed. This mode has a processing time of 0 periods and does not require the renewable resources corresponding to the container space. Next, we introduce a nonrenewable resource. The request of each of the new modes (which indicate that the related box is not packed) for this nonrenewable resource is equal to the value of that box. For the remaining modes (which imply that the related box is selected to be packed), we define a nonrenewable resource request of 0 units. As we have only one container, we redefine the renewable resource capacities as being constant and equal to 1 if we are dealing with two or three dimensions (in the one-dimensional case, we keep the constant capacity of L units). The width of the container is secured by imposing a deadline on the dummy sink activity. In the one-dimensional case, we set $\overline{\delta}_{J+1} = 1$, otherwise we have $\overline{\delta}_{J+1} = W$. Now we use objective (2.21) with $c_k^\nu = 1$ to minimize the consumption of the nonrenewable resource k. Note that this minimizes the sum of the values of the boxes not being packed, which is equivalent to the original value maximization of the knapsack packing problem.

Summing up the transformations given above, the knapsack packing problem (with up to three dimensions) has been shown to be a special case of the MRCPSP with a deadline and a nonrenewable resource based objective (and with constant renewable resource availabilities). Clearly, the knapsack packing problem can be extended by allowing more than one container (but still a limited number of containers). This can be modeled by using the time-varying renewable resource capacities as for the bin packing problem, but with zero capacities for periods later than those corresponding to the given containers.

Note that in the one-dimensional case, the knapsack packing problem coincides with the classical knapsack problem (where we would speak of weights instead of lengths). This implies that also the classical knapsack problem is a special case of multi-mode project scheduling with resource-based objective. It should be emphasized, however, that the more general multi-dimensional knapsack problem (see Chu and Beasley [32]) is not a packing problem in our sense because there the multiple knapsack constraints are independent and not linked like the spatial dimensions in the packing problems discussed here.

Strip Packing Problem

In the strip packing problem (cf. Wottawa [212]), we have one container of infinite length. In the two-dimensional case, the width W of the container is given; in the three-dimensional case, also its height H is given. The objective is to pack a given number of boxes such that the used length of the container is minimal. As in the bin packing problem, all boxes have to be packed. Note that this problem type is considered only for two or three dimensions because the one-dimensional case is trivial: There, the used container length would be equal to the sum of the lengths of the boxes.

In the two and three-dimensional cases, the boxes correspond to activities that are defined as for the bin packing problem. Again, one coordinate is related to the start times while the remaining one or two coordinates are reflected by modes. In contrast to the bin packing problem, the renewable resources have a constant availability of one unit per period. Now the makespan corresponds to the used container length. Consequently, the strip packing problem can be modeled by the standard MRCPSP (with constant resource capacities).

Table 2.2 summarizes the transformations of packing problems into project scheduling problems sketched out in this and the previous subsection. For each of the three considered packing problem types and each related (non-trivial) dimension, we state which of the variants and extensions of the basic RCPSP are needed to capture the constraints and objective. So far, we have shown that the major packing problem types are special cases of project scheduling models. Recall that this implies that also the related non-guillotine cutting problem types are included in the respective project scheduling models.

2.3.4 Additional Features

Having discussed the basic packing problem types and dimensions, we now consider some extensions of the basic problems which frequently occur in practice.

If some box is heavy, it may be required that it is not packed on top of some other box. This case is relevant especially in the three-dimensional bin packing and knapsack packing problems. We reflect this requirement by considering only those modes that are associated with a position on the bottom of the container.

Problem	*dim.*	*modes*	*deadline*	*capacities*	*objective*
bin packing	1	single	no	constant	makespan
	2	multi	no	time-varying	makespan
	3	multi	no	time-varying	makespan
knapsack packing	1	multi	yes	constant	resource
	2	multi	yes	constant	resource
	3	multi	yes	constant	resource
strip packing	2	multi	no	constant	makespan
	3	multi	no	constant	makespan

Table 2.2: Packing problems as special cases of project scheduling models

Similarly to the previous situation, it may not be allowed to pack other boxes on top of some box, e.g., because of its fragile content. This can be modeled by adjusting the resource requests of the activity corresponding to that box. This activity would require not only the resources that correspond to the space filled by this box but also the resources reflecting the space above it.

Considering knapsack packing problems, each box may be associated with a certain weight, and a weight limit for the container may have to be observed. Such a weight limit can easily be incorporated by introducing a nonrenewable resource with a capacity corresponding to the weight limit. The request of an activity for that resource is defined as follows: The mode corresponding to the related box not being packed is associated with a request of zero units. All other modes obtain a request corresponding to the weight of the box.

Chapter 3

Exact Multi-Mode Algorithms

Having discussed several models for resource-constrained project scheduling in the previous chapter, we now deal with scheduling algorithms which compute optimal schedules for given projects. Due to the NP-hardness of the RCPSP and its extensions, however, we cannot expect the exact algorithms to determine optimal solutions for problems of larger size in reasonable computation times. Consequently, heuristic procedures are needed for application to real-world projects. Nevertheless, there are two important reasons for dealing with exact approaches: First, they allow to determine optimal solutions for (smaller) test problems which provide a basis for the evaluation of heuristics. Second, the knowledge gained from designing efficient exact procedures is useful when developing heuristics, as will be demonstrated in the remainder of this work.

Our main motivation for considering exact algorithms here is to obtain benchmark solutions for test instances. In the following chapters, we will evaluate heuristics for both the single-mode and the multi-mode case. In this chapter, we deal with exact procedures for the multi-mode case that provide us with optimal solutions for test instances of the MRCPSP. As the single-mode RCPSP is a special case of the MRCPSP, these algorithms can also be used to compute optimal schedules for test instances of the RCPSP. Therefore, we only deal with the MRCPSP here and do not separately consider the single-mode case. We present a comparison of exact solution methodologies for the MRCPSP. Clearly, due to the NP-hardness of the MRCPSP, computing optimal (benchmark) solutions for large test instance sets can be a very time-consuming task. Hence, our goal is to determine the most efficient exact procedure.

The first and straightforward idea to obtain optimal solutions is to implement the integer programming formulation of the MRCPSP given by (2.7)–(2.12) in a modeling language and to solve it using mathematical standard software. Such an approach is documented in Appendix B. Unfortunately, however, the preliminary computational test results on the basis of standard instances were very disappointing. This mathematical programming approach is not at all well suited for computing benchmark solutions because even for very small project instances the computation times are much too high. As a consequence, we consider tailored exact algorithms of the branch-and-bound type. Generally speaking, branch-and-bound methods enumerate the set of solutions by "branching," which essentially means to successively fix decision variables. The branching schemes are accelerated by "bounding rules" which state conditions under which certain parts of the search space need not be (explicitly) enumerated without missing an optimal solution.

A broad variety of branch-and-bound procedures have been proposed for optimally solving the single-mode RCPSP, we refer to Bartusch et al. [12], Brucker et al. [29], Christofides et al. [31] (cf. also the comments on that approach in Demeulemeester et al. [53]), Demeulemeester and Herroelen [48, 51], Dorndorf et al. [58], Klein and Scholl [116], Mingozzi et al. [145], Möhring et al. [147], Radermacher [170], Sprecher [191], Stinson et al. [195], and Talbot and Patterson [198]. For the multi-mode case, exact algorithms have been suggested by Patterson et al. [163], Speranza and Vercellis [188], Sprecher and Drexl [192], Sprecher et al. [193], and Talbot [197]. We remark here that Hartmann and Sprecher [96] have shown that the procedure proposed in Speranza and Vercellis [188] is not correct, that is, in some cases, it finds only suboptimal solutions or even fails to determine an existing feasible solution.

This chapter starts with the discussion of existing enumeration methods for the MRCPSP as well as a new approach in Section 3.1. The algorithms are presented in a unified framework that allows to point out the similarities and differences between the algorithms. Section 3.2 then gives an overview of acceleration schemes that enable us to make the enumeration methods more efficient. In Section 3.3, we analyze the sets of schedules that are enumerated by the different procedures. Finally, Section 3.4 summarizes our computational experience with the algorithms and points out the currently most promising branch-and-bound algorithm for the MRCPSP.[1]

3.1 Enumeration Schemes

This section is devoted to enumeration procedures for the MRCPSP. In the first two subsections, we summarize the two algorithms that have been proposed in the literature for this problem. Then we present a new algorithm

[1]The comparison study of this chapter can also be found in Hartmann and Drexl [93].

in Subsection 3.1.3 using a description which points out the similarities and differences to the former procedures.

3.1.1 The Precedence Tree

Patterson et al. [163] proposed an algorithm guided by the so-called precedence tree. The basic ideas of this approach date back to the earlier work of Talbot [197]. Restructuring this methodology, Sprecher [190] and Sprecher and Drexl [192] developed a new procedure based on the precedence tree and improved it by including new bounding criteria (cf. Section 3.2).

We present a simplified formulation of the precedence tree algorithm as given by Sprecher [190] and Sprecher and Drexl [192]. The procedure begins with starting the dummy source activity at time 0. At each level g of the branch-and-bound tree, we determine the set SJ_g of the currently scheduled activities and the set EJ_g of the eligible activities, that is, those activities the predecessors of which are already scheduled. Then we select an eligible activity j_g and, subsequently, a mode m_{j_g} of this activity. Now we compute the earliest precedence and resource feasible start time s_{j_g} that is not less than the start time assigned on the previous level of the search tree. Then we branch to the next level. If the dummy sink activity is eligible, we have found a complete schedule. In this case, backtracking to the previous level occurs. Here, we select the next untested mode. If none exists, we select the next untested eligible activity. If we have tested all eligible activities in all available modes, we track another step back. More formally, we have:

Algorithm 3.1 *(Precedence tree)*

Step 1: (Initialization)
$g := 0;\ j_0 := 0;\ m_{j_0} := 1;\ s_{j_0} := 0;\ SJ_0 := \emptyset;$

Step 2: (Compute eligible activities)
$g := g + 1;\ SJ_g := SJ_{g-1} \cup \{j_{g-1}\};$
$EJ_g := \{j \in \{1, \ldots, J+1\} \backslash SJ_g \mid \mathcal{P}_j \subseteq SJ_g\};$
if $J + 1 \in EJ_g$ then store current solution and go to Step 5;

Step 3: (Select next activity)
if no untested eligible activity is left in EJ_g then go to Step 5,
else select untested activity $j_g \in EJ_g$;

Step 4: (Select next mode and compute start time)
if no untested mode is left in $\mathcal{M}_{j_g}$ then go to Step 3,
else select untested $m_{j_g} \in \mathcal{M}_{j_g}$;
if a conflict w.r.t. a nonrenewable resource occurs
then go to Step 4;
compute earliest precedence and resource feasible start time s_{j_g}
with $s_{j_g} \geq s_{j_{g-1}}$;
go to Step 2;

Step 5: (Backtracking)
$g := g - 1$; if $g = 0$ then STOP, else go to Step 4.

Note that each combination of an eligible activity and a related mode corresponds to a descendant of the current node in the branch-and-bound tree or, as it is called here, precedence tree. Each branch from the root to a leaf of the precedence tree corresponds to a permutation of the set of activities $j_1, \dots, j_J$ which is precedence feasible in the sense that each predecessor of a job j_g has a smaller index in the sequence than j_g.

The above algorithmic formulation using steps together with "go to" commands is common practice for branch-and-bound methods in the operations research literature. It is, however, also possible to reformulate it as a recursive procedure without "go to" commands, as it would be done in computer science:

```
PROCEDURE BranchToNextLevel;
BEGIN
    g := g + 1; SJ_g := SJ_{g-1} ∪ {j_{g-1}};
    EJ_g := {j ∈ {1, ..., J + 1}\SJ_g | P_j ⊆ SJ_g};
    IF J + 1 ∈ EJ_g THEN
    BEGIN
        g := g - 1;
        RETURN;
    END;
    WHILE untested eligible activity is left in EJ_g DO
    BEGIN
        select untested activity j_g ∈ EJ_g;
        WHILE untested mode is left in M_{j_g} DO
        BEGIN
            select untested mode m_{j_g} ∈ M_{j_g};
            compute earliest precedence and resource feasible
            start time s_{j_g} with s_{j_g} ≥ s_{j_{g-1}};
            IF NOT conflict w.r.t. a nonrenewable resource THEN
                BranchToNextLevel;
        END;
    END;
    g := g - 1;
END;
```

BEGIN
$g := 0$; $j_0 := 0$; $m_{j_0} := 1$; $s_{j_0} := 0$; $SJ_0 := \emptyset$;
BranchToNextLevel;
END.

Note that this formulation is equivalent to the stepwise notation of Algorithm 3.1. In the following subsections, we will restrict ourselves to formulations using steps and "go to" commands.

Finally, we remark that the precedence tree algorithm can also be applied to the MRCPSP generalized by time-varying renewable resource availabilities without having to modify the procedure (cf. Sprecher [190]). This does not hold for the two enumeration schemes presented next. Furthermore, Sprecher [190] has shown that the precedence tree procedure as described above is not applicable to two other model extensions, namely maximal time lags and renewable resource requests varying with time.

3.1.2 Mode and Delay Alternatives

In this subsection we summarize the branch-and-bound approach proposed by Sprecher et al. [193]. Introducing the notion of a mode alternative, it extends the concept of delay alternatives used by Demeulemeester and Herroelen [48] for the (single-mode) RCPSP.

In contrast to Algorithm 3.1, here each level g of the branch-and-bound tree is associated with a fixed time instant t_g (decision point) at which activities may be started. Consequently, we use a different definition of eligible activities in this algorithm: A currently unscheduled activity j is called eligible at time t_g if all of its predecessors $i \in \mathcal{P}_j$ are scheduled with a finish time $f_i \leq t_g$. Furthermore, an activity j scheduled in mode m_j with start time s_j is said to be in process at time t_g if we have $s_j \leq t_g < s_j + p_{jm_j}$.

The proceeding at the current level g of the branch-and-bound tree is as follows: We determine the new decision point t_g as the earliest finish time of the activities currently in process. Note that, due to the constant availability levels of the renewable resources, only finish times of scheduled activities need to be considered for starting unscheduled ones. Using the set FJ_g of the activities that are finished at or before the decision point, we compute the set EJ_g of the eligible activities. Then we (temporarily) start those eligible activities at the decision point that have already been assigned a mode at a previous level of the search tree. If there are eligible jobs that have not yet been assigned a mode, that is, if $EJ_g \backslash EJ_{g-1}$ is not empty, then we compute the set $\mathcal{SOMA}_g$ of mode alternatives: A *mode alternative* is a mapping $\mathcal{MA}_g$ which assigns each activity $j \in EJ_g \backslash EJ_{g-1}$ a mode $\mathcal{MA}_g(j) = m_j \in \mathcal{M}_j$. Selecting a mode alternative, we can (temporarily) start the remaining eligible activities at the decision point as well. Having started all eligible activities by adding them to the set JIP_g of the activities in process, we may have caused a resource conflict. Thus, we compute the set $\mathcal{SODA}_g$ of the minimal delay alternatives according to the following definition: A *delay alternative* $\mathcal{DA}_g$ is a subset of JIP_g such that for each renewable resource $k \in \mathcal{K}^\rho$ it is

$$\sum_{j \in JIP_g \setminus \mathcal{DA}_g} r_{jm_jk} \leq R_k^\rho.$$

A delay alternative $\mathcal{DA}_g$ is called *minimal* if no proper subset of $\mathcal{DA}_g$ is a delay alternative. We select a minimal delay alternative and remove the activities to be delayed from the current partial schedule. Note, if no resource conflict occurs, the only minimal delay alternative is the empty set. We store the start time s_j of an activity j to be delayed in s_{gj}^{old} because we have to restore the information during backtracking. Then we branch to the next level and compute the next decision point. If we have completed a schedule, we perform a backtracking step and test the next minimal delay alternative or, if all have been tested, the next mode alternative. Formally, the algorithm can be described as follows:

Algorithm 3.2 *(Mode and delay alternatives)*

Step 1: (Initialization)
$g := 0$; $t_0 := 0$; $JIP_0 := \{0\}; FJ_0 := \emptyset$; $m_0 := 1$; $s_0 := 0$;
$EJ_0 := \emptyset$; $\mathcal{DA}_0 := \emptyset$;

Step 2: (Compute new decision point and eligible activities)
$g := g + 1$; $t_g := \min\{s_j + d_{jm_j} \mid j \in JIP_{g-1}\}$;
$FJ_g := FJ_{g-1} \cup \{j \in JIP_{g-1} \mid s_j + d_{jm_j} = t_g\}$;
$EJ_g := \{j \in \{1, \ldots, J+1\} \setminus (FJ_g \cup JIP_{g-1}) \mid \mathcal{P}_j \subseteq FJ_g\}$;
$JIP_g := JIP_{g-1} \setminus FJ_g \cup EJ_g$;
if $J + 1 \in EJ_g$ then store current solution and go to Step 7;
for each $j \in \mathcal{DA}_{g-1}$ update $s_j := t_g$;

Step 3: (Compute mode alternatives)
if $EJ_g \setminus EJ_{g-1} = \emptyset$ then $\mathcal{SOMA}_g := \emptyset$ and go to Step 5,
else $\mathcal{SOMA}_g := SetOfModeAlternatives(EJ_g \setminus EJ_{g-1})$;

Step 4: (Select next mode alternative)
if no untested mode alternative is left in $\mathcal{SOMA}_g$
then go to Step 7,
else select untested $\mathcal{MA}_g \in \mathcal{SOMA}_g$;
for each $j \in EJ_g \setminus EJ_{g-1}$ update $m_j := \mathcal{MA}_g(j)$ and $s_j := t_g$;
if a conflict w.r.t. a nonrenewable resource occurs
then go to Step 4;

Step 5: (Compute delay alternatives)
$\mathcal{SODA}_g := SetOfMinimalDelayAlternatives(JIP_g)$;

Step 6: (Select next delay alternative)
if no untested minimal delay alternative is left in $\mathcal{SODA}_g$
then go to Step 4,
else select untested $\mathcal{DA}_g \in \mathcal{SODA}_g$; $JIP_g := JIP_g \backslash \mathcal{DA}_g$;
for each $j \in \mathcal{DA}_g$ store $s_{gj}^{old} := s_j$; go to Step 2;

Step 7: (Backtracking)
$g := g - 1$; if $g = 0$ then STOP,
else for each $j \in \mathcal{DA}_g$ restore $s_j := s_{gj}^{old}$; $JIP_g := JIP_g \cup \mathcal{DA}_g$;
go to Step 6.

Observe that each combination of a mode alternative and a related minimal delay alternative corresponds to a descendant of the current node in the branch-and-bound tree. Clearly, this procedure is different from Algorithm 3.1 in that sets of activities instead of (single) activities are started at each level of the branch-and-bound tree. Moreover, here the time instant at which activities may be started is determined before the activities themselves are selected. Finally, in contrast to Algorithm 3.1, this approach allows to withdraw scheduling decisions at the current level that have been made at a lower level.

3.1.3 Mode and Extension Alternatives

This subsection is devoted to a new branch-and-bound approach for solving the MRCPSP. Using again the concept of mode alternatives developed by Sprecher et al. [193], we introduce extension alternatives to construct partial schedules. A similar way to extend partial schedules has been proposed by Stinson et al. [195] for the single-mode case.

As in Algorithm 3.2, each level g of the branch-and-bound tree is associated with a decision point t_g, a set JIP_g of the activities in process, a set FJ_g of the finished activities, and a set EJ_g of the eligible activities. Again, we use a mode alternative to fix the modes of those eligible activities that have not yet been assigned a mode. Then we extend the current partial schedule by starting a subset of the eligible activities at the decision point without violating the renewable resource constraints. More precisely, an *extension alternative* $\mathcal{EA}_g$ is a subset of the eligible set for which we have

$$\sum_{j \in JIP_g \cup \mathcal{EA}_g} r_{jm_jk} \leq R_k^\rho$$

for each renewable resource $k \in \mathcal{K}^\rho$ and, moreover, $\mathcal{EA}_g \neq \emptyset$ if $JIP_g = \emptyset$. Note, in order to secure that the algorithm terminates, we may only have nonempty extension alternatives if no activities are in process. However, if there are currently activities in process, the empty set is always an extension alternative which must be tested in order to guarantee optimality.

At the current level g of the branch-and-bound tree we proceed as follows: We determine the new decision point and compute the set of the eligible activities. Then we determine the set of mode alternatives $\mathcal{SOMA}_g$ for fixing the modes of the eligible activities that have not been eligible before, that is, those activities the modes of which have not yet been fixed. After selecting a mode alternative $\mathcal{MA}_g$, we compute the set of extension alternatives $\mathcal{SOEA}_g$. Finally, we select an extension alternative $\mathcal{EA}_g$ and start the corresponding activities before branching to the next level. The backtracking mechanism equals the one of Algorithm 3.2. Formally, we can describe the algorithm as follows:

Algorithm 3.3 *(Mode and extension alternatives)*

Step 1: (Initialization)
$g := 0;\ t_0 := 0;\ JIP_0 := \{0\}; FJ_0 := \emptyset;\ m_0 := 1;\ s_0 := 0;$
$EJ_0 := \emptyset;$

Step 2: (Compute new decision point and eligible activities)
$g := g + 1;\ t_g := \min\{s_j + d_{jm_j} \mid j \in JIP_{g-1}\};$
$FJ_g := FJ_{g-1} \cup \{j \in JIP_{g-1} \mid s_j + d_{jm_j} = t_g\};$
$EJ_g := \{j \in \{1, \ldots, J+1\} \backslash (FJ_g \cup JIP_{g-1}) \mid \mathcal{P}_j \subseteq FJ_g\};$
$JIP_g := JIP_{g-1} \backslash FJ_g;$
if $J + 1 \in EJ_g$ then store current solution and go to Step 7;

Step 3: (Compute mode alternatives)
if $EJ_g \backslash EJ_{g-1} = \emptyset$ then $\mathcal{SOMA}_g := \emptyset$ and go to Step 5,
else $\mathcal{SOMA}_g := \mathit{SetOfModeAlternatives}(EJ_g \backslash EJ_{g-1});$

Step 4: (Select next mode alternative)
if no untested mode alternative is left in $\mathcal{SOMA}_g$
then go to Step 7,
else select untested $\mathcal{MA}_g \in \mathcal{SOMA}_g;$
for each $j \in EJ_g \backslash EJ_{g-1}$ update $m_j := \mathcal{MA}_g(j);$
if a conflict w.r.t. a nonrenewable resource occurs
then go to Step 4;

Step 5: (Compute extension alternatives)
$\mathcal{SOEA}_g := \mathit{SetOfExtensionAlternatives}(EJ_g, JIP_g);$

Step 6: (Select next extension alternative)
if no untested extension alternative is left in $\mathcal{SOEA}_g$
then go to Step 4,
else select untested $\mathcal{EA}_g \in \mathcal{SOEA}_g;\ JIP_g := JIP_g \cup \mathcal{EA}_g;$
for each $j \in \mathcal{EA}_g$ update $s_j := t_g$; go to Step 2;

Step 7: (Backtracking)
$g := g - 1$; if $g = 0$ then STOP, else $JIP_g := JIP_g \backslash \mathcal{EA}_g$;
go to Step 6.

Each combination of a mode alternative and a related extension alternative corresponds to a descendant of the current node in the branch-and-bound tree. Note that this procedure is different from Algorithm 3.2: Whereas the latter includes the possibility to delay activities that have been started on a lower than the current level, the new approach does not allow to withdraw a scheduling decision of a lower level. As a consequence, we may not restrict the search to maximal extension alternatives while we do not lose optimality when considering only minimal delay alternatives.

3.2 Bounding Rules

This section summarizes bounding criteria which speed up the enumeration procedures of the previous section. While most of the rules are known from the literature, we also present a new one and transfer some well-known ones to those enumeration schemes they have not yet been defined for. For the sake of shortness, we have omitted the correctness proofs of those rules that are known from the literature.

3.2.1 Time Window Based Rules

The first bounding criterion makes use of time windows as determined in Subsection 2.1.2 (cf. also the remarks on modifications for the multi-mode case in Subsection 2.2.1). Sprecher [190] and Sprecher et al. [193] have employed this rule in their algorithms for solving the MRCPSP. Given an upper bound on the makespan of the project, we use the modes of shortest duration and derive the latest finish time LF_j for each activity j by backward recursion. If a procedure has found the first or an improved schedule with a makespan Z, the latest finish times are recalculated by $LF_j := LF_j - (LF_{J+1} - Z + 1)$ for $j = 1, \ldots, J+1$. From the definition of the latest finish times we can derive the following bounding rule:

Bounding Rule 3.1 *(Basic Time Window Rule) If there is a scheduled activity the assigned finish time of which exceeds the latest finish time, then the current partial schedule cannot be completed with a makespan less than the best currently known.*

Using the definition of the time window and explicitly considering multiple modes, Sprecher [190] has developed the following rule for the precedence tree algorithm:

Bounding Rule 3.2 *(Non-Delayability Rule for Algorithm 3.1) If an eligible activity cannot be feasibly scheduled in any mode in the current partial schedule wit out exceeding its latest finish time, then no other eligible activity needs to be examined on this level.*

Taking into account the differences between the precedence tree procedure on one hand and the algorithms based on mode alternatives on the other, we can adapt Bounding Rule 3.2 as follows:

Remark 3.1 *(Non-Delayability Rule for Algorithms 3.2 and 3.3) If an eligible activity the mode of which has not yet been fixed cannot be started in the mode with the shortest duration at the current decision point without exceeding its latest finish time, then no mode alternative needs to be examined at the current level.*

3.2.2 Preprocessing

This subsection is devoted to two bounding rules which can be implemented by preprocessing. The first one has originally been proposed by Sprecher et al. [193]. It uses the following definitions: A mode is called *non-executable* if its execution would violate the renewable or nonrenewable resource constraints in any schedule. A mode is called *inefficient* if its duration is not shorter and its resource requests are not less than those of another mode of the same activity. A nonrenewable resource is called *redundant* if the sum of the maximal requests of the activities for this resource does not exceed its availability. Clearly, non-executable and inefficient modes as well as redundant nonrenewable resources may be excluded from the project data without loosing optimality. Sprecher et al. [193] describe several interaction effects appearing when modes or nonrenewable resources are removed. E.g., eliminating a redundant nonrenewable resource may cause inefficiency of a mode. Hence, they propose the following way to prepare the input data:

Bounding Rule 3.3 *(Data Reduction) The project data can be adapted as follows:*
Step 1: Remove all non-executable modes from the project data.
Step 2: Delete the redundant nonrenewable resources.
Step 3: Eliminate all inefficient modes.
Step 4: If any mode has been erased within Step 3, go to Step 2.

The next bounding rule has especially been designed for instances with nonrenewable resources. It has been proposed by Drexl [59] for a less general framework.

Bounding Rule 3.4 *(Nonrenewable Resource Rule) If scheduling each currently unscheduled activity in the mode with the lowest request for a nonrenewable resource would exceed the capacity of this nonrenewable resource, then the current partial schedule cannot be feasibly completed.*

Sprecher [190] adapted the rule to the MRCPSP and improved the effect by reformulating it as a static rule. Before an algorithm is executed, the project data is adjusted as follows: Defining $r_{jk}^{\min}$ as the minimal request of activity j for nonrenewable resource k, we update

$$r_{jmk} := r_{jmk} - r_{jk}^{\min} \qquad \text{for } j \in \mathcal{J},\ m \in \mathcal{M}_j,\ k \in \mathcal{K}^{\nu} \tag{3.1}$$

$$R_k^{\nu} := R_k^{\nu} - \sum_{j=1}^{J} r_{jk}^{\min} \qquad \text{for } k \in \mathcal{K}^{\nu}. \tag{3.2}$$

3.2.3 Dominating Sets of Schedules

The following three bounding rules make use of a classification of the set of schedules. Using schedule properties, they essentially state conditions under which a partial schedule that does not fulfill such a property can be skipped without completing it.

Semi-Active Schedules

The notion of semi-active schedules as formally defined by Sprecher et al. [194] for the single-mode case can be straightforwardly extended to the multi-mode case: A *left shift* of an activity within a given schedule is a reduction of its finish time without changing its mode and without changing the modes or finish times of the other activities, such that the resulting schedule is both precedence and resource feasible. A *local left shift* is a left shift which is obtainable by one or more successively applied left shifts of one period. A schedule is called *semi-active* if none of the activities can be locally left shifted. Following French [82], we can state that if there is an optimal schedule for a given instance, then there is an optimal semi-active schedule. This result is exploited by the following rule which has been employed by Sprecher [190] and Sprecher et al. [193] for the multi-mode case.

Bounding Rule 3.5 *(Local Left Shift Rule) If an activity that has been started at the current level of the branch-and-bound tree can be locally left shifted without changing its mode, then the current partial schedule needs not be completed.*

Tight and Mode-Minimal Schedules

Additionally allowing a mode change of the activity to be shifted, Sprecher et al. [193] defined the notion of a multi-mode left shift: Within a given schedule, a *multi-mode left shift* is a reduction of an activity's finish time without changing the modes or finish times of the other activities, such that the resulting schedule is feasible. A schedule is called *tight* if no multi-mode left shift can be performed. The notion of tight schedules has been introduced by Speranza and Vercellis [188].

Another operation on a schedule of an MRCPSP instance has been introduced by Sprecher et al. [193]: A *mode reduction* on an activity is a reduction of its mode number without changing its finish time and without violating the constraints or changing the modes and finish times of the other activities. A schedule is called *mode-minimal* if there is no activity a mode reduction can be performed on.

Note that there are tight schedules which are not mode-minimal and vice versa. Obviously, if there is an optimal schedule for a given instance, then there is an optimal schedule which is both tight and mode-minimal. Consequently, the following rule proposed by Sprecher et al. [193] induces backtracking when it is certain that no tight or mode-minimal schedule can be obtained from the current partial schedule.

Bounding Rule 3.6 *(Multi-Mode Rule) Assume that no currently unscheduled activity will be started before the finish time of a scheduled activity j when the current partial schedule is completed. If a multi-mode left shift or a mode reduction of activity j with resulting mode $m'_j \in \mathcal{M}_j$ can be performed on the current partial schedule and, moreover, if $r_{jm'_jk} \leq r_{jm_jk}$ holds for each nonrenewable resource $k \in \mathcal{K}^\nu$, then the current partial schedule needs not be completed.*

Clearly, if no multi-mode left shift can be applied, then a local left shift cannot be applied either. Nevertheless, it is useful to check for both types of left shifts separately according to the previous two bounding rules. Observe that we check for a local left shift when the corresponding activity has just been started. However, we can only check for a multi-mode left shift if the corresponding activity has already finished. Otherwise, as outlined by Hartmann and Sprecher [96], we would lose optimality. Consequently, the Local Left Shift Rule is not superflous as the exclusion of a partial schedule due to a feasible local left shift can be detected on a lower level of the branch-and-bound tree than the same (mode-preserving) multi-mode left-shift.

Order-Monotonous Schedules

The next operation and the related category of schedules are new: Denoting the finish time of a scheduled activity j with $f_j = s_j + p_{jm_j}$, we consider two activities i and j with $i > j$ that are successively processed within a schedule, that is, $f_i = s_j$. Now an *order swap* is defined as the interchange of these two activities by assigning new start and finish times $s'_j := s_i$ and

$f_i' := f_j$, respectively. Thereby, the precedence and resource constraints may not be violated, and the modes and start times of the other activities may not be changed. A schedule in which no order swap can be performed is called *order monotonous*. Clearly, it is sufficient to enumerate only order monotonous schedules. It should be noted that there are schedules which are tight and mode-minimal but not order monotonous and vice versa. We apply the following bounding criterion:

Bounding Rule 3.7 *(Order Swap Rule) Consider a scheduled activity the finish time of which is less than or equal to any start time that may be assigned when completing the current partial schedule. If an order swap on this activity together with any of those activities that finish at its start time can be performed, then the current partial schedule needs not be completed.*

Proof. Obvious. □

In analogy to the extension of the left shift concept to the multi-mode case, the definition of the order swap can easily be generalized by allowing a mode change of the activities to be swapped. However, preliminary computational results have shown that the additional effort that would be necessary to check the assumptions completely consumes the acceleration effect.

3.2.4 The Cutset Rule

The following bounding method stores information about already evaluated partial schedules. During the search process, the rule compares the current partial schedule with the stored data. If it can be proven that any solution obtainable from the current partial schedule cannot be better than a solution obtainable from a previously evaluated partial schedule the information of which has been stored, then backtracking may be performed.

Bounding criteria based on stored information of already evaluated partial schedules have been employed by Stinson et al. [195] and Demeulemeester and Herroelen [48] for the single-mode case. Defining a *cutset* of a partial schedule PS as the set of the activities scheduled in PS, Sprecher and Drexl [192] proposed the following rule for their algorithm for the MRCPSP:

Bounding Rule 3.8 *(Cutset Rule for Algorithm 3.1) Let $\overline{PS}$ denote a previously evaluated partial schedule with cutset $CS(\overline{PS})$, maximal finish time $f^{\max}(\overline{PS})$ and leftover capacities $R_k^\nu(\overline{PS})$ of the nonrenewable resources $k \in \mathcal{K}^\nu$. Let PS be the current partial schedule considered to be extended by scheduling some activity j with start time s_j. If we have $CS(PS) = CS(\overline{PS})$, $s_j \geq f^{\max}(\overline{PS})$ and $R_k^\nu(PS) \leq R_k^\nu(\overline{PS})$ for all $k \in \mathcal{K}^\nu$, then PS needs not be completed.*

When all continuations of the current partial schedule have been examined, the cutset information related to the partial schedule that is required for Bounding Rule 3.8 is stored.

If the concept of mode alternatives is used, the rule has to be adapted. Clearly, each scheduling decision made in the current partial schedule has to be reflected in the data to be stored. Having selected an extension alternative in Algorithm 3.3, the modes of some activities that are not contained in the current partial schedule may be fixed within each of its continuations. Consequently, we must store the set of those activities the modes of which are fixed and the related modes in addition to the data that is stored according to Bounding Rule 3.8 for the precedence tree procedure. The cutset rule proposed by Demeulemeester and Herroelen [48] can be generalized to the multi-mode case in a similar way and can then be employed in Algorithm 3.2. Unfortunately, however, adapting the Cutset Rule to Algorithms 3.2 and 3.3 does not speed up these procedures. Roughly speaking, this is due to the fact that we have to store much more data while each cutset information unit is less general when the concept of mode alternatives is used. That is, the effort of storing and comparing the data increases while backtracking due to some stored information becomes less probable. Therefore, we do not give the detailed formal descriptions of the variants of Bounding Rule 3.8 for the procedures based on mode alternatives.

3.2.5 Immediate Selection

The following bounding rule has been developed by Demeulemeester and Herroelen [48] for the RCPSP and generalized by Sprecher et al. [193] to the multi-mode case. It states assumptions under which we are allowed to consider only one branching alternative instead of testing all. We first give a formulation that can be employed if the decision point and mode alternative concepts are used.

Bounding Rule 3.9 *(Immediate Selection for Algorithms 3.2 and 3.3) We assume the following situation: All activities that start before the current decision point t_g finish at or before t_g. After selecting a mode alternative, there is an eligible activity j with fixed mode m_j which cannot be simultaneously processed with any other eligible activity i in its fixed mode m_i. Moreover, activity j in mode m_j cannot be simultaneously processed with any unscheduled activity h in any mode $m_h \in \mathcal{M}_h$. Then $\mathcal{DA}_g = JIP_g \backslash \{j\}$ $(= EJ_g \backslash \{j\})$ is the only minimal delay alternative that has to be examined, and $\mathcal{EA}_g = \{j\}$ is the only extension alternative that has to be examined.*

This rule can be adapted to the precedence tree guided enumeration procedure in several ways. We consider the following variant:

Remark 3.2 *(Immediate Selection for Algorithm 3.1) Consider an eligible activity j no mode of which is simultaneously performable with any currently unscheduled activity in any mode. If the earliest feasible start time of each other eligible activity in any mode is equal to the maximal finish time of the currently scheduled activities, then j is the only eligible activity that needs to be selected for being scheduled on the current level of the branch-and-bound tree.*

As described by Demeulemeester and Herroelen [48] for the single-mode and Sprecher et al. [193] for the multi-mode case, a similar immediate selection strategy for scheduling two activities and delaying all other eligible activities can be stated. Preliminary computational results, however, revealed that this rule does not speed up the algorithm when the other rules are employed. Consequently, we do not consider it here.

3.2.6 A Precedence Tree Specific Rule

Due to the construction of the precedence tree, Algorithm 3.1 may enumerate one schedule several times. This is the case in the following situation: Consider some partial schedule PS which is extended by scheduling some activity i in mode m_i on level $g-1$ and activity j in mode m_j on level g with identical start times $s_i = s_j$. If we return to PS later in the search process, and if scheduling activity j in mode m_j on level $g-1$ and activity i in mode m_i on level g results in the same start times, then we will obtain a schedule that has previously been enumerated. To avoid duplicate consideration of a schedule, Sprecher [190] has proposed the so-called Single Enumeration Rule which uses a three-dimensional array to check the assumptions mentioned above. We present an alternative rule to exclude duplicate enumeration. Clearly, it can only be used within Algorithm 3.1 since in the other two procedures a schedule can only be considered once.

Bounding Rule 3.10 *(Precedence Tree Rule for Algorithm 3.1) Consider two activities i and j scheduled on the previous and on the current level of the branch-and-bound tree, respectively. If we have $s_i = s_j$ and $i > j$ then the current partial schedule needs not be completed.*

Proof. Let PS be a partial schedule extended by scheduling activities i and j on levels $g-1$ and g, respectively, with $i > j$ and $s_i = s_j$. We assume that extending PS by scheduling j before i, both in the same modes as before, results in start times s'_j and s'_i. Clearly, we have $s'_i = s_i$ and $s'_j \leq s_j$. Thus, extending PS by scheduling i before j cannot lead to a schedule with a shorter makespan than by scheduling j before i. It should be observed that the extension of PS obtained from scheduling j before i cannot be excluded by Bounding Rule 3.10. □

The new rule is not only simpler, but also more general than the original Single-Enumeration Rule in that it additionally contains a portion of the Local Left Shift Rule. This can be seen in the proof given above: If we have $s'_j < s_j$, then the Local Left Shift Rule would also induce backtracking. Nevertheless, the Local Left Shift Rule is still necessary as the Precedence Tree Rule does not exclude partial schedules that are not semi-active if we have $i < j$.

3.3 Theoretical Comparison of Schedule Enumeration

This section analyzes the search spaces of the three branch-and-bound approaches described in Section 3.1. As we will see, the sets of schedules enumerated by the branching schemes are different. Moreover, we show that the effect of the bounding rules of Section 3.2 on the search spaces also depends on the underlying enumeration schemes.

3.3.1 Complete Enumeration

In this subsection we compare the sets of schedules enumerated by the pure branching algorithms without considering any of the bounding rules. For notational convenience, we will refer to the sets of schedules enumerated by Algorithms 3.1, 3.2, and 3.3 with $\mathcal{SS}_1$, $\mathcal{SS}_2$, and $\mathcal{SS}_3$, respectively.

We start our investigation comparing Algorithms 3.1 and 3.2. The first theorem states that for some instances schedules that are enumerated by the precedence tree algorithm are not enumerated by the algorithm based on mode and delay alternatives and vice versa.

Theorem 3.1 *There are instances for which we have* $\mathcal{SS}_1 \not\subseteq \mathcal{SS}_2$ *and* $\mathcal{SS}_2 \not\subseteq \mathcal{SS}_1$.

Proof. We consider the project instance given in Figure 3.1 as a counterexample. Note that it is a single-mode instance (thus, the mode index and the set of the nonrenewable resources have been omitted). Consequently, the results obtained hold for the single-mode RCPSP as well. It can be easily verified that the schedule shown in Figure 3.2 (a) is enumerated by Algorithm 3.1 but not by Algorithm 3.2. Schedule (b) is enumerated by Algorithm 3.2 but not by Algorithm 3.1. □

Next, we compare Algorithms 3.1 and 3.3. For each instance, any schedule enumerated by the precedence tree algorithm is also found by the algorithm based on mode and extension alternatives. The reverse, however, does not hold in general.

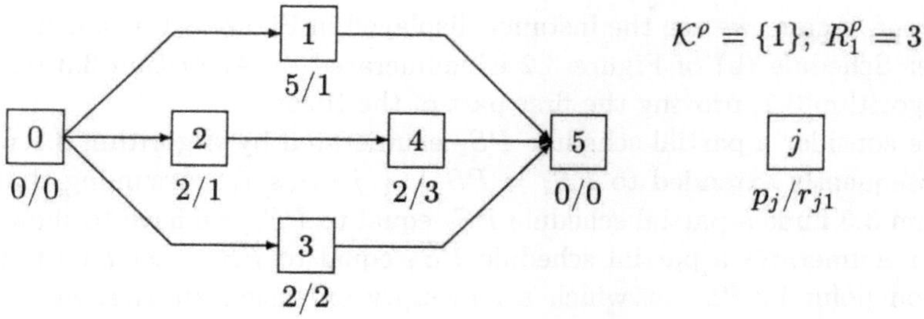

Figure 3.1: Project Instance

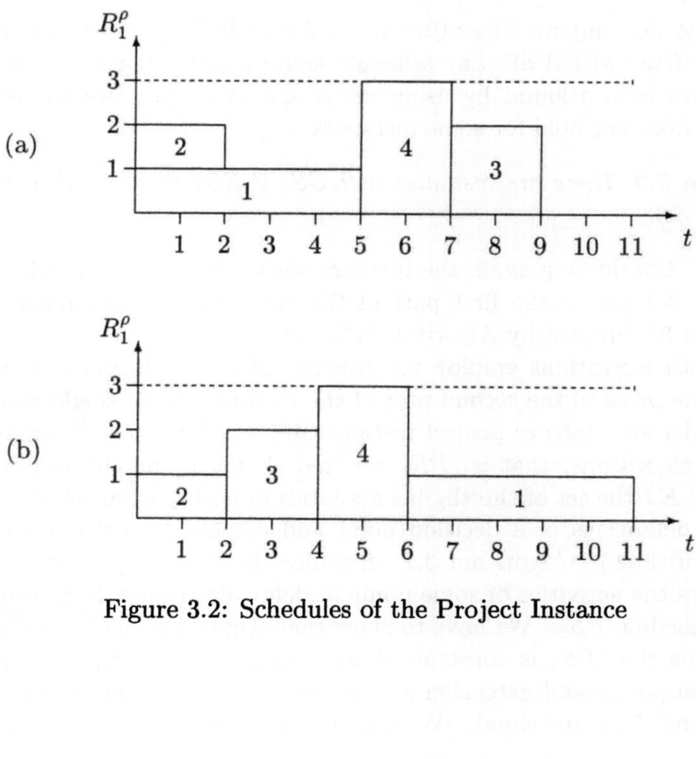

Figure 3.2: Schedules of the Project Instance

Theorem 3.2 *There are instances with $\mathcal{SS}_3 \not\subseteq \mathcal{SS}_1$, but for all instances it is $\mathcal{SS}_1 \subseteq \mathcal{SS}_3$.*

Proof. Again, we use the instance displayed in Figure 3.1 as a counterexample: Schedule (b) of Figure 3.2 is enumerated by Algorithm 3.3 but not by Algorithm 3.1, proving the first part of the theorem.

We consider a partial schedule PS_1 enumerated by Algorithm 3.1 which is subsequently extended to $\overline{PS}_1 = PS_1 \cup \{(j, m_j, s_j)\}$. Assuming that Algorithm 3.3 finds a partial schedule PS_3 equal to PS_1, we have to show that it also enumerates a partial schedule $\overline{PS}_3$ equal to $\overline{PS}_1$. Let t be the last decision point in PS_3 at which a nonempty extension alternative $\mathcal{EA}$ has been scheduled. We have $t \leq s_j$ (otherwise s_j would not be a start time considered by Algorithm 3.1). If we have $t = s_j$, we define $\overline{PS}_3$ as the result of scheduling $\overline{\mathcal{EA}} := \mathcal{EA} \cup \{j\}$ at time t instead of $\mathcal{EA}$. Note that $\overline{\mathcal{EA}}$ is a feasible extension alternative. Otherwise, we extend PS_3 by scheduling the empty extension alternative at all decision points t' with $t < t' < s_j$ (if any). Then we obtain $\overline{PS}_3$ by scheduling extension alternative $\{j\}$ at time s_j which is a decision point (i.e., a finish time of an activity scheduled in PS_3). In both cases, mode m_j can be chosen using a mode alternative, and we have $\overline{PS}_3 = \overline{PS}_1$. □

Finally, we compare Algorithm 3.2 to Algorithm 3.3. Given an arbitrary instance of the MRCPSP, any schedule enumerated using mode and delay alternatives is also found by using mode and extension alternatives. The inversion does not hold for some instances.

Theorem 3.3 *There are instances with $\mathcal{SS}_3 \not\subseteq \mathcal{SS}_2$, but for all instances it is $\mathcal{SS}_2 \subseteq \mathcal{SS}_3$.*

Proof. Considering again the instance shown in Figure 3.1, schedule (a) of Figure 3.2 proves the first part of the theorem as it is enumerated by Algorithm 3.3 but not by Algorithm 3.2.

As both algorithms employ the concept of mode alternatives, we may restrict the proof of the second part of the theorem to the single-mode case. We consider an arbitrary project instance and a partial schedule enumerated by both algorithms, that is, $PS_2 = PS_3$. Let t_{g+1} be the next decision point and EJ the set of the eligible activities in both partial schedules (note that the definitions of a decision point and eligible activities are equal in both algorithms). Algorithm 3.2 schedules the eligible jobs at time t_{g+1} and delays the activities of some minimal delay alternative $\mathcal{DA}$, resulting in partial schedule $\overline{PS}_2$. We have to show that Algorithm 3.3 finds $\overline{PS}_2$, too. We assume that PS_3 is constructed by a sequence $(t_0, \mathcal{EA}_0), \ldots, (t_g, \mathcal{EA}_g)$ of decision points and extension alternatives. Note that the decision points in PS_2 and PS_3 are equal. We set $A_i := \{j \in \mathcal{DA} \mid s_j = t_i \text{ in } \overline{PS}_2\}$

for $i = 0, \ldots, g+1$ and have $\mathcal{DA} = \cup_{i=0}^{g+1} A_i$. Now we define $\overline{\mathcal{EA}}_{g+1} := EJ \backslash A_{g+1}$ and $\overline{\mathcal{EA}}_i := \mathcal{EA}_i \backslash A_i$ for $i = 0, \ldots, g$. Observe that the sequence of decision points is not affected as all delayed activities have a finish time greater than t_{g+1}. Moreover, each $\overline{\mathcal{EA}}_i$ with $0 \leq i \leq g+1$ is a feasible extension alternative. Hence the extension algorithm enumerates a sequence $(t_0, \overline{\mathcal{EA}}_0), \ldots, (t_{g+1}, \overline{\mathcal{EA}}_{g+1})$ which corresponds to a partial schedule $\overline{PS}_3$. With $\overline{PS}_3 = \overline{PS}_2$ by construction we complete the proof. □

The results of this subsection can be summarized as follows: None of the complete enumeration schemes currently available for the MRCPSP is dominant in a sense that the set of the schedules enumerated by one algorithm is less than or equal to the sets enumerated by the other two procedures. However, combining the theorems above, we have

$$\mathcal{SS}_1 \cup \mathcal{SS}_2 \subseteq \mathcal{SS}_3.$$

3.3.2 Enumeration with Bounding Rules

In this subsection, we examine the sets of schedules enumerated by the algorithms of Section 3.1 including the bounding rules of Section 3.2. The focus will be on the Local Left Shift Rule (Bounding Rule 3.5) since this allows us to characterize the enumerated set of schedules with respect to the set of semi-active schedules. Similarly to the previous subsection, we denote the sets of schedules enumerated by Algorithms 3.1, 3.2, and 3.3 with the Local Left Shift Rule as $\mathcal{SS}_1^{LS}$, $\mathcal{SS}_2^{LS}$, and $\mathcal{SS}_3^{LS}$, respectively. Finally, the set of the semi-active schedules is referred to as $\mathcal{SAS}$.

We start our investigation with an analysis of the impact of the Local Left Shift Rule. The following theorem states that the precedence tree algorithm in accordance with the Local Left Shift Rule enumerates exactly the set of the semi-active schedules.

Theorem 3.4 *For all instances, we have* $\mathcal{SS}_1^{LS} = \mathcal{SAS}$.

Proof. The Local Left Shift Rule is applied to activity j that is started at time s_j at the current node of the branch-and-bound tree. No scheduling decision at a successor node of the search tree can free renewable resources before s_j, thus, if a local left shift is not possible when starting an activity, it is not possible in any (enumerated) completion of the partial schedule.

Let $S \in \mathcal{SAS}$ be a semi-active schedule for an arbitrary instance. We can construct a sequence $(j_0, m_0, s_0), \ldots, (j_i, m_i, s_i), \ldots, (j_J, m_J, s_J)$ with $s_i \leq s_{i+1}$ for $1 \leq i < J$ representing S. We show by induction that the sequence related to S corresponds to a branch in the search tree built up by Algorithm 3.1. Let $(j_0, m_0, s_0), \ldots, (j_g, m_g, s_g)$ with $1 \leq g < J$ correspond to a partial schedule PS_1^{LS} found by Algorithm 3.1. We consider activity

j_{g+1} which is eligible in PS_1^{LS} and can therefore be scheduled in mode m_{g+1}. Let t denote the start time assigned to activity j_{g+1} by Algorithm 3.1 and let $\overline{PS}_1^{LS} = PS_1^{LS} \cup \{(j_{g+1}, m_{g+1}, t)\}$ be the corresponding next partial schedule. We have $t \geq s_{g+1}$, otherwise S could not be semi-active. For the same reason, the left shift rule cannot be applied to activity j_{g+1}. Moreover, it is $t \leq s_{g+1}$ because the precedence tree algorithm assigns the earliest feasible start time and it is $s_g \leq s_{g+1}$. Hence, we deduce $t = s_{g+1}$, that is, $(j_0, m_0, s_0), \dots, (j_{g+1}, m_{g+1}, s_{g+1})$ corresponds to partial schedule $\overline{PS}_1^{LS}$. □

The next theorem shows that an analogous result cannot be obtained for the algorithm based on mode and delay alternatives including the Local Left Shift Rule: It may enumerate schedules which are not semi-active while on the other hand there may exist semi-active schedules which are not enumerated.

Theorem 3.5 *There are instances for which we have $\mathcal{SS}_2^{LS} \not\subseteq \mathcal{SAS}$ and $\mathcal{SAS} \not\subseteq \mathcal{SS}_2^{LS}$.*

Proof. We consider the instance shown in Figure 3.1. Schedule (b) of Figure 3.2 is not semi-active, but it is enumerated by Algorithm 3.2 with Local Left Shift Rule: At time 0, activities 1, 2, and 3 are started. Since a resource conflict occurs, we may select $\{3\}$ as minimal delay alternative. At time 2, activities 3 and 4 are started. This resource conflict may be solved by delaying activity 4 which is then rescheduled at time 4. The resulting resource conflict can be solved delaying activity 1. According to the formulation of the Local Left Shift Rule, only activity 4 is tested for a left shift. However, activity 3 may now be locally left shifted to time 0 due to the delay of activity 1. This possible local left shift is not detected by the Local Left Shift Rule. Consequently, activity 1 is started at time 6 completing the (non semi-active) schedule.

Now we consider schedule (a) of Figure 3.2 which is semi-active. However, it is not enumerated by Algorithm 3.2 (no matter whether the Local Left Shift Rule is included or not): Starting activities 1, 2, and 3 at time 0, delaying activity 3, and starting activities 3 and 4 at time 2 causes a resource conflict at time 2. It can be solved by the only minimal delay alternatives $\{1,3\}$ and $\{4\}$. None of them will result in schedule (a). □

Theorem 3.5 states that the Local Left Shift Rule considered here does not prevent the algorithm based on mode and delay alternatives from enumerating schedules which are not semi-active. Note that our formulation of the left shift rule is equivalent to the one used by Demeulemeester and Herroelen [48] for the single-mode case, that is, this observation holds for their procedure as well. Clearly, a possible enumeration of schedules which are not semi-active is due to the delay of activities which start before the previous decision point. Freeing resources before the previous decision point may induce the possibility of a left shift of an activity which starts at the previous (or an earlier) decision point. Such a left shift cannot be detected by this version of the Local Left Shift Rule. However, the rule can be extended to exclude all schedules which are not semi-active:

Remark 3.3 *(Extended Local Left Shift Rule for Algorithm 3.2) Let s denote the minimal start time of those activities currently selected to be delayed, that is, $s = \min\{s_j \mid j \in \mathcal{DA}_g\}$. If there is a scheduled activity with a start time greater than s which is not selected to be delayed, and if this activity can be locally left shifted after delaying the currently selected delay alternative, then the current partial schedule needs not be completed.*

With the arguments given above, we can state that the Extended Local Left Shift Rule prevents the algorithm based on mode and delay alternatives from enumerating a schedule which is not semi-active. Thus, denoting the set of schedules enumerated by Algorithm 3.2 with the Extended Local Left Shift Rule as $\mathcal{SS}_2^{ELS}$, the result of Theorem 3.5 can be improved as follows:

Remark 3.4 *For all instances, it is $\mathcal{SS}_2^{ELS} \subseteq \mathcal{SAS}$, but there are instances for which $\mathcal{SAS} \not\subseteq \mathcal{SS}_2^{ELS}$ holds.*

Now we turn to the algorithm based on mode and extension alternatives for which we can obtain the same result as for the precedence tree procedure. When combined with the Local Left Shift Rule, also Algorithm 3.3 enumerates exactly the set of the semi-active schedules of a given instance.

Theorem 3.6 *For all instances, we have $\mathcal{SS}_3^{LS} = \mathcal{SAS}$.*

Proof. The Local Left Shift Rule is applied to the activities started at the current decision point. As no renewable resources are freed before this decision point when the corresponding partial schedule is completed, the application of the Local Left Shift Rule excludes all schedules which are not semi-active, that is, we have $\mathcal{SS}_3^{LS} \subseteq \mathcal{SAS}$.

Using Theorem 3.4, we have $\mathcal{SAS} = \mathcal{SS}_1^{LS}$. Clearly, it is $\mathcal{SS}_1^{LS} \subseteq \mathcal{SS}_1$. Furthermore we have $\mathcal{SS}_1 \subseteq \mathcal{SS}_3$ by Theorem 3.2. Consequently it is $\mathcal{SAS} \subseteq \mathcal{SS}_3$. Note that a feasible left shift of a currently started activity is possible in any continuation of the current partial schedule. That is, it cannot be prevented by further scheduling decisions as these do not affect the resource usages before the start time of that activity. Hence the Local Left Shift Rule does not exclude schedules that are not semi-active, and we deduce $\mathcal{SAS} \subseteq \mathcal{SS}_3^{LS}$. □

Combining Theorems 3.4 and 3.6, we can state that the precedence tree algorithm and the procedure based on mode and extension alternatives both enumerate the same set of schedules when combined with the Local Left Shift Rule, that is, the set of the semi-active schedules. Furthermore, it should be noted that these two theorems can also be used to prove the correctness of Algorithms 3.1 and 3.3 since we can find an optimal semi-active schedule for an instance if we can find an optimal one. Additionally considering Remark 3.4, we can summarize the results obtained so far as follows:

$$\mathcal{SS}_2^{ELS} \subseteq \mathcal{SS}_1^{LS} = \mathcal{SS}_3^{LS} = \mathcal{SAS}.$$

Next, we briefly consider the remaining bounding rules of Section 3.2. The impact of the first four rules is identical within all branching schemes, that is, including them does not change the relationships stated in Subsection 3.3.1. This can be explained as follows: The Basic Time Window Rule (Bounding Rule 3.1) prevents any procedure from completing a schedule with a makespan that is not shorter than the best found so far. If the order in which the schedules are enumerated is the same in the three procedures (which can be achieved by an appropriate branching order), the effect is independent from the specific enumeration scheme. The Non-Delayability Rule (Bounding Rule 3.2) does not exclude schedules if used together with Bounding Rule 3.1, it only induces backtracking on lower levels of the branch-and-bound tree. The Data Reduction Rule (Bounding Rule 3.3) leads to the exclusion of those schedules that contain redundant modes, which is independent from the branching scheme. The Nonrenewable Resource Rule (Bounding Rule 3.4) does not exclude schedules, it aims at an early detection of infeasible schedules.

We now discuss those two of the remaining rules which make use of dominating sets of schedules. Within Algorithms 3.1 and 3.3, the Order Swap Rule (Bounding Rule 3.7) restricts the enumeration to the set of the order monotonous schedules, while the Multi-Mode Rule (Bounding Rule 3.6) reduces the enumeration to the tight and mode-minimal schedules only if no nonrenewable resources are given. For Algorithm 3.2 the exclusion of all schedules which are not order monotonous, tight, or mode-minimal can only be obtained if the corresponding tests are performed on those activities which finish at or before the current decision point (cf. the above discussion of the Local Left Shift Rule).

Finally, the Immediate Selection Rule (Bounding Rule 3.9) has the same effect within the decision point based Algorithms 3.2 and 3.3, that is, it does not change the relationship given in Theorem 3.2. For the formulation of this rule for Algorithm 3.1 (see Remark 3.2), an analogous statement cannot be made. The Cutset Rule (Bounding Rule 3.8), and for obvious reasons also the Precedence Tree Rule (Bounding Rule 3.10), have only been defined for Algorithm 3.1 and, therefore, need not be considered in our comparison.

We close this section remarking that although the theoretical results derived here provide a deeper insight into the different solution methodologies, they do not allow to predict the solution times required by the algorithms. This is due to the fact that the different operations the procedures consist of may result in different computation times even if the same set of schedules is enumerated. Moreover, the effect of a bounding rule may depend on the algorithmic structure, that is, one algorithm may be accelerated less than another one, cf. the discussion of the different variants of the Cutset Rule. Consequently, the theoretical comparison of this section is completed by the computational comparison provided in the following section.

3.4 Computational Results

In this section, we present the results of the computational studies concerning the algorithms discussed in the previous sections. After a brief report on the effect of the bounding rules, we compare the performance of the branch-and-bound procedures. The experiments have been performed on a Pentium-based IBM-compatible personal computer with 133 MHz clock-pulse and 32 MB RAM. The procedures have been coded in ANSI C, compiled with the GNU C compiler and tested under the Linux operating system.

In order to provide a fair comparison of the algorithms, we have attempted to use identical data structures and related update operations whenever possible. Moreover, we have used the same level of implementational know-how such as use of pointer arithmetics for coding the algorithms. Finally, in contrast to the comparison of Algorithms 3.1 and 3.2 provided by Sprecher et al. [193], we have attempted to integrate each bounding criterion of Section 3.2 into each enumeration procedure (with the exception of the Precedence Tree Rule).

We used sets of test problems constructed by the project generator ProGen which has been developed by Kolisch et al. [130] (cf. Appendix A). The instances have already been employed to evaluate the precedence tree algorithm by Sprecher and Drexl [192] as well as the procedure based on mode and delay alternatives by Sprecher et al. [193]. For our study, we have used the multi-mode instance sets that are described in Appendix A.2.2. In order to keep the computation times acceptable, we restricted the investigation to the problem sets containing instances with up to 16 non-dummy activities.

3.4.1 Effects of the Bounding Rules

As the impact of most of the acceleration methods on the computation times has been thoroughly studied by Sprecher and Drexl [192] as well as Sprecher et al. [193], we only summarize some new insights.

The new Order Swap Rule (Bounding Rule 3.7) accelerates the basic variant of Algorithm 3.2 (including only the Time Window Rule) by a factor of approximately 1.9. This effect is not totally consumed when the other rules are also included.

As already mentioned, none of the tested variants of the Cutset Rule for Algorithms 3.2 and 3.3 could accelerate these procedures when the other bounding schemes were employed. However, as reported by Sprecher and Drexl [192], the Cutset Rule can be efficiently used within the precedence tree algorithm.

The immediate selection strategy of Bounding Rule 3.9 accelerates the branching schemes when applied to small instances ($J = 10$), confirming the results obtained by Sprecher et al. [193]. However, it may slow down the procedures if instances with more activities are considered. This is due to the fact that it becomes less probable that the assumptions can be fulfilled while the effort to check them increases with an increasing number of activities.

The new formulation of the precedence tree specific rule (Bounding Rule 3.10) accelerates the basic variant of Algorithm 3.1 (including the Time Window Rule) by a factor of 8.4 while Sprecher and Drexl [192] report a factor of 3.2 for their formulation. This is mainly due to the fact that the new variant includes a portion of the Local Left Shift Rule.

Finally, the Extended Local Left Shift Rule for the algorithm based on mode and delay alternatives (cf. Remark 3.3 in Section 3.3.2) is of rather theoretical interest as it does not yield further acceleration of Algorithm 3.2.

For the comparison to be summarized in the next subsection we have used the fastest variants of the algorithms. Considering the observations given above, all bounding schemes except for the Cutset Rule, the Immediate Selection Rule, and the Precedence Tree Rule have been included in Algorithms 3.2 and 3.3. Clearly, the Cutset Rule as well as the Precedence Tree Rule have been employed in Algorithm 3.1, omitting only the Immediate Selection Rule. In order to separate the effect of the Cutset Rule, we have also tested a variant of Algorithm 3.1 in which the former is not included. The variants of the procedures are summarized in Table 3.1 where '+' indicates that the corresponding bounding rule is included and '–' means that it is not.

Algorithm	*enumeration scheme*	1	2	3	4	5	6	7	8	9	10
1 (a)	precedence tree	+	+	+	+	+	+	+	+	–	+
1 (b)	precedence tree	+	+	+	+	+	+	+	–	–	+
2	mode and delay alt.	+	+	+	+	+	+	+	–	–	–
3	mode and ext. alt.	+	+	+	+	+	+	+	–	–	–

Table 3.1: Accelerated variants of the algorithms to be tested

3.4.2 Comparison of the Algorithms

We start the summary of our numerical results with a comparison of the average computation times given in Table 3.2. Algorithm 3.1 with the Cutset Rule is the fastest procedure on the average. It is 2.0 times faster than Algorithm 3.2 when 10 activities are considered and 7.0 times faster for projects with 16 activities, that is, the comparison factor increases with an increasing number of jobs. Algorithm 3.2 is at most 1.4 times faster than Algorithm 3.3. The precedence tree algorithm is faster than the other two procedures even if the Cutset Rule is not included.

Table 3.3 shows that Algorithm 3.1 has the lowest maximal computation times, no matter whether the Cutset Rule is employed or not. For two project sizes, the maximal computation times of Algorithm 3.2 are lower than those of Algorithm 3.3. In the other two cases, the reverse holds.

Next, we have examined the impact of the renewable resource characteristics on the computation times. The resource characteristics are reflected by the resource strength RS^ρ which measures the scarceness of the resources and the resource factor RF^ρ which denotes the average number of resources requested per activity (cf. Appendix A.2). The results, summarized in Table 3.4 for the instances with $J = 16$ activities, show that Algorithm 3.1 is the fastest procedure for the so-called hard instances with high computation times, that is, if the resource factor is high or the resource strength is low. However, on the easiest instances with a high resource strength Algorithm 3.2 performs best. This indicates that none of the procedures is dominant in the sense that it is faster than the other two on each instance.

Finally, the distributions of the computation times are listed in Table 3.5. Algorithm 3.1 solves 21.5 % of the instances with 16 activities in less then 0.01 seconds while Algorithm 3.2 solves 23.8 % within this time. On the other hand, Algorithm 3.2 cannot solve 0.5 % of the instances in 1000 seconds while Algorithm 3.3 fails to solve only 0.2 % within this time.

Summing up the observations made above, the new approach based on mode and extension alternatives is outperformed by the other two algorithms with respect to average computation times. This seems to be due to the fact that, as already outlined, branching may not be restricted to "maximal" extension alternatives. This drawback cannot be fully compensated by the Local Left Shift Rule. The procedure based on mode and delay alternatives is the fastest on the easy instances. However, it is outperformed by the precedence tree guided algorithm on the hard instances, and even by the new approach on some hard instances. This is due to the possibility of cancelling previous scheduling decisions by delaying activities: On one branch of the search tree, one activity may be delayed and rescheduled several times. Clearly, the lower the renewable resource strength, the more activities have to be delayed due to the scarceness of the renewable resources, resulting

Algorithm	$J = 10$	$J = 12$	$J = 14$	$J = 16$
1 (a)	0.04	0.12	0.75	3.26
1 (b)	0.05	0.20	1.66	10.60
2	0.08	0.33	4.55	22.81
3	0.11	0.45	4.86	28.08

Table 3.2: Average computation times (sec) — all instances

Algorithm	$J = 10$	$J = 12$	$J = 14$	$J = 16$
1 (a)	0.77	2.69	22.87	165.11
1 (b)	1.25	5.14	78.91	1601.81
2	2.96	17.29	709.37	4523.44
3	2.87	20.57	529.92	6043.12

Table 3.3: Maximal computation times (sec) — all instances

Algorithm	RF^{ρ}:	0.50	1.00	RS^{ρ}:	0.25	0.50	0.75	1.00
1 (a)		0.83	5.58		8.34	2.90	1.20	0.58
1 (b)		1.30	19.51		34.81	5.32	1.77	0.68
2		1.35	43.37		81.24	9.17	1.13	0.23
3		4.07	51.08		94.63	11.75	4.80	1.72

Table 3.4: Average computation times for resource classes (sec) — $J = 16$

Algorithm	< 0.01	< 0.1	< 1	< 10	< 100	< 1000	< 10000
1 (a)	21.5	43.5	70.2	92.4	99.6	100.0	100.0
1 (b)	21.6	41.8	67.1	90.2	97.8	99.8	100.0
2	23.8	42.3	70.1	88.1	96.8	99.5	100.0
3	16.5	33.4	58.1	82.1	96.5	99.8	100.0

Table 3.5: Distribution of the computation times (%) — $J = 16$

in a high computational effort for this problem class. The precedence tree approach is the fastest with respect to average and maximal computation times. The new order swap rule and the new formulation of the precedence tree specific rule further improved its performance. The latter rule is capable of neutralizing its main disadvantage, namely the duplicate enumeration of a schedule. Moreover, the precedence tree method currently is the only multi-mode procedure in which an efficient variant of the powerful Cutset Rule can be employed, leading to further reduced computation times. Finally, according to our experience, the precedence tree algorithm seems to be easier to implement as at each node of the branch-and-bound tree a single activity is scheduled instead of a set of activities.

Hence, we conclude that the precedence tree guided enumeration scheme currently is the algorithm of choice when solving larger test instances. Still, however, optimally solving project scheduling problems of real-world size in reasonable computation times remains a rather hopeless task.

Chapter 4

Classification of Single-Mode Heuristics

The computational results reported in the previous chapter demonstrated that exact solution algorithms are of no use when scheduling projects of real-world size. From a theoretical point of view, this outcome is no surprise due to the NP-hardness of the RCPSP and its extensions. But, considering the data uncertainty often occuring in practice such as unpredictable delays, perfectly accurate planning would not be needed anyway. For that reason, schedules which are close to the optimum are sufficient in most cases. Such good but not necessarily optimal schedules are constructed by heuristics. Since 1963 when Kelley [111] introduced a schedule generation scheme, a large number of different heuristic algorithms have been suggested in the project scheduling literature.

This chapter gives an appraising survey of heuristic approaches for the RCPSP, providing an overview of the current state of the art in the literature. Due to the vast amount of literature on project scheduling heuristics, we restrict ourselves to the single-mode case here. This should be sufficient as the single-mode approaches already contain many of the main concepts that are used in heuristics for more complex project scheduling models. Based on a classification scheme, we examine the characteristics of the heuristics, such as underlying schedule generation scheme, priority rules, sampling methods, metaheuristic strategies, representations, and operators. These concepts will be used when developing new genetic algorithm heuristics in Chapter 5.

The outline of this chapter is as follows: We start in Section 4.1 with schedule generation schemes which are essential to construct feasible schedules. In Section 4.2 we show how these schemes are employed in priority rule based methods. Section 4.3 is devoted to metaheuristic approaches such as simulated annealing, tabu search, and genetic algorithms. Heuristics which do neither belong to the class of priority rule based methods nor to meta-heuristic approaches are summarized in Section 4.4.[1]

4.1 Schedule Generation Schemes

Schedule generation schemes (SGS) are the core of most heuristic solution procedures for the RCPSP. SGS start from scratch and build a feasible schedule by stepwise extension of a partial schedule. A partial schedule is a schedule where only a subset of the J non-dummy activities have been scheduled. There are two different SGS available. They can be distinguished w.r.t. the type of incrementation. While the so-called serial SGS performs activity incrementation, the so-called parallel SGS performs time incrementation.

4.1.1 Serial Schedule Generation Scheme

For a description of the serial SGS we use again the notation introduced in Chapter 3. After starting the dummy source activity at time 0, the serial SGS runs through J stages of activity incrementation. In each stage $g = 1, \ldots, J$, the set SJ_g of the currently scheduled activities is determined. Then the set EJ_g of the eligible activities, i.e., those activities the predecessors of which are already scheduled, is computed. From this set, one eligible activity j_g is selected and scheduled at the earliest possible start time s_{j_g} that does not violate the precedence or resource constraints. Criteria for the decision which activity should be scheduled next will be dealt with later in this chapter. The scheduling process is completed by assigning to the dummy sink activity $J+1$ the earliest possible start (or, due to $p_{J+1} = 0$, finish) time which determines the makespan of the project. We can now give the following formal description of the serial SGS:

Algorithm 4.1 *(Serial SGS)*

$j_0 := 0$; $s_{j_0} := 0$; $SJ_0 := \{0\}$;
FOR $g := 1$ TO J DO
BEGIN
  $SJ_g := SJ_{g-1}$; $EJ_g := \{j \in \mathcal{J} \backslash SJ_g \mid \mathcal{P}_j \subseteq SJ_g\}$;
  select $j_g \in EJ_g$;
  compute earliest precedence and resource feasible start time s_{j_g};
  $SJ_g := SJ_g \cup \{j_g\}$;
END;
$s_{J+1} := \max\{s_h + p_h \mid h \in \mathcal{P}_{J+1}\}$.

[1] Apart from minor modifications, the classification of heuristics discussed in this chapter can also be found in Kolisch and Hartmann [126].

The time complexity of the serial SGS as given above is $\mathcal{O}(J^2 \cdot |\mathcal{K}^\rho|)$ (cf. Pinson et al. [165]). In order to illustrate the serial SGS, we consider again the example project of Figure 2.1. Table 4.1 lists the eligible sets and selected activities when generating the schedule given in Figure 2.2.

g	1	2	3	4	5	6
EJ_g	{1,2}	{1,4}	{1,6}	{3,6}	{3}	{5}
j_g	2	4	1	6	3	5

Table 4.1: Example for serial SGS

The serial SGS generates always feasible schedules which are optimal for the resource-unconstrained scheduling problem. Kolisch [122] has shown that the serial SGS generates active schedules, i.e., schedules where none of the activities can be started earlier without delaying some other activity. For scheduling problems with regular performance measure (for a definition of the latter cf. Sprecher et al. [194]) such as makespan minimization, there will always be an optimal solution in the set of the active schedules.

Observe that there is a correspondence between the serial SGS and the exact precedence tree algorithm of Chapter 3. Roughly speaking, an execution of the serial SGS corresponds to one branch in the search tree of Algorithm 3.1. In other words, the serial technique of selecting an activity and scheduling it as early as possible is also part of the (exact) precedence tree algorithm. The only difference lies in the restriction within the branch-and-bound procedure that the start time at the current level may not be less than that at the previous level. This restriction is due to efficiency reasons in the exact approach but would lead to deteriorated results if used in a heuristic.

Finally, we briefly address a special case of the serial SGS. Basically, we can select an activity from the eligible set using some decision criterion such as a priority rule (cf. Section 4.2). Alternatively, the order in which the activities are selected can be directly prescribed by a so-called activity list $\lambda = (j_1, \ldots, j_J)$. Clearly, when an activity is next in the list and therefore selected for scheduling, it must be eligible, i.e., all is predecessors must have occured earlier in the activity list. Given an activity list $\lambda = (j_1, \ldots, j_J)$, Algorithm 4.1 simply selects activity j_1 on stage 1, j_2 on stage 2, and so on. The eligible set needs not be computed. Note that an activity list can be constructed by the serial SGS in accordance with a decision rule; one simply has to record the order in which the activities are selected. An activity list leading to the schedule of Figure 2.2 in the above given example is $\lambda = (2, 4, 1, 6, 3, 5)$. Since the serial SGS for activity lists is a special case of the serial SGS, it generates active schedules, too. Moreover, there is always a list λ^* for which list scheduling will generate an optimal schedule. The serial

SGS for activity lists plays an important role in classical machine scheduling where it is referred to as list scheduling (cf. Kim [112] and Schutten [179]).

4.1.2 Parallel Schedule Generation Scheme

The parallel SGS starts with scheduling the dummy source activity at time 0. Then it runs through at most J stages of time incrementation. Each stage g is associated with a decision point t_g as defined in Subsection 3.1.2, reflecting the time at which all activities selected at stage g are started. For notational convenience, we use the set SJ_g of the currently scheduled jobs and the set JIP_g of the activities in process at the current decision point. At each new stage, the related new decision point is computed as the earliest finish time of the activities that are in process at the previous decision point t_{g-1}. Next, we compute the eligible set EJ_j. Here, an eligible activity is a currently unscheduled activity that could be started at the current decision point without violating the precedence and resource constraints. Now we successively select an eligible activity j_g, start it at time t_g, and update the eligible set. Note that there may be more activities than just j_g that have to be removed from EJ_g due to the resources required for scheduling j_g. If there is no activity left that can be feasibly started at time t_g, the parallel SGS moves on to the next stage. If all non-dummy activities have been scheduled, the dummy sink activity $J+1$ is scheduled as early as possible, completing the project schedule. In algorithmic notation, we have:

Algorithm 4.2 *(Parallel SGS)*

$g := 0$; $t_0 := 0$; $j_0 := 0$; $s_{j_0} := 0$; $SJ_0 := \{0\}$; $JIP_0 := \{0\}$;
WHILE $SJ_g \neq \mathcal{J} \cup \{0\}$ DO
BEGIN
    $g := g + 1$; $SJ_g := SJ_{g-1}$;
    $t_g := \min\{s_h + p_h \mid h \in JIP_{g-1}\}$;
    $JIP_g := JIP_{g-1} \setminus \{h \in JIP_{g-1} \mid s_h + p_h = t_g\}$;
    compute EJ_g;
    WHILE $EJ_g \neq \emptyset$
    BEGIN
        select $j_g \in EJ_g$;
        $s_{j_g} := t_g$; $SJ_g := SJ_g \cup \{j_g\}$;
        $JIP_g := JIP_g \cup \{j_g\}$; update EJ_g;
    END;
END;
$s_{J+1} := \max\{s_h + p_h \mid h \in \mathcal{P}_{J+1}\}$.

The time complexity of the parallel SGS is $\mathcal{O}(J^2 \cdot |\mathcal{K}^\rho|)$. Note that the parallel SGS might have less than J stages but that there are exactly J selection decisions which have to be made. Table 4.2 reports the parallel SGS when generating the schedule given in Figure 2.2 for our example project.

g	1	2	3	3	4	5	6
t_g	0	4	6	6	9	10	12
EJ_g	{1,2}	{1,4}	{1,6}	{6}	{}	{3}	{5}
j_g	2	4	1	6		3	5

Table 4.2: Example for parallel SGS

As the serial, so does the parallel SGS always generate feasible schedules which are optimal for the resource-unconstrained case. It has been shown by Kolisch [122] that the parallel SGS constructs non-delay schedules. A non-delay schedule is a schedule where, even if activity preemption is allowed, none of the activities can be started earlier without delaying some other activity. The set of non-delay schedules is a subset of the set of active schedules. It thus has, on average, a smaller cardinality. But it has the severe drawback that it might not contain an optimal schedule with a regular performance measure. E.g., in Kolisch [122] it is shown that only 59.7 % of the instances of a standard set of projects have an optimal solution which is in the set of the non-delay schedules.

Finally, we remark that the time-incrementation mechanism which makes up the parallel SGS is also contained in two exact procedures of Chapter 3, namely Algorithms 3.2 and 3.3. Recall that we mentioned that a restriction to maximal extension alternatives in Algorithm 3.3 is not possible as we would lose the guarantee to enumerate an optimal solution. But this is exactly what the parallel SGS does: At each decision point, as many eligible activities as possible are successively selected and scheduled. Clearly, scheduling as many eligible activities as possible corresponds to selecting a maximal extension alternative. The result in both cases is the restriction to the set of non-delay schedules—which must be avoided by considering also non-maximal extension alternatives in a branch-and-bound algorithm.

4.2 Priority Rule Based Heuristics

Priority rule based methods are an important class of heuristics for project scheduling. They employ one or both of the SGS in order to construct one or more schedules. The priority rule itself is used in order to select an activity j from the eligible set EJ_g. We first give a survey of different priority rules.

Thereafter we show how schedule generation schemes and priority rules can be combined in order to obtain different priority rule based heuristics.

4.2.1 Priority Rules

A priority rule is a mapping which assigns each activity j in the eligible set EJ_g a priority value $v(j)$, along with the information whether the activity with the minimum or the maximum priority value is selected. In case of ties, one or several tie breaking rules have to be employed. The easiest ways to resolve ties is to choose the activity with the smallest activity label. There has been an overwhelming amount of research on priority rules for the RCPSP, cf. Alvarez-Valdes and Tamarit [6], Boctor [20], Cooper [35, 36], Davies [37], Davis and Patterson [38], Elsayed [74], Kolisch [121, 122], Lawrence [132], Özdamar and Ulusoy [155, 157], Patterson [160, 161], Thesen [199], Thomas and Salhi [200], Ulusoy and Özdamar [202], Valls et al. [204], and Whitehouse and Brown [209].

Priority rules can be classified according to different criteria. W.r.t. to the type of information employed to calculate $v(j)$, we can distinguish network, time, and resource based rules (cf. Alvarez-Valdes and Tamarit [6] and Lawrence [132]) as well as lower and upper bound rules. Lower bound rules calculate for each activity a lower bound of the objective function value, upper bound rules calculate for each activity an upper bound of the objective function value. W.r.t. the amount of information employed we distinguish local and global rules. Local rules employ only information from the activity under consideration such as the processing time while global rules make use of a wider range of information. A distinction into static and dynamic rules is made w.r.t. the fact whether the value $v(j)$ remains constant or changes during the iterations of the SGS. Finally, we can distinguish rules which can be employed in the serial, the parallel, or both SGS.

Table 4.3 gives an overview of the well known priority rules GRPW (greatest rank positional weight), LFT (latest finish time), LST (latest start time), MSLK (minimum slack), MTS (most total successors), and WRUP (weighted resource utilization and precedence). In the MSLK rule, the earliest feasible finish time ef_j of activity j in the current partial schedule is calculated. Note that this makes MSLK a dynamic rule while the other five rules are static ones. The priority values of static rules can be computed in a preprocessing step which saves computation time if more than one schedule is constructed for a given project instance with the same rule (cf. especially the sampling methods described in the following subsection). Observe that the weights of the WRUP rule as given in Table 4.3 are those that lead to the best results in the study of Ulusoy and Özdamar [202].

Recently, more elaborate priority rules have been developed. Kolisch [121] proposed, among other rules, the so-called WCS (worst case slack) rule for

Reference	*rule*		$v(j)$
Alvarez-Valdes, Tamarit [6]	GRPW	max	$p_j + \sum_{i \in S_j} p_i$
	MTS	max	$\lvert\overline{S}_j\rvert$
Davis, Patterson [38]	LFT	min	LF_j
	MSLK	min	$LF_j - ef_j$
Kolisch [120]	LST	min	$LF_j - p_j$
Ulusoy, Özdamar [202]	WRUP	max	$0.7\,\lvert S_j\rvert + 0.3 \sum_{k \in \mathcal{K}^\rho} \frac{r_{jk}}{R_k^\rho}$

Table 4.3: Priority Rules

the parallel SGS. Özdamar and Ulusoy [157] as well as Ulusoy and Özdamar [203] introduced the so-called local constraint based analysis (LCBA). LCBA employs the parallel SGS and decides via feasibility checks and so-called essential conditions which activities have to be selected and which activities have to be delayed. Like MSLK, these two rules can be classified as dynamic.

4.2.2 Proposed Methods

A specific priority rule based heuristic combines priority rules and schedule generation schemes. If the heuristic generates a single schedule, it is called a *single pass method.* Single pass methods are the oldest heuristics for the RCPSP. They employ one SGS and one priority rule in order to obtain one feasible schedule. Examples are the heuristics of Alvarez-Valdes and Tamarit [6], Boctor [20], Cooper [35, 36], Davies [37], Davis and Patterson [38], Elsayed [74], Kolisch [121, 122], Lawrence [132], Patterson [160, 161], Thesen [199], Valls et al. [204], and Whitehouse and Brown [209].

A method which generates more than one schedule is referred to as a *multi pass method.* There are many possibilities to combine SGS and priority rules to a multi pass method. The most common ones are multi priority rule methods, forward-backward scheduling methods, sampling methods, and adaptive methods. In what follows, these four types of multi pass methods will be outlined.

Multi Priority Rule Methods

Multi priority rule methods employ the SGS several times. Each time a different priority rule is used. Often, the rules are used in the order of descending solution quality. Boctor [20] employed 7 different rules in his experimental study.

Instead of using n priority rules in order to generate n schedules, a much larger number of schedules can be generated by using convex combinations of n priority rules. That is, we define $v(j) = \sum_{i=1}^{n} \Omega_i \cdot v_i(j)$ with $\Omega_i \geq 0$

for all i and $\sum_{i=1}^{n} \Omega_i = 1$. Examples of such approaches are given by Ulusoy and Özdamar [202] and Thomas and Salhi [200]. Ulusoy and Özdamar [202] employed a convex combination of $n = 2$ rules in order to generate 10 different schedules.

Forward-Backward Scheduling Methods

Forward-backward scheduling methods employ an SGS in order to iteratively schedule the project by alternating between forward and backward scheduling. Forward scheduling is done as outlined in Section 4.1. Backward scheduling applies one of the SGS to the reversed precedence network where the former end activity $J + 1$ has become the new start activity. The priority values are usually obtained from the start or finish times of the last generated schedule. Forward-backward scheduling methods have been proposed by, e.g., Li and Willis [135] as well as Özdamar and Ulusoy [157, 158].

Instead of independently generating complete schedules either by forward or by backward scheduling, Klein [115] proposes a so-called bidirectional scheduling method which uses forward and backward scheduling steps simultaneously. After scheduling both the source and sink activity (the latter at the end of the planning horizon), the next activity to be scheduled is selected either by the forward or the backward scheduling part, depending on some priority rule. The final schedule is obtained from left shifting the activities that were scheduled by the backward method.

Sampling Methods

Sampling methods generally make use of one SGS and one priority rule. Different schedules are obtained from randomized activity selection. The probability to select an eligible activity can be biased by a priority rule. For each selection decision of the SGS, $p(j)$ is the probability that activity j will be selected from the eligible set EJ_g. Dependent on how the probabilities are computed, one can distinguish random sampling, biased random sampling, and regret based biased random sampling (cf. Kolisch [122]).

Random sampling (RS) assigns each activity in the eligible set the same probability

$$p(j) = \frac{1}{|EJ_g|}.$$

Biased random sampling (BRS) employs the priority values computed by a priority rule directly in order to obtain the selection probabilities. If the priority rule selects the activity with the highest priority value, then the probability is calculated by

$$p(j) = \frac{v(j)}{\sum_{i \in EJ_g} v(i)}.$$

Biased random sampling methods have been applied by Alvarez-Valdes and Tamarit [5] and Cooper [35]. Schirmer and Riesenberg [176] propose a modification called normalized biased random sampling (NBRS) which essentially ensures that the selection probability of the activity with the smallest (highest) priority value is the same when seeking for the activity with the highest (smallest) priority value.

Regret based biased random sampling (RBRS) uses the priority values indirectly via regret values. If the objective is again to select the activity with the highest priority value, the regret value $r(j)$ is the absolute difference between the priority value $v(j)$ of the activity under consideration and the worst priority value of all activities in the eligible set, i.e.,

$$r(j) = v(j) - \min_{i \in EJ_g} v(i).$$

Before calculating the selection probabilities based on the regret values, the latter can be modified by

$$r'(j) = (r(j) + \epsilon)^{\alpha}$$

(cf. Drexl [59]). Adding the constant $\epsilon > 0$ to the regret value assures that the selection probability for each activity in the eligible set is greater than zero and thus every schedule of the search space can be generated. With the choice of the parameter α the strength of bias can be controlled. A high α will cause no bias and thus deterministic activity selection while an α of zero will cause maximum bias and hence random activity selection. Kolisch [120] has found out that, in general, $\epsilon = \alpha = 1$ will provide good results. Drexl [59] uses $\epsilon = \min_{i \in EJ_g} v(i)$. Schirmer and Riesenberg [176] propose a modified regret based biased random sampling (MRBRS) where ϵ is determined dynamically. Experimental comparisons performed by Kolisch [120] as well as Schirmer and Riesenberg [176] revealed (modified) regret based biased random sampling as the best sampling approach.

Illustrating the impact of the different sampling approaches, Table 4.4 gives exemplary selection probabilities for $EJ_g = \{1, 2, 3\}$, $\epsilon = 1$, and $\alpha = 1$.

Adaptive Methods

Adaptive methods analyze the project instance at hand in order to decide which SGS, which priority rule, and which sampling approach is employed. The decision is usually based on instance characteristics such as resource

$j \in EJ_g$	1	2	3
$v(j)$	11	13	20
random sampling	0.33	0.33	0.33
biased random sampling	0.25	0.30	0.45
regret based biased random sampling	0.07	0.21	0.72

Table 4.4: Selection probabilities $p(j)$ for different sampling methods

scarceness and the number of activities. Also further information such as the number of schedules to be generated can be employed for the decision on the solution methodology.

An adaptive multi pass approach has been proposed by Kolisch and Drexl [124]. The heuristic applies the serial SGS with the LFT-priority rule and the parallel SGS with the WCS-priority rule while employing deterministic and regret based sampling activity selection. Partial schedules are discarded by the use of lower bounds. Schirmer and Riesenberg [177] as well as Schirmer [174] have extended this approach by employing both schedule generation schemes together with three different priority rules (LFT, LST, WCS) and two different sampling schemes (MRBRS, RBRS).

Table 4.5 gives a survey of priority rule based heuristics for the RCPSP. For each reference, we mention the algorithmic features used therein, such as the employed SGS and priority rules. Moreover, we characterize it as a single or a multi pass method and give information about sampling techniques.

4.3 Metaheuristic Approaches

This section gives an overview of the two main components of metaheuristic solution procedures, namely the underlying metaheuristic strategies and the problem representations on which the algorithms operate. Afterwards, a literature review of metaheuristic methods proposed for the RCPSP follows.

4.3.1 General Metaheuristic Strategies

Several metaheuristic strategies have been developed to solve hard optimization problems. Overviews of such techniques can be found in Franck and Zimmermann [81], Glover and Greenberg [87], and Pirlot [166].

Simulated Annealing

Simulated annealing (SA), introduced by Kirkpatrick et al. [114], originates from the physical annealing process in which a melted solid is cooled down to

Reference	*SGS*	*priority rule(s)*	*passes*	*sampling*
Alvarez-Valdes, Tamarit [5]	parallel	several rules	multi	BRS
Alvarez-Valdes, Tamarit [6]	parallel	GRPW, MTS and other	single	—
Boctor [20]	both	several rules	multi	—
Cooper [35]	serial	several rules	multi	BRS
Davis, Patterson [38]	parallel	MSLK, LFT and other	single	—
Klein [115]	both	several rules	multi	—
Kolisch [120]	both	LST and other	multi	RS, BRS, RBRS
Kolisch [121]	parallel	WCS and other	single	—
Kolisch [122]	both	several rules	multi	RBRS
Kolisch, Drexl [124]	both	LFT, WCS	multi	RBRS
Li, Willis [135]	parallel	start and finish times	multi	—
Özdamar, Ulusoy [155]	parallel	LCBA	single	—
Özdamar, Ulusoy [157, 158]	parallel	LCBA	multi	—
Schirmer [174]	both	LST, LFT, WCS	multi	RBRS, MRBRS
Schirmer, Riesenberg [176]	both	several rules	multi	NBRS, MRBRS
Schirmer, Riesenberg [177]	both	several rules	multi	RBRS, MRBRS
Thomas, Salhi [200]	parallel	convex combination	multi	—
Ulusoy, Özdamar [202]	parallel	convex combination	multi	—

Table 4.5: Survey of priority rule based heuristics for the RCPSP

a low-energy state. Starting with some initial solution, a so-called neighbor solution is generated by slightly perturbing the current one. If this new solution is better than the current one, it is accepted, and the search proceeds from this new solution. Otherwise, if it is worse, the new solution is only accepted with a probability that depends on the magnitude of the deterioration as well as on a parameter called temperature. The acceptance of solutions with a worse objective function value is motivated by the intention to escape local optima and eventually reach a global optimum. As the algorithm proceeds, this temperature is reduced in order to lower the probability to accept worse neighbors.

Clearly, SA can be viewed as an extension of a simple greedy procedure, sometimes called *first fit strategy* (FFS), which immediately accepts a better neighbor solution but rejects any deterioration.

Several methods similar to SA have been suggested which mainly introduce alternative criteria to control the acceptance of worse neighbor solutions, namely the *threshold accepting* algorithm of Dueck and Scheuer [67] and the *great deluge algorithm* and *record-to-record travel* algorithm of Dueck [66].

Tabu Search

Tabu search (TS), developed by Glover [85, 86], is essentially a steepest descent/mildest ascent method. That is, it evaluates all solutions of the neighborhood and chooses the best one, from which it proceeds further. This concept, however, bears the possibility of cycling because one may always move back to the same local optimum one has just left. In order to avoid this problem, a tabu list is set up as a form of memory for the search process. Usually, the tabu list is employed to forbid those neighborhood moves that might cancel the effect of recently performed moves and might thus lead back to a recently visited solution. Typically, such a tabu status is overrun if the corresponding neighborhood move would lead to a new overall best solution (aspiration criterion).

It is obvious that TS extends the simple steepest descent search, often called *best fit strategy* (BFS), which scans the neighborhood and then accepts the best neighbor solution, until none of the neighbors improves the current objective function value.

Genetic Algorithms

Genetic algorithms (GAs), inspired by the process of biological evolution, have been introduced by Holland [103]. In contrast to the local search strategies above, a GA simultaneously considers a set or population of solutions instead of only one. Having generated an initial population, new solutions are produced by mating two existing ones (crossover) and/or by altering an existing one (mutation). After producing new solutions, the fittest solutions "survive" and make up the next generation while the others are deleted by means of the so-called selection. The fitness value measures the quality of a solution, usually based on the objective function value of the optimization problem to be solved. In Chapter 5, GAs are discussed in more detail.

As mentioned by Eiben et al. [70], GAs generalize the SA concept: The neighbor solution of the current one is obtained from performing mutation on the only solution in the population, and the acceptance mechanism can be viewed as a special case of the selection operator which decides if the search will proceed from the new or the old solution.

Further Metaheuristics

The simulated annealing, tabu search, and genetic algorithm strategies summarized above have been successfully applied to project scheduling problems. There are, however, several general purpose optimization techniques that still await their application to solve the RCPSP. Dorigo et al. [56] proposed the so-called *ant system* which constructs and improves solutions for combinatorial optimization problems by simulating a colony of ants. *Neural networks*, which can be traced back to the work of McCulloch and Pitts [143], imitate the behavior of neurons which transmit information via synapses. The applicability of neural networks to optimization problems has been demonstrated by Hopfield and Tank [104].

4.3.2 Representations

Once a metaheuristic strategy has been chosen, one has to select a suitable representation for solutions. In most cases, metaheuristic approaches for the RCPSP rather operate on representations of schedules than on schedules themselves. Then, an appropriate decoding procedure must be selected to transform the representation into a schedule. Finally, operators are needed to produce new solutions w.r.t. the selected representation. A unary operator constructs a new solution from a single existing solution. Unary operators make up the neighborhood move in local search procedure such as SA and TS as well as the mutation in a GA. A binary operator constructs a new solution from two existing ones. This is done by crossover in a GA.

This subsection summarizes five representations reported in the literature that have been used within metaheuristic approaches to solve the RCPSP. For each representation, we give the related decoding procedures and operators. Another representation, based on a sequence of priority rules, which is known from other scheduling problems will be employed for the standard RCPSP in Chapter 5.

Activity List Representation

In the activity list representation, a schedule is represented by a precedence feasible activity list

$$\lambda = (j_1, j_2, \dots, j_J)$$

in which each activity j_i must have a higher index i than each of its predecessors in $\mathcal{P}_{j_i}$. That is, we have $\mathcal{P}_{j_i} \subseteq \{0, j_1, \dots, j_{i-1}\}$ for $i = 1, \dots, J$. As shown in Section 4.1, the serial SGS can be used as a decoding procedure to obtain a schedule from an activity list. It successively selects the next activity from the list and schedules it as early as possible. Note, however, that the parallel SGS cannot be applied without modification. For illustration, consider the project instance of Figure 2.1 and example activity list

$$\lambda^E = (2, 4, 6, 1, 3, 5)$$

which is transformed by the parallel SGS into the schedule of Figure 2.2.

An initial solution can be generated by randomly selecting an activity from the eligible set in each step of the serial SGS. To obtain better solution quality, one can also use a priority rule or priority rule based sampling scheme for choosing an eligible activity. In either case, recording the activities in the order of their selection results in a (precedence feasible) activity list.

Several unary operators have been proposed for the activity list representation, see, e.g., Della Croce [44]. The so-called pairwise interchange is defined as swapping two activities j_q and j_s, $q, s \in \{1, \ldots, J\}$ with $q \neq s$, if the resulting activity list is precedence feasible. As a special case, the adjacent pairwise interchange swaps two activities j_q and j_{q+1}, $q \in \{1, \ldots, J-1\}$, that are adjacent in λ but not precedence related. Considering again the example project of Figure 2.1, we could apply the adjacent pairwise interchange for $q = 3$ to λ^E as given above and obtain

$$\lambda^N = (2, 4, 1, 6, 3, 5).$$

Furthermore, the simple shift operator selects some activity j_q and inserts it immediately after some other activity j_s, if the precedence constraints are not violated. In our example, shifting activity 6 immediately after activity 3 in λ^E results in neighbor activity list

$$\lambda^{N'} = (2, 4, 1, 3, 6, 5).$$

More sophisticated shift operators have been proposed by Baar et al. [8] for the RCPSP. They make use of the schedule $S(\lambda)$ that is represented by the current activity list λ. The operators are based on the notion of a critical arc which is defined as a pair of successively scheduled activities (i, j), that is, $s_i + p_i = s_j$ in $S(\lambda)$. The underlying idea is that at least one critical arc must become non-critical to improve the current schedule. Hence, Baar et al. [8] define three shift operators that may cancel a critical arc. They extend the simple shift by allowing more than one activity to be shifted. Without giving the formal definitions here, we illustrate such a shift operator on the critical arc (4,1) in the schedule $S(\lambda^E)$ shown in Figure 2.2: Shifting activity 4 and its successor activity 6 immediately after activity 1 leads to neighbor activity list

$$\lambda^{N''} = (2, 1, 4, 6, 3, 5).$$

Another shift operator as well as a binary operator for crossover in an activity list based GA will be developed in Chapter 5.

Random Key Representation

We now turn to the random key representation. Several researchers employed a representation which makes use of an array

$$\rho = (\rho_1, \rho_2, \ldots, \rho_J)$$

that assigns a (typically real-valued) number ρ_j to each activity $j \in \mathcal{J}$. Following Bean [13], we will call such an encoding random key representation. It is similar to the priority value representation of Lee and Kim [133] and Cho and Kim [30] and the problem-space based representation of Storer et al. [196], Leon and Ramamoorthy [134], and Naphade et al. [150]. Therefore, we will discuss these three approaches in a unified framework here.

For an initial solution, the random keys are usually chosen randomly (see, e.g., Lee and Kim [133]) or computed by some priority rule (see, e.g., Leon and Ramamoorthy [134]).

Both the parallel and the serial SGS can be used to derive a schedule from ρ: On each stage g, we can select activity j with the highest random key $\rho_j = \max\{\rho_i \mid i \in EJ_g\}$ from the eligible set EJ_g (clearly, if initialized with, e.g., the latest finish time, one would select the activity with the minimum random key). In other words, the random keys play the role of priority values. Considering again our example project, we obtain the schedule of Figure 2.2 from applying either the parallel or the serial SGS to

$$\rho^E = (0.58, 0.64, 0.31, 0.87, 0.09, 0.34).$$

An alternative approach is proposed by Naphade et al. [150]. Here, the random keys are used to perturb activity slacks which serve as priority values.

While both the parallel and the serial SGS as decoding procedures guarantee that only feasible schedules are found, only the serial one ensures the existence of at least one optimal schedule in the solution space, as discussed in Section 4.1. In order to overcome the drawback of possible exclusion of all optimal solutions by the parallel SGS, several researchers (see Cho and Kim [30], Naphade et al. [150], and Leon and Ramamoorthy [134]) introduced different modifications of the parallel SGS as decoding procedures for the random key representation. These essentially allow to delay a schedulable activity such that the search is no longer restricted to non-delay schedules.

As a unary operator, any pairwise interchange of ρ_j and ρ_i can be employed to the random key representation, including the adjacent pairwise interchange of ρ_j and ρ_{j+1}. Considering a pairwise interchange with $j = 2$ and $i = 4$, an example neighbor of ρ^E is

$$\rho^N = (0.58, 0.87, 0.31, 0.64, 0.09, 0.34).$$

In an approach for the job shop problem, Storer et al. [196] proposed the so-called problem-space based neighborhood which randomly reselects $\rho_j^{\text{new}} \in [(1-\varepsilon) \cdot \rho_j^{\text{old}}, (1+\varepsilon) \cdot \rho_j^{\text{old}}]$ from a uniform distribution, where ε is a positive real-valued constant. For this neighborhood definition with $\varepsilon = 0.1$ an example neighbor of ρ^E is given by

$$\rho^{N'} = (0.59, 0.62, 0.34, 0.89, 0.09, 0.33).$$

The random key representation allows the application of the standard one-point crossover as binary operator (cf. Lee and Kim [133]): Given a random integer q with $1 \leq q < J$, a new random key array $\rho^D = (\rho_1^D, \dots, \rho_J^D)$ is derived by taking the first q positions from a "mother" random key array $\rho^M = (\rho_1^M, \dots, \rho_J^M)$ and the remaining ones from a "father" array $\rho^F = (\rho_1^F, \dots, \rho_J^F)$. We obtain $\rho_i^D = \rho_i^M$ for $i = 1, \dots, q$ and $\rho_i^D = \rho_i^F$ for $i = q+1, \dots, J$. An example for $q = 3$ is

$$\begin{aligned} \rho^M &= (0.58, 0.64, 0.31, 0.87, 0.09, 0.34), \\ \rho^F &= (0.12, 0.43, 0.99, 0.65, 0.19, 0.22), \\ \rho^D &= (0.58, 0.64, 0.31, 0.65, 0.19, 0.22). \end{aligned}$$

Further crossover operators for this representation will be examined in Chapter 5.

Shift Vector Representation

The shift vector representation has been proposed by Sampson and Weiss [173] for the RCPSP. A solution is represented by a shift vector

$$\sigma = (\sigma_1, \sigma_2, \dots, \sigma_J),$$

where σ_j is a nonnegative integer. As a decoding procedure, an extension of the classical forward recursion (see Subsection 2.1.2) is used, in which the start time s_j of an activity $j \in \mathcal{J}$ is calculated as the maximum of the finish times of its predecessors plus the shift σ_j of activity j, that is, $s_0 = 0$ and $s_j = \max\{s_h + p_h \mid h \in \mathcal{P}_j\} + \sigma_j$ for $j = 1, \dots, J$. The following shift vector for our example project leads to the schedule of Figure 2.2:

$$\sigma^E = (6, 0, 1, 0, 0, 0)$$

As this decoding procedure does not consider the resource constraints, a schedule derived from a shift vector may be infeasible. This is illustrated by the following shift vector which forces activities 1 and 4 to be simultaneously in process, thus exceeding the resource capacity by 2 units:

$$\sigma^I = (4, 0, 1, 0, 0, 0)$$

Consequently, the objective function is extended by penalizing the violation of the resource constraints.

The neighborhood of a shift vector σ is given by those vectors that differ from σ in exactly one position and do not lead to a project makespan that exceeds some given upper bound. An example neighbor for shift vector σ^E above is

$$\sigma^N = (6, 0, 1, 0, 1, 0).$$

Schedule Scheme Representation

The schedule scheme representation has been introduced by Brucker et al. [29] for a branch-and-bound algorithm for the RCPSP, see also Brucker and Knust [28]. In what follows we give a brief and rather informal description. A schedule scheme

$$SS = (C, D, N, F)$$

consists of four disjoint relations. $(i,j) \in C$ implies that activity i must be finished before activity j can be started (conjunctions). $(i,j) \in D$ implies that activities i and j may not overlap (disjunctions). $(i,j) \in N$ implies that activities i and j must be processed in parallel in at least one period (parallelity relations). For activities i and j with $(i,j) \in F$ there are no restrictions (flexibility relations). A schedule scheme represents those (not necessarily feasible) schedules in which the related relations are maintained. As a decoding procedure, Baar et al. [8] develop a heuristic that constructs a feasible schedule in which all relations of C and D and a "large" number of parallelity relations in N are satisfied.

Baar et al. [8] introduce a neighborhood definition which basically consists of moves that transform flexibility relations into parallelity relations and parallelity relations into flexibility relations. The neighborhood size is reduced by a critical path calculation and impact estimations for the moves.

Direct Schedule Representation

The recently proposed metaheuristic of Thomas and Salhi [201] is the first attempt for the RCPSP to define a neighborhood that operates directly on schedules instead of a representation which would have to be transformed into a schedule. Hence, a solution is given by a schedule

$$S = (s_1, s_2, \ldots, s_J),$$

that is, a vector that assigns a start time s_j to each activity $j \in \mathcal{J}$.

Thomas and Salhi [201] define a neighborhood which is made up by three different unary operators: First, two activities i and j with $s_i \neq s_j$ which are not precedence related are swapped in the schedule by exchanging their start times, i.e., $s'_i := s_j$ and $s'_j := s_i$. Second, given again i and j as above, activity i is shifted to the start time of activity j, i.e., $s'_i := s_j$. Third, given two non-precedence related activities i and j, activity i is shifted to the finish time of activity j, i.e., $s'_i := s_j + p_j$.

Clearly, these three moves may produce schedules that violate the constraints. Therefore, Thomas and Salhi [201] proceed as follows: For each newly constructed schedule, the level of resource infeasibility as well as the objective function value are estimated. If, based on this estimation, the new schedule is decided to be accepted, it is transformed into a feasible schedule by means of an auxiliary procedure.

4.3.3 Proposed Methods

In this subsection, we briefly summarize the metaheuristic approaches which have been proposed for the RCPSP. A summarizing overview is given in Table 4.6. The references are listed in alphabetical order. For each reference, we denote the employed metaheuristic strategies together with the underlying representation, the decoding procedure, and the used operator. In case of a GA, we only mention the crossover operator.

Reference	*type*	*representation*	*SGS*	*operator*
Baar et al. [8]	TS	activity list	serial	critical path shifts
	TS	sched. scheme	related	related moves
Boctor [22]	SA	activity list	serial	shift
Bouleimen, Lecocq [25]	SA	activity list	serial	shift
Cho, Kim [30]	SA	random key	mod. par.	pairwise interchange
Kohlmorgen et al. [118]	GA	random key	serial	two-point crossover
Lee, Kim [133]	SA	random key	parallel	pairwise interchange
	TS	random key	parallel	pairwise interchange
	GA	random key	parallel	one-point crossover
Leon, Ramamoorthy [134]	FFS	random key	mod. par.	problem-space
	BFS	random key	mod. par.	problem-space
	GA	random key	mod. par.	one-point crossover
Naphade et al. [150]	BFS	random key	mod. par.	problem-space
Pinson et al. [165]	TS	activity list	serial	adjacent pairwise interchange
	TS	activity list	serial	pairwise interchange
	TS	activity list	serial	shift
Sampson, Weiss [173]	(SA)	shift vector	recursion	related move
Thomas, Salhi [201]	TS	schedule	—	related moves

Table 4.6: Survey of metaheuristic approaches for the RCPSP

Baar et al. [8] develop two TS algorithms. The first one is based on the activity list representation in accordance with the serial SGS. The neighborhood is defined by three kinds of critical path based moves. Their second TS approach employs the schedule scheme representation with the related decoding procedure and neighborhood definition. Both TS algorithms use dynamic tabu lists as well as priority based start heuristics.

Boctor [22] proposes an SA procedure based on the activity list representation together with the serial SGS. For neighborhood moves, the shift operator is used.

Bouleimen and Lecocq [25] propose an SA approach similar to that of Boctor [22]. It makes use of the activity list representation, the serial SGS, and the shift operator.

Cho and Kim [30] modify the SA algorithm of Lee and Kim [133] (see below) by extending the random key representation in order to allow the delay of schedulable activities within an adapted parallel SGS.

Kohlmorgen et al. [118] develop a GA which employs the random key representation with standard two-point crossover. They test their approach on a massively parallel computer.

Lee and Kim [133] propose an SA algorithm, a TS procedure and a GA. These three approaches are based on the random key representation with the parallel SGS as decoding procedure. While SA and TS make use of a restricted version of the pairwise interchange move, the GA employs the standard one-point crossover.

Leon and Ramamoorthy [134] test an FFS and a BFS approach as well as a GA. They employ the problem-space based version of the random key representation. The random keys are initialized with values computed by a priority rule. A modified variant of the parallel SGS serves as decoding procedure. The unary operator is defined by the problem-space based neighborhood, and the binary operator is the standard one-point crossover.

Naphade et al. [150] use the BFS concept with the problem-space based variant of the random key representation. The random keys are initialized with the latest finish times of the activities and then modified according to the problem-space based neighborhood. As decoding procedure, they employ a modified parallel SGS, where the random keys are used to calculate slack based priority values.

Pinson et al. [165] suggest several variants of a TS approach based on the activity list representation, the serial SGS, and a priority rule procedure for computing a start solution. The variants differ in the neighborhood definitions, using the adjacent pairwise interchange, the (general) pairwise interchange, and the shift move, respectively.

Sampson and Weiss [173] propose a local search procedure which can be viewed as a variant of SA. Their approach is based on the shift vector representation and the related neighborhood definition.

Finally, Thomas and Salhi [201] introduce a TS method which operates on schedules. They define three different moves. As these may result in infeasible neighbor schedules, they employ a procedure to turn an infeasible schedule into a feasible one.

4.4 Other Heuristics

This section summarizes heuristics that can neither be classified as priority rule methods nor as metaheuristics. We consider truncated exact methods, disjunctive arc based procedures, and two further approaches.

4.4.1 Truncated Branch-and-Bound Methods

In order to limit the notoriously long computation times of exact methods (cf. Chapter 3), truncated branch-and-bound approaches essentially abort enumeration before an optimal solution or an optimality proof of the best solution found so far can be achieved and hence produce heuristic solutions in appropriate computation times.

Pollack-Johnson [167] introduces a so-called jumptracking branch-and-bound procedure which partially searches a solution tree in a depth-first manner. The algorithm is essentially a parallel scheduling heuristic. Instead of scheduling the activity with the highest priority value it branches on certain occasions such that one branch has the activity with the highest priority value and the other branch has the activity with the second highest priority value, which is scheduled next. Note, due to use of the parallel SGS the optimal solution might be excluded from the search space.

Sprecher [191] employs his depth-first search branch-and-bound procedure as a heuristic by imposing a time limit. The enumeration process is guided by the so-called precedence tree which essentially branches on the activities in the eligible set of the serial SGS (cf. Subsection 3.1.1). Via backtracking, all precedence feasible activity lists are (implicitly) enumerated. In order to obtain good solutions early in the search process (and thus within the time limit), priority rules are applied to select the most promising activity from the eligible set for branching first.

4.4.2 Disjunctive Arc Based Methods

The basic idea of the disjunctive-arc-based approaches is to extend the precedence relations (the set of conjunctive arcs) by adding additional arcs (the disjunctive arcs) such that the so-called minimal forbidden sets are considered ("destroyed") and thus the earliest start schedule is feasible with respect to (precedence and) resource constraints. The minimal forbidden sets are sets of activities which are independent w.r.t. the precedence relations but cannot be scheduled simultaneously due to resource constraints.

Shaffer et al. [182] develop the so-called "resource scheduling method." They restrict the scope to those forbidden sets for which all activities in the earliest finish schedule are processed at the same time. The disjunctive arc which produces the smallest increase in the earliest finish time of the unique sink is introduced and the earliest finish schedule is recalculated. The algorithm terminates as soon as a (precedence- and) resource-feasible earliest finish schedule is found. Note that this approach can be transformed into a single-pass priority rule method based on the parallel SGS, cf. Kolisch [120].

Alvarez-Valdes and Tamarit [6] propose four different ways of destroying the minimal forbidden sets. The best results are achieved by applying the following strategy: Beginning with the minimal forbidden sets of lowest cardinality, one set is arbitrarily chosen and destroyed by adding the disjunctive arc for which the earliest finish time of the unique dummy sink is minimal.

Bell and Han [15] present a two-phase algorithm. The first phase is very similar to the approach of Shaffer et al. [182]. However, the second phase tries to improve the feasible solution obtained by phase one as follows: After removing redundant arcs, each disjunctive arc that is part of the critical path(s) is temporarily cancelled and the first phase is applied again.

Note that the schedule scheme based tabu search procedure of Baar et al. [8] is a disjunctive arc based approach as well (cf. Section 4.3).

4.4.3 Further Approaches

An integer programming based heuristic has been used by Oguz and Bala [153]. The method employs the integer programming formulation originally proposed by Pritsker et al. [169], cf. also Subsection 2.1.3.

Mausser and Lawrence [142] use so-called block structures to improve the makespan of projects. They start by generating a feasible solution with the parallel SGS. Following this, they identify blocks which represent contiguous time spans that completely contain all activities processed within them. Each such block can be considered independently of the other blocks. The method essentially reschedules individual blocks in order to shorten the overall project length.

Chapter 5

Single-Mode Genetic Algorithms

In this chapter, we discuss genetic algorithm (GA) heuristics for the RCPSP. The GAs make use of many of the concepts that were discussed in the previous chapter, such as schedule generation schemes, problem representations, and priority rule methods. We will also introduce some new approaches such as new operators, generalized representations, and a local search extension. In particular, we will introduce a representation which allows the GA to adapt itself by learning which algorithmic component should be used.

We proceed as follows: Section 5.1 summarizes the basic principles of evolution and leads to a general GA scheme. Sections 5.2 – 5.4 define three GAs based on different problem representations, namely the activity list, the random key, and the priority rule representation. In Section 5.5, these three GA approaches are analyzed; the most promising representation (and hence the most promising GA) is determined in thorough computational tests. Finally, Section 5.6 considers various extensions of the most promising GA in order to further improve the solution quality.[1]

5.1 Evolution and Optimization

This section gives a more detailed introduction into GAs than could be provided in Subsection 4.3.1. We begin with a brief discussion of those elements of the theory of evolution that are exploited in genetic algorithms. Subsequently, we describe the basic GA scheme that will be the backbone of the GAs that are developed in this chapter.

---

[1]With the exception of Section 5.6, the approaches and results of this chapter can also be found in Hartmann [92].

5.1.1 The Theory of Evolution

In his book "On the Origin of the Species by Means of Natural Selection," Charles R. Darwin (1809-1882) laid the foundation of the theory of evolution. It has later been extended and confirmed by various researchers such as Gregor Mendel (1822-1884) who developed a theory of genetic inheritance.

We will now describe those aspects of the process of evolution that will be important for fully understanding the motivation behind the genetic algorithms developed in this and the following chapters. An individual, or more precisely, its phenotype, consists of basic characteristics contained in its genes, the genotype, and further acquired characterictics. The individuals of a species are similar but differ both in their genotypes and phenotypes. New individuals are produced by crossover, that is, usually two parent individuals mate. The genotype of a child individual is determined by a recombination of the parents' genes and mutation, that is, random changes of some genes.

In the struggle for life, the individuals of a species compete for food and mating partners. The fittest individuals of the population survive and may pass on their genes, the others die before they can have offspring. This principle of selection leads to an increasing level of adaptation to the species' environment.

Populations may be separated from each other by mountains, deserts, or water. Isolated populations of the same species may develop differently. Nevertheless, some fit individuals may eventually migrate between populations and spread their genes.

The adaptation of a species to its environment is called phylogenetic learning. In addition, each individual of a species may learn individually. This process is referred to as ontogenetic learning. The results of phylogenetic learning are passed on to the following generations by means of recombination of the genes as described above. In contrast, the results of ontogenetic learning are not hereditary, that is, changes within the phenotype do not have an influence on the genotype. A possible explanation for this is that there seems to be no mechanism to decide whether a change is useful or not, such as, e.g., injuries or changes due to old age. Only random changes within the genotype by means of mutation may be passed on; together with recombination and selection this forms the process of phylogenetic learning. This contradicts the theory of Jean-Baptiste de Monet Chevalier de Lamarck (1744-1829) who claimed that physical changes of an individual occur if and because they are useful, and that these changes are passed on to its offspring. His teleological theory of evolution, however, has been disproved.

5.1.2 Basic Genetic Algorithm Scheme

Genetic algorithms have been developed by Holland [103]. For an introduction into GAs we refer to Goldberg [88]. GAs are inspired by the theory of biological evolution and serve as a meta strategy within the fields of, e.g., continuous and discrete optimization, machine learning, and game theory. Viewing the sequence of generations produced by a GA as a Markov chain, Eiben et al. [70] examine the general GA characteristics that make GAs suitable to solve combinatorial optimization problems. They state some simple sufficient conditions under which a GA "almost surely" finds an optimum (i.e., finds an optimum with probability one within an infinite number of generations).

Given an optimization problem, individuals correspond to solutions (or their representations) while populations are sets of solutions. The fitness of an individual corresponds to the objective function value of the solution related to that individual. The crossover operator recombines parts of two fit individuals to form new ones. These parts, the genes or gene combinations, are assumed to have contributed to the fitness of the parent individuals. The mutation operator alters single solutions and may produce genes or gene combinations that had not occured in the population before (and could therefore not have been produced by crossover).

We will use the following general GA scheme: The GA starts by computing an initial population, i.e., the first generation. We assume that the initial population contains POP individuals where POP is an even integer. After computing the fitness values of the individuals, the population is randomly partitioned into pairs of individuals. To each resulting pair of individuals (parents), we apply the crossover operator to produce two new individuals (children). Subsequently, we apply the mutation operator to the genotypes of the newly produced children. After determining the fitness of each child individual, we add the children to the current population, leading to a population size of $2 \cdot POP$. Finally, applying the selection operator to reduce the population to its former size, we obtain the next generation. The algorithm stops if the generation counter G is equal to the prespecified number of generations which is denoted as GEN or if a given time limit is reached. Clearly, at most $POP \cdot GEN$ different individuals (and related schedules) are calculated.

In each generation, the population is given by a list of individuals $\mathcal{POP}$. In contrast to a set of individuals, a list structure allows us to keep identical individuals in the population. This is useful because identical individuals can be assumed to represent "fit" information which should be given all chances to be hereditary. Moreover, this way we save the additional computation time that would be needed for checking whether a newly produced child and an already existing individual of the population are identical. Analogously,

$\mathcal{CHI}$ denotes the list of the children produced from the current generation. In algorithmic notation, the basic GA scheme described above can be given as follows:

Algorithm 5.1 *(Basic Genetic Algorithm Scheme)*

$G := 1$;
generate initial population $\mathcal{POP}$;
compute fitness for individuals $I \in \mathcal{POP}$;
WHILE $G < GEN$ AND time limit is not reached DO
BEGIN
    $G := G + 1$;
    produce children $\mathcal{CHI}$ from $\mathcal{POP}$ by crossover;
    apply mutation to children $I \in \mathcal{CHI}$;
    compute fitness for children $I \in \mathcal{CHI}$;
    $\mathcal{POP} := \mathcal{POP} \cup \mathcal{CHI}$;
    reduce population $\mathcal{POP}$ by means of selection;
END.

5.2 Activity List Based Genetic Algorithm

The first GA variant to be examined employs the activity list representation that has been described in Subsection 4.3.2. As underlying scheme we use that of Subsection 5.1.2.

5.2.1 Individuals and Fitness

In the first GA variant to be examined, an individual is given by a precedence feasible activity list

$$\lambda = (j_1, j_2, \dots, j_J).$$

Each such genotype is related to a uniquely determined schedule (phenotype) which is computed using serial SGS of Subsection 4.1.1: First, the dummy source activity is started at time 0. Then we schedule the activities in the order that is prescribed by the list $(j_1, \dots, j_J)$. Thereby, each activity is assigned the earliest feasible start time.

The fitness $f(\lambda)$ of an individual λ is given by the makespan of the related schedule. For determining the initial population, we have tested two alternative approaches that have been described in Section 4.2: First, we use a simple random sampling method which successively determines the eligible activities within the serial SGS, randomly selects an activity, and puts it into the list. Second, we employ the regret based biased random sampling method together with the LFT priority rule. Here, the probabilities for activity selection are biased w.r.t. the latest finish times of the eligible activities.

Notice that, while each individual is related to a unique schedule, a schedule can be related to more than one individual. In other words, there is some redundancy in the search space as distinct elements of the search space (i.e., genotypes) may be related to the same schedule. For demonstration, we consider again the project instance of Figure 2.1 and borrow example individual $\lambda^E = (2, 4, 6, 1, 3, 5)$ from Subsection 4.3.2. Obviously, exchanging activities 6 and 1 in this activity list, we obtain a different precedence feasible genotype, i.e., $\lambda^N = (2, 4, 1, 6, 3, 5)$. However, both genotypes are related to the same schedule, i.e., the schedule displayed in Figure 2.2.

5.2.2 Crossover and Mutation

We consider three different crossover variants for the activity list based encoding. They are similar to the general crossover technique described by Reeves [171] for permutation based genotypes, with the difference that our encoding takes precedence relations into account.

One-Point Crossover

The first crossover operator is called one-point crossover. We consider two individuals selected for crossover, a mother $\lambda^M = (j_1^M, \dots, j_J^M)$ and a father $\lambda^F = (j_1^F, \dots, j_J^F)$. Then we draw a random integer q with $1 \leq q < J$. Now two new individuals, a daughter $\lambda^D = (j_1^D, \dots, j_J^D)$ and a son $\lambda^S = (j_1^S, \dots, j_J^S)$, are produced from the parents. We first consider λ^D which is defined as follows: The positions $i = 1, \dots, q$ in λ^D are taken from the mother, that is,

$$j_i^D := j_i^M.$$

The activity list of positions $i = q+1, \dots, J$ in λ^D is taken from the father. However, the jobs that have already been taken from the mother may not be considered again. We obtain

$$j_i^D := j_k^F \text{ where } k \text{ is the lowest index such that } j_k^F \notin \{j_1^D, \dots, j_{i-1}^D\}.$$

As a result, the relative positions in the parents' activity lists are preserved. This way, the parents contribute to the child's fitness. For illustration, we consider again the example project of Figure 2.1 and parent individuals

$$\lambda^M = (1, 3, 2, 5, 4, 6), \quad \lambda^F = (2, 4, 6, 1, 3, 5). \tag{5.1}$$

With $q = 3$, we obtain daughter individual

$$\lambda^D = (1,3,2,4,6,5). \tag{5.2}$$

While the above definition obviously ensures that each activity appears exactly once in the resulting activity list, the following theorem shows that also the precedence assumption is fulfilled.

Theorem 5.1 *If applied to precedence feasible parent individuals, the one-point crossover operator for the activity list based genetic encoding results in a precedence feasible offspring genotype.*

Proof. Let the genotypes of the parents λ^M and λ^F fulfill the precedence assumption. We assume that the child individual λ^D produced by the crossover operator is not precedence feasible. That is, there are two activities j_i^D and j_k^D with $1 \leq i < k \leq J$ and $j_k^D \in \mathcal{P}_{j_i^D}$. Three cases can be distinguished:

Case 1: We have $i, k \leq q$. Then activity j_i^D is before activity j_k^D in the activity list of λ^M, a contradiction to the precedence feasibility of λ^M.

Case 2: We have $i, k > q$. As the relative positions are maintained by the crossover operator, activity j_i^D is before activity j_k^D in the activity list of λ^F, contradicting the precedence feasibility of λ^F.

Case 3: We have $i \leq q$ and $k > q$. Then activity j_i^D is before activity j_k^D in the activity list of λ^M, again a contradiction to the precedence feasibility of λ^M. □

The son λ^S of the individuals λ^M and λ^F is computed similarly. However, the positions $1, \ldots, q$ of the son's activity list are taken from the father and the remaining positions are determined by the mother. Obviously, Theorem 5.1 holds for both offspring individuals λ^D and λ^S.

Two-Point Crossover

The second crossover operator is an extension of the one-point variant, called two-point crossover. Here, we draw two random integers q_1 and q_2 with $1 \leq q_1 < q_2 \leq J$. Now the daughter individual λ^D is determined by taking the activity list of the positions $i = 1, \ldots, q_1$ from the mother, that is,

$$j_i^D := j_i^M.$$

The positions $i = q_1 + 1, \ldots, q_2$ are derived from the father:

$$j_i^D := j_k^F \text{ where } k \text{ is the lowest index such that } j_k^F \notin \{j_1^D, \ldots, j_{i-1}^D\}.$$

The remaining positions $i = q_2 + 1, \ldots, J$ are again taken from the mother, that is,

$$j_i^D := j_k^M \text{ where } k \text{ is the lowest index such that } j_k^M \notin \{j_1^D, \ldots, j_{i-1}^D\}.$$

Considering again Figure 2.1 and the example parents λ^M and λ^F given in (5.1), we obtain for $q_1 = 1$ and $q_2 = 3$ daughter

$$\lambda^D = (1, 2, 4, 3, 5, 6).$$

The son individual is computed analogously, taking the first and third part from the father and the second one from the mother. Obviously, Theorem 5.1 can easily be extended to the two-point crossover. Observe also that fixing $q_2 = J$ leads to the one-point variant which therefore is a special case of the two-point crossover.

Uniform Crossover

The third crossover type is called uniform crossover. Here, the daughter λ^D is determined as follows: We draw a sequence of random numbers $\xi_i \in \{0, 1\}$, $i = 1, \ldots, J$. Then we successively fill positions $i = 1, \ldots, J$ in λ^D. If we have $\xi_i = 1$, we take that activity from the mother's activity list which has the lowest index among the currently unselected activities, that is,

$$j_i^D := j_k^M \text{ where } k \text{ is the lowest index such that } j_k^M \notin \{j_1^D, \ldots, j_{i-1}^D\}.$$

Otherwise, if $\xi_i = 0$, the activity is analogously derived from the father's activity list:

$$j_i^D := j_k^F \text{ where } k \text{ is the lowest index such that } j_k^F \notin \{j_1^D, \ldots, j_{i-1}^D\}.$$

For the example parent individuals λ^M and λ^F of (5.1) and random number sequence $0, 1, 1, 0, 1, 1$, we obtain daughter

$$\lambda^D = (2, 1, 3, 4, 5, 6).$$

The son S is computed using an analogous procedure which takes the i-th job from the father if $p_1 = 1$ and from the mother otherwise. Note that the uniform crossover generalizes the two-point variant: Fixing $\xi_i = 1$ for $i \in \{1, \ldots, q_1, q_2 + 1, \ldots, J\}$ and $\xi_i = 0$ for $i \in \{q_1 + 1, \ldots, q_2\}$ leads to the definition of the daughter in the two-point crossover. With arguments similar to those used in the proof of Theorem 5.1, one can show that also the uniform crossover produces precedence feasible offspring.

Mutation

Finally, we turn to the mutation operator. Given an activity list based individual λ, the mutation operator modifies the related activity list as follows: For all positions $i = 1, \dots, J-1$, activities j_i and j_{i+1} are exchanged with a probability of p_{mutation}, if the result is a activity list which fulfills the precedence assumption. Observe that this is essentially the adjacent pairwise interchange for activity lists described in Subsection 4.3.2.

The mutation operator may create activity lists (i.e., gene combinations) that could not have been produced by the crossover operator. However, it should be noted that performing a mutation on an individual does not necessarily change the related schedule. This is due to the redundancy in the genetic representation mentioned above. For example, interchanging two activities in the activity list which have the same start time changes the individual, but not the related schedule.

5.2.3 Selection

We consider three alternative types of selection operators which follow a survival-of-the-fittest strategy as similarly described by, e.g., Michalewicz [144].

Ranking

The first selection approach considered here is a simple ranking method. We keep the *POP* best individuals and remove the remaining ones from the population (ties are broken arbitrarily).

Proportional Selection

The second variant, the proportional selection, can be viewed as a randomized version of the previously described ranking technique. Let $f(\lambda)$ be the fitness of an individual λ, and let $f_{\text{best}} = \min\{f(\lambda) \mid \lambda \in \mathcal{POP}\}$ denote the best fitness in the current population. We restore the original population size by successively removing individuals from the population $\mathcal{POP}$ until *POP* individuals are left, using the following probability: The probability to "die" (i.e., to be removed) for an individual λ is given by

$$p_{\text{death}}(\lambda) = \frac{(f(\lambda) - f_{\text{best}} + 1)^2}{\sum_{\lambda' \in \mathcal{POP}} (f(\lambda') - f_{\text{best}} + 1)^2} \,.$$

Tournament Selection

Next, we consider two versions of the tournament technique. In the 2-tournament selection, two different randomly chosen individuals λ_1 and λ_2

compete for (temporary) survival. If individual λ_1 is not better than individual λ_2, i.e., if $f(\lambda_1) \geq f(\lambda_2)$, then it dies and is removed from the population (again, ties are broken arbitrarily). This process is repeated until *POP* individuals are left. Recall that a lower fitness value implies a better quality of the individual.

Finally, the 3-tournament selection extends the previously described approach by randomly selecting three individuals λ_1, λ_2, and λ_3. If we have $f(\lambda_1) \geq f(\lambda_2)$ and $f(\lambda_1) \geq f(\lambda_3)$, individual λ_1 is removed from the population. Again, this step is repeated until *POP* individuals are left.

5.3 Random Key Based Genetic Algorithm

This section is devoted to a GA which makes use of a random key based encoding that has been described in Subsection 4.3.2. We employ the basic GA scheme of Subsection 5.1.2 that was used for the activity list GA. Moreover, we make use of the selection operator variants here that have been defined for the activity list GA as they are not encoding specific. This allows us to obtain comparable results when evaluating the GA approaches. In the following, the random key based representation and the related crossover and mutation operators are discussed in more detail.

5.3.1 Individuals and Fitness

In this GA approach, an individual is represented by an array of random keys

$$\rho = (\rho_1, \rho_2, \ldots, \rho_J).$$

For each random key of activity $j = 1, \ldots, J$, we have $\rho_j \in [0,1]$. Using the serial SGS (cf. Subsection 4.1.1), we obtain the schedule related to an individual. More precisely, we treat the random keys as priority values, that is, we successively select the eligible activity with the highest random key and start it as early as possible. Note that this distinguishes our random key GA from that of Lee and Kim [133] who employ the parallel SGS (cf. Subsection 4.1.2). Clearly, using the serial SGS allows us to compare the results obtained from the random key representation with those of the activity list encoding for which we use the serial SGS as well.

Again, the fitness $f(\rho)$ of an individual ρ is defined as the makespan of the related schedule. Each individual ρ of the initial population is determined by randomly drawing a random key $\rho_j \in [0,1]$ with a uniform distribution for each activity $j = 1, \ldots, J$.

As was the case for the activity list based encoding, there is some redundancy in the search space also for the random key based representation. We consider again example individual

$$\rho^E = (0.58, 0.64, 0.31, 0.87, 0.09, 0.34)$$

of Subsection 4.3.2 for the project instance of Figure 2.1. Setting for example $\rho_2 = 0.93$ instead of 0.64 in ρ^E, we obtain a different individual. However, both individuals are related to the same schedule, namely the one of Figure 2.2.

5.3.2 Crossover and Mutation

The random key encoding allows us to employ standard crossover operators. Again, we consider two individuals selected for crossover, a mother $\rho^M = (\rho_1^M, \dots, \rho_J^M)$ and a father $\rho^F = (\rho_1^F, \dots, \rho_J^F)$, from which two offspring individuals are computed. In the following, we only define the daughter $\rho^D = (\rho_1^D, \dots, \rho_J^D)$. As for the activity list representation, the son ρ^S is computed analogously to the daughter's definition.

For the one-point crossover, we draw a random integer q with $1 \leq q < J$. The first q positions of daughter individual ρ^D are taken from the mother while the remaining ones are defined by the father, that is, we have for each $i = 1, \dots, J$

$$\rho_i^D = \begin{cases} \rho_i^M, & \text{if } i \in \{1, \dots, q\} \\ \rho_i^F, & \text{if } i \in \{q+1, \dots, J\}. \end{cases}$$

For an illustration of this definition, we refer to the example given in Subsection 4.3.2.

Similarly to the activity list based encoding, we have considered the two-point crossover in addition to the one-point variant defined above. We draw two random integers q_1 and q_2 with $1 \leq q_1 < q_2 \leq J$ and obtain for each $i = 1, \dots, J$

$$\rho_i^D = \begin{cases} \rho_i^M, & \text{if } i \in \{1, \dots, q_1\} \\ \rho_i^F, & \text{if } i \in \{q_1+1, \dots, q_2\} \\ \rho_i^M, & \text{if } i \in \{q_2+1, \dots, J\}. \end{cases}$$

Finally, for the uniform crossover, we draw a sequence of random numbers $\xi_i \in \{0, 1\}$, $i = 1, \dots, J$. Then we set for each $i = 1, \dots, J$

$$\rho_i^D = \begin{cases} \rho_i^M, & \text{if } \xi_i = 1 \\ \rho_i^F, & \text{otherwise.} \end{cases}$$

The mutation for the random key based encoding is defined as follows: Given an individual ρ, we modify the related random key sequence as follows: For all positions $i = 1, \dots, J$, a new random key $\rho_i \in [0, 1]$ is drawn with a probability of p_{mutation}. Clearly, the result is always a feasible random key sequence. Obviously, the mutation operator may create random keys (i.e., genes) that did not occur in the population before. Again, however, performing a mutation on an individual does not necessarily change the related schedule due to the redundancy discussed above.

5.4 Priority Rule Based Genetic Algorithm

In this section, we describe a GA based on a representation consisting of a priority rule list. This representation type has been proposed by Dorndorf and Pesch [57] and Herrmann et al. [100] for the job shop scheduling problem. Özdamar [154] employed it for the multi-mode extension of the RCPSP. Like the random key based one, also this GA employs the basic scheme and the selection operator variants that have been used for the activity list GA. Next, the priority rule encoding and the related crossover and mutation operators are provided.

5.4.1 Individuals and Fitness

In this GA variant, an individual is given by a list of priority rules

$$\pi = (\pi_1, \pi_2, \ldots, \pi_J)$$

where we have for each position $i = 1, \ldots, J$

$$\pi_i \in \{\text{LFT, LST, MTS, MSLK, WRUP, GRPW}\}.$$

Each of these six priority rules has been suggested in the literature and shown to produce good schedules for the RCPSP, we refer to the study recently performed by Kolisch [122]. Table 4.3 in Section 4.2 contains a brief mathematical definition for each priority rule.

Using the serial SGS, we transform an individual into a schedule. We successively select an eligible activity and start it as early as possible. Thereby, the g-th decision which activity to select next is made by the g-th priority rule in the list. Considering the project instance of Figure 2.1, the schedule related to example individual

$$\pi^E = (\text{LST, GRPW, MTS, LST, MSLK, LFT})$$

is again the one of Figure 2.2. The use of the serial SGS is motivated by the intention to compare the results of this representation to those of the two encodings described in the previous sections. In contrast, Özdamar [154] employed the parallel SGS in her priority rule based GA for the multi-mode case.

The fitness of an individual is again given by the makespan of the related schedule. Each individual π of the initial generation is determined by randomly selecting one of the six priority rules for π_i, $i = 1, \ldots, J$.

Like the two previously described genetic representations, also the priority rule based encoding contains some redundancy. Consider again example individual π^E given above. Replacing the first priority rule in the list (LFT) with the GRPW rule, we obtain a different genotype which is, however, also related to the schedule of Figure 2.2.

While the search spaces for the other two encodings always contain an optimal solution, this is not the case for the priority rule based representation. For the sake of shortness, we do not give a detailed counterexample, mentioning only that in some cases none of the employed priority rules may select an activity that must be scheduled next in order to obtain an optimal schedule from the current partial schedule. This drawback could be overcome by adding a priority rule which allows any eligible activity to be selected, namely the random rule (RAND). However, we did not employ the RAND priority rule because it seems to be incompatible with the GA paradigm: Obviously, selecting an activity with the RAND rule may contribute to the fitness if, by chance, this activity continues the current partial schedule in an advantageous way. However, the RAND rule itself does not contain specific information that is worth to be inherited.

5.4.2 Crossover and Mutation

We can employ standard crossover operators similar to those used for the random key encoding. The definitions of the one-point, two-point, and uniform crossover for the priority rule representation are obtained from replacing ρ_i by π_i in the respective definitions for the priority value encoding.

The mutation operator for the priority rule based encoding is defined as follows: For each position $i = 1, \ldots, J$ of an individual π, a new priority rule

$$\pi_i \in \{\text{LFT}, \text{LST}, \text{MTS}, \text{MSLK}, \text{WRUP}, \text{GRPW}\}$$

is randomly drawn with a probability of p_{mutation}. Again, due to the redundancy described above, performing a mutation on a genotype does not necessarily change the related schedule.

5.5 Computational Results

This section examines the three GAs introduced in the previous sections in order to determine the most promising representation. The best representation will then be extended in the next section. Like the comparison of the exact procedures in Chapter 3, the experiments have been conducted on a

Pentium-based IBM-compatible personal computer with 133 MHz clock-pulse and 32 MB RAM. The three GAs have been coded in ANSI C, compiled with the GNU C compiler, and run under Linux.

As test instances, we have used standard sets constructed by the project instance generator ProGen of Kolisch et al. [130] (see Appendix A). We considered the two sets with 30 and 60 non-dummy actvities to be sufficient to determine the best representation (more in-depth computational tests which also employ the remaining single-mode instance sets mentioned in Appendix A as well as other heuristics will follow in Chapter 6).

As mentioned in Appendix A.2.1, for the set with 30 non-dummy activities all optimal objective function values are known. Therefore, we report the average percentage deviation from the optimal makespan for these instances. However, for some of the instances with 60 activities, only heuristic solutions are known. In these cases, we give the average percentage deviation from the best lower and upper bounds as reported in the library PSPLIB (cf. Kolisch and Sprecher [129]) at the time this research was performed. The lower bounds were computed by Baar et al. [8] and Heilmann and Schwindt [99]. The upper bounds were obtained by Kolisch and Drexl [124], Kohlmorgen et al. [118], and Baar et al. [8].

This section is organized as follows: In Subsection 5.5.1, we configure the GAs, that is, we determine the best operators and parameter settings. Subsection 5.5.2 then provides the results of the computational comparison of the three approaches. Finally, Subsection 5.5.3 examines the impact of the genetic inheritance mechanisms on the solution quality for the three representations.

5.5.1 Configuration of the Genetic Algorithms

Crucial for the success of a GA is an appropriate choice of good genetic operators and adequate parameter settings, usually on the basis of computational experiments. We report the outcome of our study to determine the best GA configuration only for the suggested activity list GA approach of Section 5.2 and for the ProGen instance set with 30 non-dummy activities, because the results for the other GAs and the other instance sets are similar. For each instance, 1000 schedules were computed.

Table 5.1 reports the average deviation from the optimum, the percentage of instances for which an optimal solution was found, and the computation time in seconds for different combinations of alternative genetic operators. We have tested all possible GA configurations that arise from combining three mutation probability levels, the three crossover variants, and the four selection variants. The best configuration turned out to be a mutation probability of 0.05, the two-point crossover strategy, and the ranking method for selection. For the sake of shortness, Table 5.1 contains only those configurations that vary this best one in only one point. The two-point crossover operator appears to be capable of inheriting building blocks that contributed to the parents' fitness (for much larger projects, even more than two cuts may probably be advisable). In contrast, the uniform crossover operator (which yields good results for problems with a different structure such as, e.g., the multidimensional knapsack problem, cf. Chu and Beasley [32]) does not seem to be well suited for sequencing problems. A randomized selection strategy seems to be advantageous only if a much larger number of individuals is considered.

p_{mutation}	*crossover*	*selection*	*av. dev.*	*optimal*	*CPU-sec*
0.01	two-point	ranking	0.64 %	77.5 %	0.54
0.05	two-point	ranking	0.54 %	81.5 %	0.54
0.10	two-point	ranking	0.56 %	80.4 %	0.55
0.05	one-point	ranking	0.65 %	77.5 %	0.54
0.05	two-point	ranking	0.54 %	81.5 %	0.54
0.05	uniform	ranking	0.66 %	79.6 %	0.76
0.05	two-point	ranking	0.54 %	81.5 %	0.54
0.05	two-point	proportional	0.62 %	78.5 %	0.60
0.05	two-point	2-tournament	0.63 %	79.0 %	0.54
0.05	two-point	3-tournament	0.59 %	80.9 %	0.54

Table 5.1: Alternative genetic operators — activity list GA, 1000 schedules, $J = 30$

Table 5.2 shows that a population size of 40 and 25 generations is the best parameter relationship when calculating 1000 individuals (i.e., schedules). Finally, Table 5.3 shows that it pays to use a sampling method instead of a pure random procedure to determine the initial population.

POP	*GEN*	*av. dev.*	*optimal*	*CPU-sec*
50	20	0.56 %	80.8 %	0.54
40	25	0.54 %	81.5 %	0.54
20	50	0.79 %	76.5 %	0.54

Table 5.2: Impact of population size — activity list GA, 1000 schedules, $J = 30$

The results for the other two representations are similar to those of the activity list based encoding. That is, for all three representations, the best results are obtained from a mutation probability of 0.05, a two-point crossover, the ranking selection, and the relationship of population size and number of

Initial population	*av. dev.*	*optimal*	*CPU-sec*
sampling — LFT	0.54 %	81.5 %	0.54
sampling — random	0.99 %	70.8 %	0.52

Table 5.3: Impact of initial population — activity list GA, 1000 schedules, $J = 30$

generations given above. In the further computational studies, the three GAs make use of the best configuration determined here.

5.5.2 Comparison of the Genetic Algorithms

In this subsection, we present the experimental results obtained from the comparison of the new activity list based GA of Section 5.2 with the GA approaches described in Sections 5.3 and 5.4. Our goal is to determine the best representation.

The first numerical results to be presented are obtained from the ProGen project instance set with 30 activities where 1000 individuals (i.e., schedules) are computed for each instance. Table 5.4 gives the average and the maximal deviation from the optimum, the percentage of instances for which an optimal solution was found, and the computation time in seconds. The activity list based encoding yields better results than the random key based representation while both outperform the priority rule encoding.

GA	*av. dev.*	*max. dev.*	*optimal*	*CPU-sec*
activity list	0.54 %	7.9 %	81.5 %	0.54
random key	1.03 %	10.8 %	70.6 %	0.64
priority rule	1.38 %	17.7 %	70.6 %	0.91

Table 5.4: Comparison of genetic algorithms — 1000 schedules, $J = 30$

Table 5.4 also shows that the activity list GA results in the lowest computation times. This is because we have to determine eligible activities and apply priority rules only when computing the initial population. Clearly, when using a heuristic procedure in practice, it is important to obtain good schedules within a reasonable amount of CPU time. Therefore, we have additionally tested the three GA variants with time limits instead of fixing the number of schedules to be computed.

Table 5.5 displays the average deviations from the optimum obtained for the instances with $J = 30$ from four different time limits. The activity list GA performs best for all time limits while the priority rule based GA yields the worst results. Note especially that the deviation of the activity list GA is two times lower than that of the priority rule based GA for a time limit of 0.5 seconds while it is more than four times lower for 4 seconds. That is, the new activity list based GA is not only the best for small time limits, its superiority also further increases when the time limit is increased.

GA	*0.50 sec*	*1.00 sec*	*2.00 sec*	*4.00 sec*
activity list	0.71 %	0.45 %	0.37 %	0.24 %
random key	1.16 %	0.88 %	0.69 %	0.54 %
priority rule	1.51 %	1.33 %	1.21 %	1.13 %

Table 5.5: Average deviations w.r.t. time limit — $J = 30$

Next, we have performed the same experiment on the set of instances with 60 activities. As for some of the instances optimal solutions are currently unknown, we measure the deviations from the best known lower and upper bound here. The results can be found in Tables 5.6 and 5.7, respectively. Again, the activity list GA performs best for all time limits. In contrast to the instances with $J = 30$, however, here the priority rule based GA outperforms the random key GA. This observation can be explained as follows: Selecting $J = 60$ instead of $J = 30$ results in a much larger search space. Within the same time limit, only a much smaller portion of the search space can be examined. Therefore, the strategy to combine several good priority rules corresponds to examining only potentially promising regions of the search space. However, the restriction to the regions identified by the priority rules is disadvantageous for smaller projects and/or higher computation times (or, of course, faster computers).

GA	*0.50 sec*	*1.00 sec*	*2.00 sec*	*4.00 sec*
activity list	5.30 %	4.73 %	4.37 %	4.16 %
random key	7.60 %	6.60 %	6.17 %	5.70%
priority rule	5.92 %	5.50 %	5.18 %	4.96 %

Table 5.6: Average deviations from lower bound w.r.t. time limit — $J = 60$

We remark here that most of the best known upper bounds for the hard instances were computed by Kohlmorgen et al. [118] with their parallel GA approach. Using a massively parallel computer with 16384 processing units, they could generate 16384 individuals per generation, while our GA could not evaluate more than 4000 individuals altogether within 4 seconds when applied to the instances with 60 activities. Thus, it is not surprising that the best known upper bounds are on the average 0.59 % better than our results (cf. Table 5.7). Nevertheless, it should be mentioned that the schedules for 3

GA	0.50 sec	1.00 sec	2.00 sec	4.00 sec
activity list	1.42 %	1.10 %	0.79 %	0.59 %
random key	3.61 %	2.88 %	2.24 %	1.79 %
priority rule	2.07 %	1.80 %	1.52 %	1.34 %

Table 5.7: Average deviations from best upper bound w.r.t. time limit — $J = 60$

of the 480 instances with 60 activities found by our GA (within a time limit of 4 seconds) were better than those reported in the library PSPLIB at the time this research was performed.

The results can be summarized as follows: The activity list GA outperforms the other two GA approaches. Considering again Subsection 5.5.1, we observe that the choice of an appropriate representation is far more important than other configuration decisions such as crossover and selection type or mutation rate.

5.5.3 Impact of Genetic Operators

In what follows, we examine the question whether the three representations are well suited for application in genetic algorithms. In other words, we want to know if they benefit from the application of genetic operators. Thus, for each encoding, we compare the related GA which computes 1000 schedules by applying the genetic operators on 40 individuals over 25 generations with what we will call a "random procedure." For each encoding, this random procedure generates 1000 schedules independently, that is, without applying the genetic operators. Note that it can be viewed as a GA with a population size of 1000 and only one generation (i.e., the initial one).

For the three encodings, the average deviations from the optimal solutions for both the "real" GAs and the random procedures are listed in Table 5.8. We observe that the GAs clearly outperform the corresponding random procedures if the activity list and random key encodings are considered. However, for the priority rule encoding, there are only slight differences between randomly generating 1000 priority rule lists (and thus schedules) on the one hand and randomly generating only 40 and applying the genetic operators over 25 generations on the other hand. Hence we can deduce that the priority rule encoding does not exploit the potential of the GA paradigm when applied to solve the RCPSP. In contrast, the other two representations are well suited for application in a GA.

Recall that the initial population of the activity list GA is computed using a sampling method. That is, the random procedure for the activity list encoding listed in Table 5.8 is in fact a sampling algorithm. Table 5.8 shows that it is better to determine only 40 schedules using the sampling procedure and then apply the genetic operators over 25 generations, than to compute all 1000 schedules with the sampling method.

Encoding	*GA*	*random*
activity list	0.54 %	0.82 %
random key	1.03 %	1.69 %
priority rule	1.38 %	1.41 %

Table 5.8: Impact of genetic operators — 1000 schedules, $J = 30$

5.6 Extending the Genetic Algorithm

The computational study of the previous section revealed that the activity list representation yields the most promising result in a genetic algorithm. This section deals with several possibilities to extend the activity list based GA in order to further improve the computational results. We consider a generalization of the basic genetic metaphor, an extended activity list representation, a new method to determine the initial population, genetic operators for the new representation, and the incorporation of a local search method. These changes lead to an extended GA approach which will be thoroughly examined in the experimental analysis reported in Chapter 6.

5.6.1 Generalized Genetic Algorithm Paradigm

The basic genetic algorithm is a powerful optimization tool, using biological mechanisms such as mating (crossover), mutation, and survival-of-the-fittest based selection. This leads to the question if there are further phenomena known from the field of biology that are applicable within an optimization algorithm and, moreover, capable of improving the solution quality.

Several approaches of extending the basic GA concept are reported in the literature. For example, Kohlmorgen et al. [118] employed the concept of isolated development of several populations which takes place on independent "islands." Mattfeld [141] extended the basic GA scheme by a psychological component: Each individual has an "attitude" which influences its behavior towards crossover.

Here, we will study the island model which is reminiscent of Darwin's observations concerning the isolated development of diverse species on the different Galapagos islands (cf. Subsection 5.1.1). This approach is employed into the algorithmic scheme as follows: We divide our population of size POP into a given number of islands, denoted as ISL. Each individual of the initial population is assigned to one of the islands, such that the subpopulations on the islands are of the same size. Only individuals living on the same island can mate and produce children by crossover. The children are assigned to their parents' island. So far, the evolution according to the basic GA scheme simply takes place ISL times. Now the different island populations are connected by means of migration. We assume that in each generation the fittest individual leaves his home island with a probability of $p_{\text{migration}}$ and "swims" to another island where it is added to the subpopulation. This allows to spread genes of fit individuals into other subpopulations with a different gene pool.

Unfortunately, however, in our computational tests the island model did not perform well. A possible explanation lies in the relatively small numbers of individuals allowed to be computed for a project instance in our experiments. We consider only up to 5000 individuals for a project instance because, otherwise, we would obtain huge computation times for large project sizes. This leads to a small number of individuals per generation (in fact we typically have $POP \leq 100$, cf. the discussion of the parameter settings in Subsection 5.5.1). Splitting small populations into several islands may lead to a too small gene pool on each island, causing inferior results. On a parallel computer, however, the island model has shown favorable results as a huge number of individuals can be computed simultaneously (cf. Kohlmorgen et al. [118]).

We have also tested another variant of the migration concept which does not require to divide the population. Explicitly considering only one island ($ISL = 1$), in each generation an individual migrates to this island with a probability of $p_{\text{migration}}$. More precisely, we generate a new individual using the same procedure that is designed to determine the initial population. With a probability of $p_{\text{migration}}$, this new individual—which can be viewed as coming from a hypothetical island—is added to the current population.

As a matter of fact, also this migration model did not improve the computational results. Again, allowing only relatively few individuals to be computed may explain this observation. Few individuals imply a small maximal number of generations GEN. Hence, migration does not occur often enough to have a measurable positive effect. As a consequence, we do not consider these GA paradigm extensions any further (that is, we keep $ISL = 1$ and $p_{\text{migration}} = 0$).

5.6.2 Extended Representation

So far, we have employed the activity list representation together with the serial SGS as decoding procedure. Computational studies (cf. Chapter 6 and Hartmann and Kolisch [95]) show, however, that for large project sizes the parallel SGS yields better results than the serial one. Roughly speaking, this is because the serial SGS constructs active schedules while the parallel one generates non-delay schedules (cf. Section 4.1). This implies that the parallel SGS searches a typically smaller solution space and may, therefore, miss all optimal schedules which can be a drawback for small instance sizes (with small solution spaces). For large project sizes, however, this restriction can be an advantage because non-delay schedules are of good average quality as they tend to exploit the available resource capacity as early as possible.

The idea is now to allow both SGS to be employed as decoding procedures. As the parallel SGS is not immediately applicable to deal with activity lists, we have to define how it constructs a feasible schedule from a given activity list. We simply adapt the activity selection mechanism of the parallel SGS: The procedure selects the eligible activity with the lowest index in the activity list. Note that if the activity list under consideration does not transform to a non-delay schedule by means of the serial SGS, then the two SGS types construct two different schedules from the same activity list, i.e., an active and a non-delay schedule.

How can we include both SGS types into our GA? We extend the representation as follows: An individual $I = (\lambda, SGS_{\text{serial}})$ now consists of an activity list λ and a boolean indicator

$$SGS_{\text{serial}} = \begin{cases} 1, & \text{if activity list } \lambda \text{ is to be decoded by the serial SGS} \\ 0, & \text{if activity list } \lambda \text{ is to be decoded by the parallel SGS.} \end{cases}$$

In order to compute a schedule and the related fitness value (which is again given by the makespan of the schedule) for an individual $I = (\lambda, SGS_{\text{serial}})$, we apply the SGS referred to by SGS_{serial} to activity list λ.

Note that this new representation does not only determine the schedule itself but also the algorithm with which it is constructed. This way, we can leave it to the GA to decide which SGS is more successful to find good schedules for the project instance under consideration. In other words, the GA will learn not only in which regions of the search space the most promising solutions can be found, it also learns which SGS is the better choice and adapts itself accordingly.

The idea behind this is quite general: Whenever it is unclear which of the alternatives for a component of a GA should be selected (in our case, which decoding procedure), all promising alternatives can be employed. The alternative to be used for an individual can be indicated by an additional gene in an extended representation. Now the survival-of-the-fittest mechanism leads to an increasing occurance of the most successful alternative in the population—and hence to the most successful GA variant. We obtain a self-adapting GA in which not only the solution of the problem but also the algorithmic structure is subject to genetic optimization. Due to its generality, this metaheuristic strategy can easily be applied to many kinds of optimization problems. The approach is promising especially if the behavior of some component's alternatives depends on the instance characteristics, that is, if the instances are heterogenous. Note that the mechanism of self-adaptation is not restricted to decoding procedures. It can also be applied to deal with other components such as different crossover operators, requiring one additional gene for each variable component in an extended representation.

5.6.3 Improved Initial Population

Having set up a representation consisting of an activity list and a decoding procedure, we have to make clear how an initial population containing *POP* individuals of this new type of representation should be determined. We will proceed in two steps. First, we will reconsider the construction of an activity list. Second, we will describe the selection of a decoding procedure, i.e., an SGS with which an already determined actity list is to be transformed into a schedule.

The basic GA of Section 5.2 constructs initial activity lists using regret-based biased random sampling together with the LFT priority rule. We extend this approach by additionally considering the LST rule (cf. Table 4.3). More precisely, before we select the next activity for the list currently under construction, we choose the priority rule for the selection of the activity. Thereby, either the LFT or the LST rule is chosen with a probability of 0.5 each. We consider two rules instead of one because using the same rule all the time will, with a high probability, lead to similar areas of the search space. Employing more than one rule should therefore lead to a more diversified initial population of activity lists, which is a good starting point for the crossover operator. The LST and LFT rules were selected for two reasons: First, in several computational studies (cf. Kolisch [122] and Schirmer and Riesenberg [177]), both rules rank among the best performing priority rules. Second, they are static rules, i.e., the related priority values can be computed by preprocessing, resulting in a fast procedure. Note that the closest competitor of these two rules, the WCS rule of Kolisch [121], is not a static rule and thus requires a higher computational effort.

Now we have to choose an SGS in order to make the current activity list a complete individual. We proceed as follows: The SGS for the first activity list is the parallel one. Then, with an increasing number of completed individuals, the probability of selecting the parallel SGS decreases and, thus, the probability of selecting the serial SGS increases. Starting with an initial probability to select the parallel SGS of $p_1^{\text{parallel}} = 1$, this probability is successively updated for the i-th selection ($i = 2, \ldots, POP$) by

$$p_i^{\text{parallel}} = p_{i-1}^{\text{parallel}} \cdot \left(1 - \frac{\eta}{J^{\vartheta}}\right)$$

where $\eta > 0$ and $\vartheta \geq 1$ are parameters that determine how fast the probability decreases. Clearly, the respective probability to select the serial SGS is 1 −

p_i^{parallel}. Computational tests revealed that the parameter choices $\eta = 100$ and $\vartheta = 2$ lead to good results (considering real-world instances as well as available test sets, we assume $J > 10$). The rationale behind this approach is that for a larger number of schedules and a smaller number of activities in the project, the serial SGS yields better results than the parallel one (cf. Schirmer [174]). These effects are due to the impact of the SGS on the search space: As already mentioned above, a large project implies a large search space, making a restriction to the non-delay schedules and hence the parallel SGS favorable. On the other hand, a larger number of schedules allowed to be constructed makes it more probable that we can get very close to an optimal solution, which we may miss if we use the parallel SGS.

For illustration, Table 5.9 gives the average percentage of the serial SGS in the initial population for different project sizes J and different (initial) population sizes POP. These test results were obtained from the settings of the parameters η and ϑ are as given above.

	$J = 30$	$J = 60$	$J = 120$
$POP = 50$	82.1 %	45.5 %	15.2 %
$POP = 100$	90.9 %	66.1 %	27.7 %

Table 5.9: Average percentage of the serial SGS in the initial population

We will now discuss the differences between our priority rule based procedure and those presented in the literature. While most priority rule based sampling methods consist of one SGS and one priority rule, the so-called adaptive sampling methods of Kolisch and Drexl [124] as well as Schirmer [174] (cf. Section 4.2) consider both SGS and more than one priority rule. These adaptive approaches, however, decide which SGS and which priority rule they will employ on the basis of parameters such as the number of schedules to be computed and the size of the project at hand. That is, for some given project instance, again only one SGS and one priority rule is used. Schirmer [174] proposes to identify equivalence classes of instances which should be solved with the same SGS and priority rule. A case library based on computational experience should contain the characterictics of these equivalence classes along with the best performing SGS and priority rule to be used for each class. This results in very strict decisions concerning the actual algorithm to be chosen to solve a specific project instance, e.g., for $J = n$ and $J = n + 1$ activities in the project different procedures may be recommended.

Clearly, our approach is different from the adaptive search methods: We make "fuzzy" rather than strict decisions on the SGS to be used, as we consider probabilities (which are influenced by the project size and the number of SGS decisions already made) for selecting an SGS. An advantage lies in the possibility to address different promising regions of the search space by using both SGS and more than one priority rule whereas adaptive methods, with only one SGS and one priority rule, tend to construct similar schedules. More important, however, is that we construct an initial population containing both SGS. This is essential because we want the GA to decide by means of selection which SGS is most promising for the specific project instance to be solved. We expect the GA to be capable of more accurately finding the better suited SGS for one instance than any case library could. In a case library, experience concerning all specific characteristics of the given instance is almost surely not reported. The SGS distribution in the initial population is guided by the probability mechanism which considers the instance to be solved, providing a good starting point for the GA.

5.6.4 Adapting the Genetic Operators

An extended representation requires an adaptation of the crossover and mutation operators. Clearly, the third genetic operator, the selection mechanism, remains unchanged as it only requires information about the fitness, but not about the representation. Therefore, we will continue to use the ranking selection which performed best in the computational experiments of Section 5.5.

The crossover operator of Subsection 5.2.2 is extended as follows: Given a mother individual $M = (\lambda^M, SGS^M_{\text{serial}})$ and a father individual $F = (\lambda^F, SGS^F_{\text{serial}})$, the daughter $D = (\lambda^D, SGS^D_{\text{serial}})$ is defined by

$$SGS^D_{\text{serial}} := SGS^M_{\text{serial}}$$

and the activity list λ^D as computed by the two-point crossover of Subsection 5.2.2. That is, the daughter inherits the information which SGS should be used from the mother. Analogously, the son $S = (\lambda^S, SGS^S_{\text{serial}})$ obtains this gene from the father, i.e., $SGS^S_{\text{serial}} := SGS^F_{\text{serial}}$. Again, the son's activity list is constructed by the two-point crossover of Subsection 5.2.2.

After crossover, the GA performs mutation on each newly generated child individual. We simply extend the mutation operator for activity lists of Subsection 5.2.2 by defining a mutation on the gene related to the SGS: With a probability of p_{mutation}, we set $SGS_{\text{serial}} := \neg SGS_{\text{serial}}$. That is, by applying mutation, the serial SGS is replaced by the parallel one in the current individual and vice versa.

5.6.5 Adding a Local Search Phase

This subsection discusses a local search extension of our genetic algorithm. We first show how the local search phase is incorporated into our GA. Then we define a new neighborhood move for the activity list representation. The most important feature will be the exploitation of problem-specific knowledge. Afterwards, we briefly outline how we attempt to avoid revisiting previously tested neighbor solutions.

Local Search Environment

Up to this point, our GA starts with a priority rule based method to construct an initial population. Then it proceeds improving the solutions found so far by repeatedly recombining parts of good solutions to new ones and deleting inferior ones. In the GA of Section 5.2, we stop after $POP \cdot GEN$ solutions have been constructed or a given time limit has been reached.

Consider the following situation: The GA has not improved the best solution found so far for a number of generations. Now, instead of continuing with the rather rough genetic search, we conjecture that we have already found a population of good solutions and begin a local search phase to improve the solutions that have survived. The idea behind this is that we expect good solutions to have similar properties, in our case similar activity lists. Exploring the neighborhood of a good solution found so far (by slightly perturbing its activity list) may therefore lead us to even better solutions. This local search principle is usually referred to as "hill climbing" (we are dealing with a minimization problem here and are rather seeking for "valleys").

We include a local search phase into our GA as follows: The GA stops if a given number of generations have not brought an improvement of the best makespan found so far, leaving us with the last population. Now the local search phase begins. We pick the best individual from the last population (ties are broken arbitrarily) and try to improve it by local search. If, during that local search execution, some stopping criterion is met, we skip to the next best individual for local search improvement and so on. If altogether $POP \cdot GEN$ schedules have been visited (i.e., by the GA itself and during the local search phase) or if a global time limit has been reached, the procedure stops. That is, denoting the last generation of the GA with G, at most $POP \cdot (GEN - G)$ schedules are generated by local search.

Next, we have to clarify how to perform local search on one individual. Our intention is to employ local search in order to get very close to an optimal solution. However, as outlined above, we may miss good or optimal solutions if we use the parallel SGS. Therefore, we want to perform local search using only the serial SGS. Thus, having selected an individual $I = (\lambda, SGS_{\text{serial}})$ based on the parallel SGS (i.e., $SGS_{\text{serial}} = 0$) for local search, we transform activity list λ into activity list λ' such that applying the parallel SGS to λ leads to the same schedule as applying the serial SGS to λ'. Note that such a transformation is always possible because the search space of the parallel SGS is a subset of the search space of the serial SGS (cf. Subsection

4.1.2). Actually, λ' is obtained from sorting the activities with respect to non-decreasing start times. Now we start the local search phase from activity list λ'. Obviously, if the selected individual is already based on the serial SGS, we do not have to modify its activity list. During the local search phase, all activity lists are decoded by means of the serial SGS.

The local search approach follows a first fit strategy (FFS, cf. Subsection 4.3.1). That is, we generate a neighbor of the current activity list by performing a move as defined below. Then we compute the related schedule with the serial SGS. If the resulting makespan is worse than the previous one, we reject the neighbor and keep the original list, for which we test the next neighbor. Otherwise, we keep the neighbor activity list and test one of its neighbors. If a maximal number of consecutive rejected moves (i.e., a maximal number of consecutively tested worse neighbors) has been reached, the next individual from the last GA population is selected for local search improvement. Moreover, if $POP \cdot GEN$ schedules have been constructed altogether during the GA and the local search phases, the heuristic stops. Clearly, we have to count all computed schedules, i.e., the accepted as well as the rejected ones, in order to check whether we have already computed $POP \cdot GEN$ solutions altogether and need to stop.

The main difference between our greedy local search procedure and simulated annealing as well as tabu search (cf. Subsection 4.3.1) is that it never accepts worse neighbors. If we cannot find a neighbor of at least equal quality for some time, we select the next best individual from the GA population. We do so because the individuals of the last population are already the product of an optimization process. This allows us to continue the search in a possibly different, but also promising region.

Neighborhood Definition

The neighborhood of our local search component is defined by right shift moves which, given $i \in \{1, \dots, J-1\}$ and $h \in \{i+1, \dots, J\}$, transform a precedence feasible activity list

$$\lambda = (j_1, \dots, j_i, \dots, j_h, \dots, j_J)$$

into a precedence feasible neighbor activity list

$$\lambda' = (j_1, \dots, j_{i-1}, j_{i+1}, \dots, j_h, j_i, j_{h+1}, \dots, j_J).$$

That is, some activity j_i is right shifted within the activity list and inserted immediately after some activity j_h without violating the precedence assumption.

Having randomly selected some position $i \in \{1, \dots, J-1\}$ of an activity to be right shifted, we need to determine between which positions activity j_i

should be allowed to be shifted. Let us first consider the most right position $\psi(i)$ which is defined as the highest index that would yield a precedence feasible neighbor activity list. If activity j_i has no (non-dummy) successor in the list, it can be shifted to the end of the list. Otherwise, we must not shift it to a position higher than one of its successors in the list. This leads to

$$\psi(i) = \begin{cases} J, & \text{if } \mathcal{S}_{j_i} \cap \mathcal{J} = \emptyset \\ \min \{k \mid j_k \in \mathcal{S}_{j_i}\} - 1, & \text{otherwise.} \end{cases} \tag{5.3}$$

Next, we consider the most left position $\varphi(i)$. As we are dealing with right shifts, we could set $\varphi(i) = i + 1$, implying that activity j_i would have to be right shifted by at least one position. Now we could randomly draw an index $h \in \{\varphi(i), \dots, \psi(i)\}$ and shift j_i immediately after j_h. This would result in a precedence feasible neighbor activity list. The drawback of this straightforward approach, however, is that this may lead us to a different activity list but eventually not to a different schedule. This is due to the redundancy discussed in Subsection 5.2.1. Actually, the example given in that subsection shows that a right shift by one position might not change the schedule.

The consequence is to adapt the definition of the most left position $\varphi(i)$ in order to exclude as many right shifts as possible that do not change the schedule. To do so, we incorporate schedule-dependent knowledge into the right shift move. The foundation for this is laid by the following theorem which examines right shifts by one position, i.e., adjacent pairwise interchanges.

Theorem 5.2 *Consider an activity list $\lambda = (j_1, \dots, j_J)$ which leads, by means of the serial SGS, to schedule $S(\lambda)$ associated with start times s_{j_i} and finish times f_{j_i}, $i = 1, \dots, J$. Let further $s_{j_i}^{\text{prec}} = \max\{f_h \mid h \in \mathcal{P}_{j_i}\}$ denote the earliest precedence feasible start time of activity j_i in schedule $S(\lambda)$. Now consider an adjacent pairwise interchange of activities j_i and j_{i+1} with $j_i \notin \mathcal{P}_{j_{i+1}}$ in λ, leading to neighbor activity list λ' with related schedule $S(\lambda')$. If at least one of the following four conditions holds, then we have $S(\lambda) = S(\lambda')$:*

$$s_{j_i} \geq s_{j_{i+1}} \tag{5.4}$$

$$f_{j_i} \leq s_{j_{i+1}}^{\text{prec}} \tag{5.5}$$

$$s_{j_{i+1}} = s_{j_{i+1}}^{\text{prec}} \tag{5.6}$$

$$f_{j_i} < s_{j_{i+1}} \text{ and } s_{j_{i+1}} - 1 - s_{j_{i+1}}^{\text{prec}} < p_{j_{i+1}} \tag{5.7}$$

Proof. Basically, we can obtain a different schedule from such an adjacent pairwise interchange only if activity j_{i+1} can be assigned an earlier start time in schedule $S(\lambda')$ than in $S(\lambda)$. Hence, the main idea is to show that activity j_{i+1} cannot be started earlier if it is scheduled before activity j_i is scheduled. With this in mind, we now examine the four conditions separately. The conditions are illustrated in Figure 5.1.

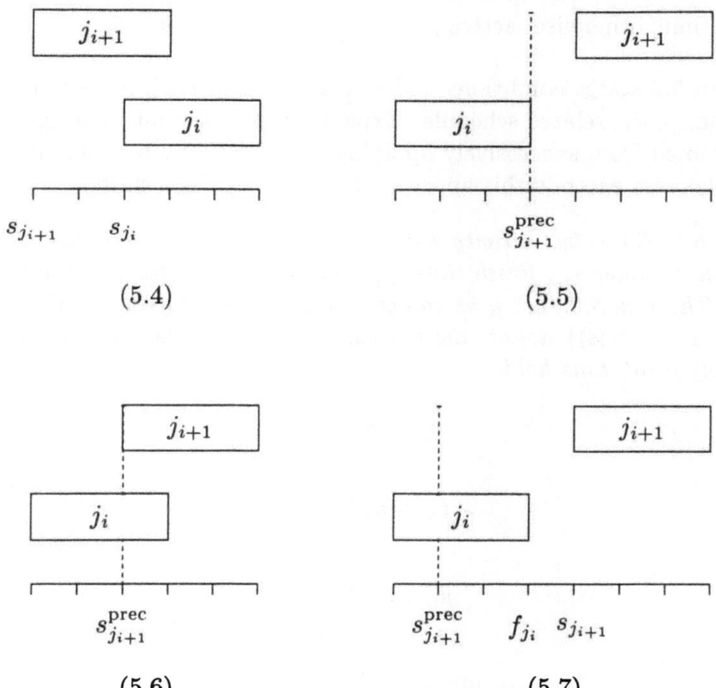

Figure 5.1: Illustration of conditions for equal neighbor schedules

Consider condition (5.4): Scheduling activity j_{i+1} before j_i cannot lead to an earlier start time of activity j_{i+1} because delaying activity j_i does not free any resources before the previous start time of activity j_{i+1}.

Condition (5.5) implies that activity j_{i+1} cannot be started before the previous finish time of activity j_i due to the precedence relations. Thus delaying activity j_i does not free resources that can be used by activity j_{i+1} to allow the latter to start earlier.

Condition (5.6) considers the case of activity j_{i+1} starting at its earliest precedence feasible start time. Clearly, it cannot be started earlier.

Finally, condition (5.7) works as follows: We assume $s_{j_{i+1}}^{\text{prec}} < s_{j_{i+1}}$ (otherwise, condition (5.6) would already be fulfilled). Activity j_{i+1} cannot be in process at $t = s_{j_{i+1}} - 1$ due to the resource constraints because delaying activity j_i would not free any resources at that time. Consequently, after the adjacent pairwise interchange, activity j_{i+1} must be finished at or before t in order to start earlier. Therefore, activity j_{i+1} must be performed within $\{s_{j_{i+1}}^{\text{prec}}, \ldots, t\}$. This time span must be at least of the same length as its processing time; otherwise, activity j_{i+1} cannot start earlier. □

Theorem 5.2 states conditions under which a right shift by one position does not change the related schedule. Exploiting the fact that each right shift can be obtained from successively applying right shifts by one position, the following theorem extends this approach to arbitrary right shifts.

Theorem 5.3 *Consider activity list $\lambda = (j_1, \ldots, j_J)$ leading to schedule $S(\lambda)$ with start times s_{j_i}, finish times f_{j_i}, and precedence feasible start times $s_{j_i}^{\text{prec}}$ as in Theorem 5.2. Let j_i be an activity to be right shifted. Furthermore, let $l \in \{i+1, \ldots, \psi(i)\}$ denote the highest position for which at least one of the following conditions holds:*

$$s_{j_i} \geq s_{j_l} \tag{5.8}$$

$$f_{j_i} \leq s_{j_l}^{\text{prec}} \tag{5.9}$$

$$s_{j_l} = s_{j_l}^{\text{prec}} \tag{5.10}$$

$$f_{j_i} < s_{j_l} \text{ and } s_{j_l} - 1 - s_{j_l}^{\text{prec}} < p_{j_l} \tag{5.11}$$

Define $\varphi(i) := l+1$. Then right shifting activity j_i behind any activity j_k with $k < \varphi(i)$ would lead to a schedule equal to $S(\lambda)$. Moreover, if $\varphi(i) > \psi(i)$, all right shifts of activity j_i lead to the same schedule.

Proof. Let l be as given in the theorem. We define λ_k to be the activity list obtained from right shifting activity j_i behind activity j_k in λ for $k = i+1, \ldots, l$. We have to show $S(\lambda_k) = S(\lambda)$ for all $k = i+1, \ldots, l$. This is done by induction: Assume that we have $S(\lambda_k) = S(\lambda)$ for some $k \in \{i+1, \ldots, l-1\}$. We want to show $S(\lambda_{k+1}) = S(\lambda)$.

Clearly, right shifting j_i after j_{k+1} can be done in two steps: First, j_i is right shifted after j_k in λ, leading to λ_k with $S(\lambda_k) = S(\lambda)$ according to the assumption of the induction. Second, in λ_k, j_k (the former activity j_i of λ) is right shifted by one position after j_{k+1}, leading to λ_{k+1}. As we have $k+1 \leq l$, at least one of the conditions (5.8)–(5.11) holds for the right shift of

j_i after j_{k+1} in λ. Then at least one of the conditions (5.4)–(5.7) of Theorem 5.2 holds for the right shift of j_k by one position after j_{k+1} in λ_k, because j_i in λ is the same activity as j_k in λ_k and $S(\lambda_k) = S(\lambda)$. That is, Theorem 5.2 leads to $S(\lambda_{k+1}) = S(\lambda_k)$. With $S(\lambda_k) = S(\lambda)$ due to the assumption of the induction, we obtain $S(\lambda_{k+1}) = S(\lambda)$.

The second part of the proof is straightforward. □

With the definition of $\varphi(i)$ in Theorem 5.3, we have completed the definition of the neighborhood moves used in the local search procedure: After randomly selecting a position $i \in \{1, \ldots, J-1\}$ of an activity to be right shifted, we determine $\psi(i)$ as defined in (5.3) and $\varphi(i)$ according to the description above. If we have $\varphi(i) > \psi(i)$, we select another position $i \in \{1, \ldots, J-1\}$ of an activity to be shifted. Otherwise, we randomly chose a position

$$h \in \{\varphi(i), \ldots, \psi(i)\}$$

in order to insert activity j_i immediately after j_h.

It should be emphasized, however, that the definition of $\varphi(i)$ does not ensure that the resulting right shift leads to a different schedule. In other words, the conditions of Theorem 5.3 (and hence also those of Theorem 5.2) are sufficient but not necessary. It does, however, exclude a large number of right shifts that would lead to the same schedule at a very low computational effort. Also excluding the remaining of such right shifts would increase the computation time needed to determine the related $\varphi(i)$ substantially. In the worst case, further excluding positions by computing an improved most left position $\varphi'(i) > \varphi(i)$ would lead to the same effort as not excluding that position and testing the respective neighbor.

Forbidden Neighborhood Moves

As long as we reject neighbor activity lists, we record the related right shifts in order to avoid to test a (worse) neighbor twice. That is, we put the right shifts into a list, indicating that they are "forbidden." Once we have accepted a new activity list, the recorded right shifts are deleted (and hence no longer forbidden).

Having accepted a neighbor of equal quality bears the possibility of cycling, that is, the next move may lead us back to the previous activity list. As we are dealing with right shifts, this may only occur if the last accepted move was a shift from some position i to $i+1$. In this case we put the same move (from i to $i+1$) into the forbidden list because this would lead us back to the previous solution. Note that this concept to avoid cycling can be viewed as some kind of simple "tabu list."

The local search procedure leaves the current individual if no allowed move is possible or a maximal number of consecutive rejected moves has been reached. Then the next individual from the last GA population is selected for local search improvement.

5.6.6 Configuration of the Extended Genetic Algorithm

We have tested the basic activity list GA of Section 5.2 with all extensions discussed in this section. The extended representation along with the related crossover and mutation operators, the new method for computing an initial population, and the local search procedure were able to improve the performance of the GA. As already mentioned in Subsection 5.6.1, this does not hold for the generalized GA paradigm, and we set $ISL = 1$ and $p_{\text{migration}} = 0$.

Based on further computational tests, we have determined the following parameter settings for the three phases of the extended GA: For generating the initial population, we have selected $\eta = 100$ and $\vartheta = 2$ (cf. Subsection 5.6.3). For the GA itself, we have chosen again a mutation probability of $p_{\text{mutation}} = 0.05$ and continue to work with the relationship of POP and GEN that has been determined in Subsection 5.5.1. Finally, we consider the local search component. We stop the GA phase and begin with the local search phase if for $\frac{1}{2} \cdot GEN$ generations of the GA the best solution found so far could not be improved. Note that this implies that, if the GA manages to continuously improve the objective function value, the local search phase may not be executed at all. The number of consecutive unsuccessful trials to accept a neighbor of at least equal quality is limited to the number of activities J.

From now on, we consider an "extended GA" which is the best performing GA variant, including the extended representation together with the related crossover and mutation operators, the new method for computing an initial population, and the local search phase. In an in-depth computational analysis in the following chapter, this extended GA will be compared with the other three GA approaches of this chapter as well as several well known heuristics from the literature.

We remark here that we have implemented two time window based methods to speed up the extended GA that have similarly been used by Kolisch [120]. First, if we have found a schedule with a makespan Z equal to the precedence based earliest finish time EF_{J+1} of the project as determined by Algorithm 2.1, we have found an optimal solution and stop the extended GA. Second, using Algorithm 2.2, we compute the latest start times LS_j for all activities $j \in \mathcal{J}$ in each generation, proceeding from the upper bound on the makespan Z given by the worst individual among the current POP individuals. If, while computing the schedule for a new child individual, an activity j is assigned a start time $s_j \geq LS_j$, we can stop the scheduling process and remove that individual from the population immediately. Clearly, this situation would lead to a schedule with a makespan $Z' \geq Z$, that is, it would be removed from the population by means of the ranking selection anyway. Observe that the latter acceleration method is very similar to the idea behind Bounding Rule 3.1 which speeds up exact algorithms.

Chapter 6

Evaluation of Single-Mode Heuristics

In the last chapter, we have only briefly reported on computational results concerning the impact of the representation within a genetic algorithm. However, we have not yet given any test results for the extended GA, and we do not yet know how our GAs perform compared to heuristics from the literature. This chapter closes these gaps. We present a computational study which gives a performance analysis of the four GAs introduced in Chapter 5 and many of the state-of-the-art heuristics which have been described in the literature survey of Chapter 4. As in the previous two chapters, the focus is again on the single-mode RCPSP. The experimental investigation is accompanied by explanations for the performance results. The goal is to point out the most promising heuristic for the RCPSP.

The testing environment and the test instances are given in Section 6.1. Section 6.2 then summarizes the computational results.[1]

6.1 Test Design

Evaluating optimization procedures means to compare the solution quality in terms of objective function values on a standard set of problem instances with respect to the computational effort. We chose the following design for comparing our GAs with heuristics from the literature: Each algorithm was tested by its author(s) using the original implementation. This allowed the authors to adjust the parameters of their algorithms in order to obtain good results. As a consequence, however, the tests were performed on different

[1]The study reported in this chapter is based on the investigation of Hartmann and Kolisch [95].

computer architectures and operating systems. Therefore, we could not impose a bound on the computation time to provide a basis for the comparison. Instead, we limited for all tested (non-single pass) heuristics the number of generated and evaluated schedules to 1000 and 5000, respectively. This decision is based on the assumption that the effort needed for generating one schedule is similar in the tested heuristics. With one exception, namely the schedule scheme based tabu search approach of Baar et al. [8], all algorithms considered for our investigation make use of an SGS as described in Section 4.1. Hence, we found this assumption justified. Note also that limiting the number of schedules as a basis for the comparison instead of imposing a time limit has the advantage that the results are independent from implementational effort such as to make the code faster. Thus, we rather measure the quality of an algorithm itself than that of its implementation. As test instances, we used the standard sets with 30, 60, and 120 non-dummy activities per project generated by ProGen (cf. Kolisch et al. [130] and Subsection A.2.1 in the appendix).

Using this design, we tested the four GA approaches of Chapter 5, i.e., the activity list, the random key, and the priority rule based GAs as well as the extended GA. The experiments were performed on a Pentium-based IBM-compatible personal computer with 133 MHz clock-pulse and 32 MB RAM. The GAs were coded in ANSI C, compiled with the GNU C compiler and tested under the Linux operating system. Furthermore, the following heuristics were included in our experimental investigation: From the priority rule methods described in Section 4.2, we have selected the pure random sampling approach of Kolisch [120] and the regret based biased random sampling procedure with the LFT priority rule of Kolisch [122]. Both were tested separately with the serial and the parallel SGS. Moreover, we considered the regret based biased random sampling method with the WCS priority rule of Kolisch [121, 122] which is only applicable within the parallel SGS. In order to gain further insight, the two LFT and the WCS priority rules were additionally tested in a deterministic single-pass environment. Finally, the adaptive sampling procedures of Kolisch and Drexl [124] and Schirmer [174] are included. From the metaheuristics summarized in Section 4.3, we considered the schedule scheme based tabu search method of Baar et al. [8], the activity list based simulated annealing procedure of Bouleimen and Lecocq [25], and the GA of Leon and Ramamoorthy [134] based on the problem-space variant of the random key representation. This gives altogether 14 multi-pass and 3 single-pass heuristics which have been tested.

Unfortunately, many heuristics proposed in the literature could not be included because neither results obtained from the test design outlined above nor their source codes or executables were available. Therefore, we have collected those computational results recently reported in the literature that were obtained on another standard set of instances, namely the classical Patterson set (cf. Section A.1 in the appendix). To allow a comparison, the four genetic algorithms of Chapter 5 were also tested on the Patterson instances. Considering the time limits reported in the literature, we chose a time limit of five seconds for our GAs on the computer mentioned above. This way, we were able to compare our heuristics with the simulated annealing (SA) procedures of Cho and Kim [30] and Lee and Kim [133], the local search approach of Sampson and Weiss [173], and the disjunctive arc based two-phase procedure of Bell and Han [15]. The results for the latter four heuristics are given as reported in the experimental study of Cho and Kim [30]. Furthermore, the local constraint based analysis (LCBA) method of Özdamar and Ulusoy [155] has been included in its iterative variant, see Özdamar and Ulusoy [157]. The results cited here are taken from the study performed by Özdamar and Ulusoy [156, 157]. Moreover, we have considered the tabu search approach based on the direct schedule representation of Thomas and Salhi [201]. Finally, we have included the results originally reported by Leon and Ramamoorthy [134] for their GA. For a description of these procedures, we refer again to Chapter 4.

6.2 Computational Results

The results of our experimental study are summarized in Tables 6.1 – 6.6. Table 6.1 gives the average percentage deviations from the optimal makespan for the ProGen instance set with 30 activities in a project obtained from the evaluation of 1000 and 5000 schedules, respectively. As for the larger two ProGen instance sets some of the optimal solutions are not known, we measured for these sets the average percentage deviation from an upper and a lower bound, respectively. The upper bound is set to the best makespan that was found by any heuristic in our study for each project; the respective results for the instances with 60 and 120 activities are provided in Tables 6.2 and 6.3.[2] As lower bound, we chose the critical path based lower bound (cf. Subsection A.2.1 in the appendix and Stinson et al. [195]). As the critical path based lower bound can be easily computed, this allows researchers to compare their future results with those reported here. The lower bound based results for the instances with 60 and 120 activities can be found in Tables 6.4 and 6.5, respectively. In each table, the heuristics are sorted according to descending performance with respect to 5000 iterations. In order to detect significant differences in the heuristic performance for 5000 iterations, we

[2]Note that the schedule scheme based tabu search heuristic of Baar et al. [8] was additionally run using the original termination criterion of the authors, which allows 2 trials each of which was terminated after no improved solution was found after 250 iterations. This way, the deviation from the upper bound was lowered to 1.14% on the ProGen set with $J = 60$.

compared the results of each heuristic with those of the next best one by means of the Wilcoxon signed-rank test using SPSS (cf. Norusis [152]). A star (*) in the last column of Tables 6.1 – 6.3 indicates that the respective heuristic performs significantly better than the next best one at the 5% level of confidence.

Finally, the results for the classical Patterson instances are provided in Table 6.6. We give the average percentage deviation from the optimal makespan, the percentage of instances for which an optimal schedule was found, and information about the computation time and the computer that was used for testing. The procedures are sorted according to increasing deviation from the optimum.

In what follows, we discuss these results. After determining the best heuristics, we analyze the behavior of the metaheuristics and the priority rule methods and describe the influence of the SGS. Then we summarize the impact of the resource characteristics and comment on the computation times.

6.2.1 Best Heuristics

The heuristic that performed best in our study is the extended genetic algorithm introduced in Section 5.6. It outperforms all other procedures on all instance sets. On the ProGen sets with 60 and 120 activities in each project, the difference to the second best heuristic is statistically significant. The next best algorithms are the simulated annealing approach of Bouleimen and Lecocq [25] and the plain activity list based GA of Section 5.2.

Considering the Patterson instance set, the extended GA and the plain activity list based GA find an optimal schedule for each project instance within 5 seconds of CPU time. Even when the different computers and computation times are taken into account, this shows the dominance of these two approaches over the other two GAs of Chapter 5 and the heuristics cited from the literature. On the other hand, these results also imply that the Patterson instances can no longer be used to find out which of the state-of-the-art heuristics perform best.

Generally, the results show that the best metaheuristics outperform the best priority rule based sampling approaches. Increasing the number of generated schedules from 1000 to 5000 results in a stronger superiority of the metaheuristic results. This is mainly because sampling procedures generate each schedule anew without considering any information given by already visited solutions while metaheuristic algorithms typically exploit the knowledge gained from the previously evaluated schedule(s). That is, for finding high-quality schedules, metaheuristics rather than priority rule based sampling methods should be used. The latter, however, play an important role in determining start solutions for metaheuristics.

Algorithm	SGS	reference	Iterations 1	1000	5000
GA – extended	ser./par.	Section 5.6	–	0.36	0.17
SA – activity list	serial	Bouleimen, Lec. [25]	–	0.38	0.23
GA – activity list	serial	Section 5.2	–	0.54	0.25*
sampling – adaptive	ser./par.	Schirmer [174]	–	0.65	0.44
TS – sched. scheme	special	Baar et al. [8]	–	0.86	0.44*
sampling – adaptive	ser./par.	Kolisch, Drexl [124]	–	0.74	0.52
priority rule – LFT	serial	Kolisch [122]	5.58	0.83	0.53
GA – random key	serial	Section 5.3	–	1.03	0.56*
sampling – random	serial	Kolisch [120]	–	1.44	1.00
GA – priority rule	serial	Section 5.4	–	1.38	1.12
priority rule – WCS	parallel	Kolisch [121, 122]	3.88	1.40	1.28
priority rule – LFT	parallel	Kolisch [122]	4.39	1.40	1.29*
sampling – random	parallel	Kolisch [120]	–	1.77	1.48*
GA – problem space	mod. par.	Leon, Ramam. [134]	–	2.08	1.59

Table 6.1: Average deviations from optimal solution — $J = 30$

Algorithm	SGS	reference	Iterations 1	1000	5000
GA – extended	ser./par.	Section 5.6	–	0.77	0.29*
GA – activity list	serial	Section 5.2	–	0.96	0.42
SA – activity list	serial	Bouleimen, Lec. [25]	–	1.13	0.46*
sampling – adaptive	ser./par.	Schirmer [174]	–	1.17	0.91
GA – priority rule	serial	Section 5.4	–	1.41	1.02*
sampling – adaptive	ser./par.	Kolisch, Drexl [124]	–	1.57	1.23*
GA – random key	serial	Section 5.3	–	2.45	1.42
TS – sched. scheme	special	Baar et al. [8]	–	1.75	1.51
priority rule – LFT	serial	Kolisch [122]	4.98	1.85	1.51*
priority rule – WCS	parallel	Kolisch [121, 122]	4.39	1.84	1.52
priority rule – LFT	parallel	Kolisch [122]	4.87	1.79	1.53*
GA – problem space	mod. par.	Leon, Ramam. [134]	–	2.44	1.79*
sampling – random	parallel	Kolisch [120]	–	2.80	2.35*
sampling – random	serial	Kolisch [120]	–	3.43	2.82

Table 6.2: Average deviations from best solution — $J = 60$

			Iterations		
Algorithm	*SGS*	*reference*	1	1000	5000
GA – extended	ser./par.	Section 5.6	–	1.66	0.49*
GA – activity list	serial	Section 5.2	–	2.83	1.13*
SA – activity list	serial	Bouleimen, Lec. [25]	–	5.98	2.10*
GA – priority rule	serial	Section 5.4	–	3.05	2.13
sampling – adaptive	ser./par.	Schirmer [174]	–	3.34	2.50
priority rule – LFT	parallel	Kolisch [122]	6.24	3.15	2.56
priority rule – WCS	parallel	Kolisch [121, 122]	6.02	3.18	2.58*
sampling – adaptive	ser./par.	Kolisch, Drexl [124]	–	4.19	3.57*
GA – problem space	mod. par.	Leon, Ramam. [134]	–	5.57	4.00*
priority rule – LFT	serial	Kolisch [122]	8.52	5.03	4.35*
GA – random key	serial	Section 5.3	–	7.35	4.79*
sampling – random	parallel	Kolisch [120]	–	6.70	5.70*
sampling – random	serial	Kolisch [120]	–	9.89	8.69

Table 6.3: Average deviations from best solution — $J = 120$

			Iterations		
Algorithm	*SGS*	*reference*	1	1000	5000
GA – extended	ser./par.	Section 5.6	–	12.35	11.70
GA – activity list	serial	Section 5.2	–	12.68	11.89
SA – activity list	serial	Bouleimen, Lec. [25]	–	12.75	11.90
sampling – adaptive	ser./par.	Schirmer [174]	–	12.94	12.59
GA – priority rule	serial	Section 5.4	–	13.30	12.74
sampling – adaptive	ser./par.	Kolisch, Drexl [124]	–	13.51	13.06
GA – random key	serial	Section 5.3	–	14.68	13.32
TS – sched. scheme	special	Baar et al. [8]	–	13.80	13.48
priority rule – LFT	serial	Kolisch [122]	18.13	13.96	13.53
priority rule – WCS	parallel	Kolisch [121, 122]	16.87	13.66	13.21
priority rule – LFT	parallel	Kolisch [122]	17.46	13.59	13.23
GA – problem space	mod. par.	Leon, Ramam. [134]	–	14.33	13.49
sampling – random	parallel	Kolisch [120]	–	14.89	14.30
sampling – random	serial	Kolisch [120]	–	15.94	15.17

Table 6.4: Average deviations from critical path lower bound — $J = 60$

			Iterations		
Algorithm	*SGS*	*reference*	1	1000	5000
GA – extended	ser./par.	Section 5.6	–	37.33	35.60
GA – activity list	serial	Section 5.2	–	39.37	36.74
SA – activity list	serial	Bouleimen, Lec. [25]	–	42.81	37.68
GA – priority rule	serial	Section 5.4	–	39.93	38.49
sampling – adaptive	ser./par.	Schirmer [174]	–	39.85	38.70
priority rule – LFT	parallel	Kolisch [122]	43.86	39.60	38.75
priority rule – WCS	parallel	Kolisch [121, 122]	43.57	39.65	38.77
sampling – adaptive	ser./par.	Kolisch, Drexl [124]	–	41.37	40.45
GA – problem space	mod. par.	Leon, Ramam. [134]	–	42.91	40.69
priority rule – LFT	serial	Kolisch [122]	48.11	42.84	41.84
GA – random key	serial	Section 5.3	–	45.82	42.25
sampling – random	parallel	Kolisch [120]	–	44.46	43.05
sampling – random	serial	Kolisch [120]	–	49.25	47.61

Table 6.5: Average deviations from critical path lower bound — $J = 120$

Algorithm	*reference*	*av. dev.*	*optimal*	*CPU-sec*
GA – extended	Section 5.6	0.00 %	100.0 %	5.0[a]
GA – activity list	Section 5.2	0.00 %	100.0 %	5.0[a]
SA – random key	Cho, Kim [30]	0.14 %	93.6 %	18.4[b]
GA – random key	Section 5.3	0.25 %	88.4 %	5.0[a]
SA – random key	Lee, Kim [133]	0.57 %	82.7 %	17.0[b]
GA – random key	Leon, Ramam. [134]	0.74 %	75.5 %	7.5[c]
GA – priority rule	Section 5.4	0.78 %	74.6 %	5.0[a]
LCBA	Özdamar, Ulusoy [157]	1.14 %	63.6 %	0–25[d]
local search	Sampson, Weiss [173]	1.98 %	55.5 %	10.2[b]
TS	Thomas, Salhi [201]	2.30 %	46.4 %	218.7[e]
two-phase	Bell, Han [15]	2.60 %	44.5 %	28.4[f]

[a] maximal CPU-time on a Pentium 133 MHz
[b] average CPU-time on a Pentium 60 MHz
[c] average CPU-time on an IBM RS 6000
[d] CPU-time range on an IBM PC 486
[e] average CPU-time on a Sun Sparc Station 10
[f] average CPU-time on a Macintosh plus

Table 6.6: Comparison of heuristics — Patterson instance set

6.2.2 Performance of Metaheuristics

A comparison of the results obtained from the metaheuristics shows that the choice of the underlying representation is crucial. The three best procedures make use of different metaheuristic strategies (GA and SA) while they all employ the activity list representation. The use of one metaheuristic paradigm itself does not necessarily lead to consistently good solutions. This can be seen from the results of the four new GAs of Chapter 5 and the GA of Leon and Ramamoorthy [134].

Considering the good results of the extended GA, we can state two more observations for metaheuristics in general and GAs in particular: First, a combination of two (or more) metaheuristic strategies can be promising. This is demonstrated by the integration of a local search phase for fine-tuning into the extended GA. Second, integrating alternative algorithmic components (in our case the two SGS types) into the representation can be beneficial, because this further exploits the inherent property of self-adaptation.

Not all metaheuristics give results of consistent quality for different project sizes. Whereas the extended GA yields the best results for all project sizes, the outcome of the random key based GA is of moderate quality on the ProGen set with $J = 30$ but of low quality on the set with $J = 120$. One reason for this is probably that the random key GA does not use priority rule based methods to compute the initial population, which is obviously a serious drawback, especially in larger search spaces. The performance of the priority rule based GA, on the other hand, improves with increasing project size. This is because combining good priority rules is an effective strategy in huge search spaces. But, as discussed in Section 5.4, it might exclude all optimal solutions from the search space which is a severe disadvantage for small project sizes. Furthermore, recall that we have shown in Subsection 5.5.3 that the priority rule based GA hardly exploits the benefits of genetic inheritance.

6.2.3 Performance of Priority Rule Based Heuristics

Considering the deterministic single pass procedures, we see that for all three ProGen instance sets the WCS priority rule with the parallel SGS performs best, followed by the LFT priority rule with the parallel SGS and the LFT priority rule with the serial SGS. This is in line with the results documented in Kolisch [121].

Analyzing the priority rule based sampling methods, we observe that the two rules WCS and LFT give almost identical results when employed within the parallel SGS. On none of the three ProGen instance sets, a significant difference could be found. On the other hand, there is a strong influence of the SGS, as will be explained below in Subsection 6.2.4. It is evident that sampling is capable of improving the results of the related deterministic single pass approaches. Moreover, using a priority rule within a sampling method improves the performance. This can be seen from comparing the priority rule based sampling procedures with the pure random sampling methods based on the same SGS (employing random sampling approaches as benchmarks is common for the evaluation of scheduling heuristics, cf., e.g., Conway et al. [34]).

Note that although the random sampling methods select the next eligible activity on a pure random basis, they contain project scheduling knowledge within the employed SGS. Due to this knowledge, their results are not as bad as one may expect from the term "random method". Nevertheless, for the instances with more than 30 activities the two random sampling procedures perform worst among all heuristics if 5000 iterations are considered.

Finally, we have a look at the adaptive sampling methods. We see that the recent approach of Schirmer [174] outperforms the one of Kolisch and Drexl [124]. This is due to the fact that the former procedure is based on a more accurate partitioning of the solution space in terms of problem parameters. The approach of Schirmer [174] makes use of the problem parameters number of activities, resource factor, and resource strength (for a description of the latter we refer to Appendix A.2). In contrast, the heuristic of Kolisch and Drexl [124] only employs the resource factor. Furthermore, the adaptive method of Kolisch and Drexl [124] was not tested on instances with more than 30 activities during the design phase. This also explains why even some of the simple (non-adaptive) sampling procedures outperform the approach of Kolisch and Drexl [124] on the set with 120 activities. Generally speaking, this shows an inherent limitation of adaptive sampling methods: It is almost impossible to consider all relevant parameters in all constellations when designing such an approach.

6.2.4 Impact of Schedule Generation Scheme

The theoretical difference between the two SGS types has already been discussed in Section 4.1. Summarizing that discussion, the search space of the serial SGS is the set of the active schedules which always contains an optimal solution. In contrast, the search space of the parallel SGS is the set of the non-delay schedules which is only a subset of the set of the active schedules and does not necessarily contain an optimal solution.

The resulting difference in the computational behavior between the two SGS types can be best shown for the LFT based and the pure random sampling approach. Both methods were tested with the serial as well as the parallel SGS. We observe a strong influence of the SGS which depends on the problem size: While the serial SGS is the better choice for these sampling approaches on the ProGen instance set with $J = 30$, the parallel one takes the lead on the set with $J = 120$. This result can be explained as follows: Restricting the search to the set of the non-delay schedules associated with the parallel SGS is a promising strategy if the search space is huge, as it is the case for the large projects with 120 activities. On the instances with 30 activities, however, the much smaller search space makes it possible to find good (or even optimal) solutions within small time limits. There, the restriction to the non-delay schedules is disadvantageous as one may exclude all optimal solutions from the search space. Hence the serial one becomes the SGS of choice. Similar findings are reported by Kolisch [120]. This project size-dependent impact of the SGS supports the idea to use both SGS types in a heuristic, as done in the extended GA. Recall that the interdependence between SGS performance and project size has been used in the method to generate the initial population in the extended GA (cf. Subsection 5.6.3). It is further exploited by the extended GA itself via self-adaptation.

The strength of the influence of the SGS compared to that of other components of the heuristics can be demonstrated as follows: We consider the ProGen instance set with $J = 30$, 5000 iterations, and the pure random sampling approach with the parallel SGS. If we replace the random activity selection with the more advanced selection based on the LFT priority rule, we reduce the average deviation from the optimal makespan from 1.48 % to 1.28 %. However, if we keep the pure random activity selection mechanism and use the serial SGS instead of the parallel one, the deviation decreases from 1.48 % to 1.00 %. This shows that the SGS can have a stronger impact than other components of heuristics such as priority rules. In other words, the two SGS types contain project scheduling knowledge that is very effective with repect to heuristic performance.

6.2.5 Impact of Resource Parameters

We now focus on the effect of the resource characteristics on the results of the heuristics. The resource characteristics are reflected by the resource strength RS^ρ which measures the resource scarcity and the resource factor RF^ρ which denotes the average number of resources requested per activity (cf. Appendix A.2). Tables 6.7 and 6.8 display the average deviations from the optimal makespan after 5000 iterations for each respective parameter setting of the ProGen set with 30 activities in each project. For all procedures, the average deviation decreases monotonically with increasing resource strength, i.e., with declining resource availability. This implies that scarce resource capacities make a problem hard to solve, which is in line with the results obtained for the exact algorithms in Chapter 3. Note that the problems with $RS^\rho = 1$ are resource-unconstrained, allowing each heuristic to find an optimal solution.

Analyzing the performance of the heuristics w.r.t. the resource factor, we can see that for a low RF^ρ value, procedures based on the serial SGS

			RS^ρ			
Algorithm	*SGS*	*reference*	0.25	0.50	0.75	1.00
GA – extended	ser./par.	Section 5.6	0.59	0.10	0.00	0.00
SA – activity list	serial	Bouleimen, Lec. [25]	0.81	0.09	0.00	0.00
GA – activity list	serial	Section 5.2	0.68	0.24	0.04	0.00
TS – sched. scheme	special	Baar et al. [8]	0.78	0.66	0.31	0.00
sampling – adaptive	ser./par.	Kolisch, Drexl [124]	1.51	0.37	1.19	0.00
sampling – LFT	serial	Kolisch [122]	1.60	0.41	0.10	0.00
GA – random key	serial	Section 5.3	1.31	0.76	0.15	0.00
sampling – random	serial	Kolisch [120]	2.58	1.15	0.26	0.00
GA – priority rule	serial	Section 5.4	3.18	1.11	0.18	0.00
sampling – WCS	parallel	Kolisch [121, 122]	2.52	1.28	1.29	0.00
sampling – LFT	parallel	Kolisch [122]	2.53	1.31	1.29	0.00
sampling – random	parallel	Kolisch [120]	2.98	1.62	1.31	0.00
GA – problem space	mod. par.	Leon, Ramam. [134]	3.08	1.85	1.42	0.00

Table 6.7: Average deviations from optimal solution w.r.t. RS^ρ — 5000 schedules, $J = 30$

			RF^ρ			
Algorithm	*SGS*	*reference*	0.25	0.50	0.75	1.00
GA – extended	ser./par.	Section 5.6	0.00	0.04	0.30	0.34
SA – activity list	serial	Bouleimen, Lec. [25]	0.12	0.09	0.40	0.28
GA – activity list	serial	Section 5.2	0.02	0.11	0.37	0.47
TS – sched. scheme	special	Baar et al. [8]	0.03	0.30	0.67	0.75
sampling – adaptive	ser./par.	Kolisch, Drexl [124]	0.00	0.18	0.83	1.04
sampling – LFT	serial	Kolisch [122]	0.00	0.18	0.83	1.10
GA – random key	serial	Section 5.3	0.01	0.13	0.89	1.18
sampling – random	serial	Kolisch [120]	0.01	0.38	1.54	2.06
GA – priority rule	serial	Section 5.4	0.26	1.33	1.45	1.43
sampling – WCS	parallel	Kolisch [121, 122]	1.44	1.60	1.00	1.04
sampling – LFT	parallel	Kolisch [122]	1.44	1.59	1.01	1.09
sampling – random	parallel	Kolisch [120]	1.44	1.63	1.21	1.63
GA – problem space	mod. par.	Leon, Ramam. [134]	1.44	1.79	1.40	1.71

Table 6.8: Average deviations from optimal solution w.r.t. RF^ρ — 5000 schedules, $J = 30$

perform much better than those based on the parallel one. Note that the extended GA which includes both SGS types seems to select the serial one for instances with a low RF^{ρ} value, because it learns that the parallel SGS yields bad results.

6.2.6 Computation Times

We close this section with a few remarks on the computation times. Let us first analyze the computational effort of the four new GAs. In order to provide a fair comparison, we have included the time window based acceleration methods described in Subsection 5.6.6 into all of the four GAs. For each project size in the ProGen sets, Table 6.9 displays the average computation times obtained from the GAs after the evaluation of at most 1000 schedules for an instance. Note that for each instance set and each heuristic, computing 5000 schedules takes approximately 5 times longer than computing 1000. Table 6.9 shows that the activity list based GA is faster than the random key GA. This is because the random key GA requires substantial computational effort for computing the eligible set and for selecting an eligible activity, which is not necessary in the activity list GA. Moreover, the random key GA is faster than the priority rule based GA because the latter employs a dynamic priority rule (MSLK) which requires additional effort. Finally, we observe that the extended GA is as fast as the activity list based GA on the small instances, but slower on the larger ones. This is due to the use of the parallel SGS in the extended GA which, as explained above, is selected more often for larger instances. For the activity list representation, the parallel SGS is slightly slower than the serial one because it cannot simply take the next activity from the list but has to determine the next eligible activity in the list.

Algorithm	*reference*	$J = 30$	$J = 60$	$J = 120$
GA – extended	Section 5.6	0.29	0.50	3.07
GA – activity list	Section 5.2	0.29	0.49	2.63
GA – random key	Section 5.3	0.41	0.75	3.42
GA – priority rule	Section 5.4	0.56	1.22	8.40

Table 6.9: Average computation times of GAs w.r.t. project size (CPU-sec) — 1000 schedules

Generally, we can state that the major portion of the computational effort results from schedule construction. Hence, the metaheuristic algorithms which make use of the activity list representation can be assumed to be the fastest heuristics, independently from the underlying metaheuristic strategy. Priority rule methods generally compute the eligible set and are thus slower.

The use of dynamic priority rules further increases the computation times. Biased random sampling approaches spend additional computational effort with the priority value based computation of selection probabilities and the random selection. Consequently, the heuristics show different computation times when constructing the same number of schedules. It is noteworthy, however, that the best performing heuristics, namely the activity list based GA, the SA procedure of Bouleimen and Lecocq [25], and with some reservation also the extended GA, can be viewed as the fastest algorithms.

Finally, we remark that the computation times obtained in our tests are encouraging. Also considering the steadily increasing computer performance, our results indicate that we can obtain high-quality schedules within relatively short computation times. We conclude that state-of-the-art heuristics should be included into software systems for project management and scheduling, as the solution quality of the latter currently is rather disappointing (cf. Kolisch [119] and Farid and Manoharan [76]).

Chapter 7

Multi-Mode Genetic Algorithm

The previous chapter has shown that our extended genetic algorithm is currently the best heuristic for the single-mode RCPSP. The goal of this chapter is to generalize and adapt the concepts used in the single-mode GA to obtain a good heuristic for multi-mode project scheduling. Therefore, we will consider those general aspects that contributed to the success of the best single-mode GA. We extend the activity list representation and associated crossover and mutation in order to make it suitable for dealing with multiple modes. Moreover, we will discuss local search extensions that further improve the behavior of the GA. The local search components for the multi-mode case are completely different from that of the single-mode RCPSP and will lead us to an analysis of different inheritance mechanisms within GAs in general.

Until today, several heuristics for the MRCPSP have been proposed in the literature. We refer to the approaches of Drexl and Grünewald [61], Kolisch and Drexl [125], Özdamar [154], and Slowinski et al. [186]. Sprecher [190] as well as Sprecher and Drexl [192] suggested to use their branch-and-bound algorithms (cf. also Chapter 3) as heuristics by stopping the enumeration when some time limit has been reached. Boctor [21, 22, 23] as well as Mori and Tseng [149] developed heuristics for the MRCPSP without nonrenewable and, hence, doubly constrained resources.

This chapter is arranged as follows: Section 7.1 deals with the basic GA components, namely the MRCPSP-specific representation, the method to generate the initial population, and the genetic operators. Section 7.2 introduces a local search method to improve schedules which exploits the multi-mode structure of the problem. Finally, Section 7.3 reports the computational results for the new GA and compares the performance of the GA to that of several other multi-mode heuristics. Throughout this chapter, we illustrate the definitions using the example project displayed in Figure 7.1.

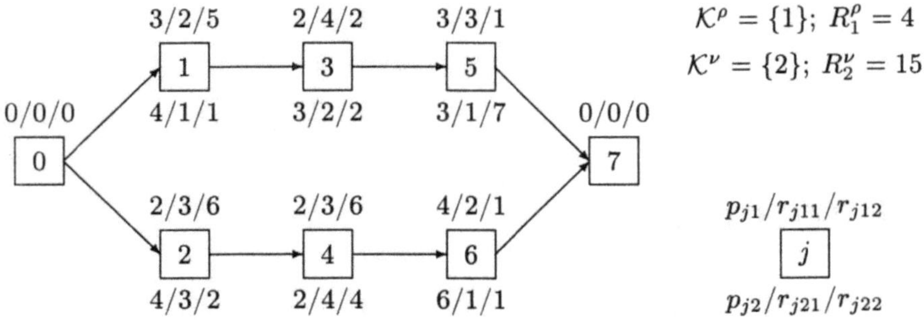

Figure 7.1: Project instance

7.1 Components of the Genetic Algorithm

In this section we present a new GA approach for the MRCPSP. The GA can be summarized as follows: First, we execute the preprocessing procedure of Bounding Rule 3.3 that was originally developed for accelerating branch-and-bound algorithms for the MRCPSP (cf. Chapter 3). This is useful because deleting nonrenewable resources will save computation time in the GA while removing modes reduces the search space. Clearly, this does not affect feasibility or optimality. Observe that this preprocessing procedure modifies the example instance of Figure 7.1. If activity 5 was performed in mode 2, the whole project would require at least 17 units of the nonrenewable resource whereas only 15 units are available. Consequently, mode 2 of activity 5 is non-executable w.r.t. to the nonrenewable resource and may therefore be deleted.

After preprocessing, we employ the basic GA scheme of Subsection 5.1.2 that has already been used for the single-mode GAs. That is, we generate an initial population with *POP* individuals and repeatedly apply crossover, mutation, and selection operators until *GEN* generations have been produced or a given time limit has been reached. With the computational results of Chapter 5 in mind, we use again the ranking method for selection as it gave the best result within the single-mode GAs (recall that the selection operator is independent from the problem-specific representation).

In the following subsections, the components of the multi-mode GA are described. Subsection 7.1.1 defines the genetic representation for the MR-CPSP. Subsection 7.1.2 describes a method to generate the initial population. Finally, Subsection 7.1.3 introduces the encoding-specific genetic operators crossover and mutation.

7.1.1 Individuals and Fitness

As we are dealing with the multi-mode extension of the standard RCPSP, our genetic representation has to reflect both the scheduling problem (which assigns start times to activities) and the mode assignment problem (which assigns modes to activities). Our goal is to deal with both problems simultaneously because of the interactions between them (e.g., there is no "good" mode assignment itself as long as we don't know how the resulting processing times and resource requirements influence possible start times and hence the makespan).

With this in mind, we extend the activity list representation of Subsection 4.3.2 as follows: In our multi-mode GA, an individual is represented by a pair $I = (\lambda, \mu)$ of a precedence feasible activity list $\lambda = (j_1, \ldots, j_J)$ and a mode assignment μ. A mode assignment μ is a mapping which assigns to each activity $j \in \{1, \ldots, J\}$ one of its modes $\mu(j) \in \mathcal{M}_j$. We will use the following alternative notation for the individuals:

$$I = \begin{pmatrix} j_1 & \cdots & j_J \\ \mu(j_1) & \cdots & \mu(j_J) \end{pmatrix}.$$

Each genotype $I = (\mu, \lambda)$ is related to a uniquely determined schedule (phenotype) which is obtained from fixing the modes according to the mode assignment μ and then applying the serial SGS (cf. Subsection 4.1.1) to activity list λ for the resulting single-mode problem.[1] Recall that the serial SGS successively takes the next unscheduled activity from the list and schedules it at the earliest precedence and resource feasible start time.

Clearly, the schedule related to an individual is feasible with respect to the precedence relations and the renewable resource constraints, but not necessarily w.r.t. the nonrenewable resource constraints. However, it is useful to include schedules that are infeasible w.r.t. the nonrenewable resources into the search space because, as proven by Kolisch and Drexl [125], already finding a feasible schedule is an NP-complete problem if at least two nonrenewable resources are given. In other words, we cannot find a procedure which constructs a nonrenewable resource feasible individual (e.g., for the initial population) in polynomial time.

---

[1] Although incorporating the SGS type to be used into the representation is generally advantageous (cf. Section 5.6 and the computational results of Chapter 6), we assumed the serial SGS to be sufficient. The reason for this is that the standard test instances used here contain only up to 20 non-dummy activities (cf. Appendix A.2.2). For this small project size, the serial SGS can be assumed to give much better results than the parallel one (cf. again the computational results of Chapter 6). Moreover, restricting ourselves to the serial SGS simplifies the description in this chapter. Nevertheless, the parallel SGS can be added by straightforwardly extending the representation to $I = (\mu, \lambda, SGS_{\text{serial}})$, where SGS_{serial} is a boolean variable which denotes the SGS to be used (cf. Subsection 5.6.2).

The fitness of an individual $I = (\lambda, \mu)$ is computed as follows: Let $L_k^\nu(\mu)$ denote the leftover capacity of nonrenewable resource $k \in \mathcal{K}^\nu$ w.r.t. the mode assignment μ, that is,

$$L_k^\nu(\mu) = R_k^\nu - \sum_{j=1}^{J} r_{j\mu(j)k}.$$

A negative leftover capacity $L_k^\nu(\mu) < 0$ implies infeasibility of mode assignment μ with respect to nonrenewable resource k. Let the number of nonrenewable resource units that exceed the capacities be given by

$$L^\nu(\mu) = \sum_{\substack{k \in \mathcal{K}^\nu \\ L_k^\nu(\mu) < 0}} |L_k^\nu(\mu)|.$$

If we have $L^\nu(\mu) > 0$, then mode assignment μ is infeasible w.r.t. the nonrenewable resource constraints. In this case, the fitness of individual $I = (\lambda, \mu)$ is given by $f(I) = T + L^\nu(\mu)$, where T is the upper bound on the project's makespan that is given by the sum of the maximal durations of the activities. Otherwise, if individual I is feasible w.r.t. the nonrenewable resources, the fitness $f(I)$ of individual I is given by the makespan of the related schedule. From the definitions given above it is clear that a lower fitness of an individual implies a better quality of the related schedule. Observe that a feasible individual always has a lower fitness than an infeasible one.

For illustration, we consider the project instance given in Figure 7.1 and the two example individuals

$$I^M = \begin{pmatrix} 2 & 4 & 1 & 6 & 3 & 5 \\ 2 & 2 & 1 & 1 & 1 & 1 \end{pmatrix}, \quad I^F = \begin{pmatrix} 1 & 3 & 2 & 5 & 4 & 6 \\ 1 & 2 & 1 & 1 & 2 & 2 \end{pmatrix}. \qquad (7.1)$$

Clearly, the mode assignment of individual I^M is feasible as 15 units of the single nonrenewable resource are requested, that is, the capacity is not exceeded. Now we derive a schedule from the genotype of I^M which can be found in Figure 7.2, where $j(m)$ stands for activity j being performed in mode m. The fitness of I^M is equal to the makespan of the schedule, that is, we have $f(I^M) = 15$. Individual I^F induces a nonrenewable resource requirement of 19 units which exceeds the availability by 4 units. Computing $T = 22$, we obtain a fitness value of $f(I^F) = 26$.

7.1.2 Initial Population

Each individual of the initial population is computed by the following three steps which are repeated until *POP* individuals are generated.

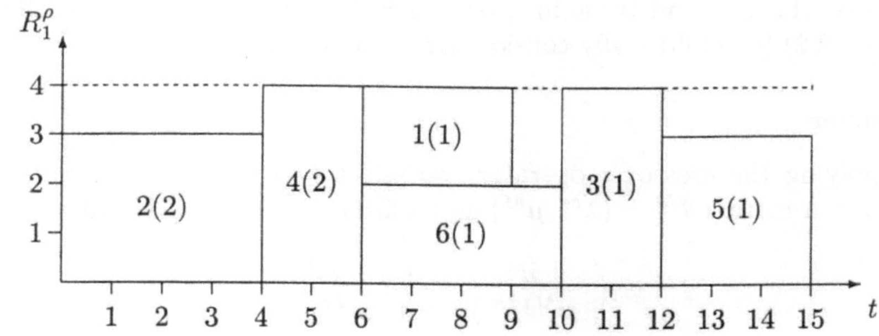

Figure 7.2: Schedule of example individual I^M

First, a mode assignment is generated by randomly selecting $\mu(j) \in \mathcal{M}_j$ for activities $j = 1, \ldots, J$.

Second, the mode assignment μ is checked for nonrenewable resource feasibility. If the capacity of a nonrenewable resource would be exceeded, i.e., if $L^\nu(\mu) > 0$, then the following simple local search procedure which follows a first fit strategy (cf. Subsection 4.3.1) tries to improve the current mode assignment: We randomly select an activity $j \in J$ with $M_j > 1$ and a mode $m_j \in \mathcal{M}_j$ with $m_j \neq \mu(j)$, leading to a new mode assignment μ'. If this new mode assignment is at least as good as the previous one, that is, if $L^\nu(\mu') \leq L^\nu(\mu)$, then we accept this new mode by setting $\mu := \mu'$, that is, $\mu(j) := m_j$. This process is repeated until J consecutive unsuccessful trials to improve the mode assignment (by reducing $L^\nu(\mu)$) have been made or until the mode assignment is feasible (i.e., $L^\nu(\mu) = 0$). Recall that there is no algorithm which guarantees the construction of feasible mode assignment in polynomial time, which is due to the NP-completeness of this problem.

Third, based on mode assignment μ, the priority rule based sampling method of Kolisch [122] for the single-mode case (cf. also Section 4.2) is employed to construct a precedence feasible activity list λ. More precisely, we (temporarily) fix the modes of the activities with respect to μ. Then, starting with the empty activity list, we obtain a precedence feasible activity list by repeatedly selecting an activity from the set of the eligible activities. The probability with which an activity is selected is derived from the latest finish times which are derived by the backward recursion of Algorithm 2.2 on the basis of the activity durations given by the mode assignment.

7.1.3 Crossover and Mutation

For our problem representation, we cannot use any of the standard crossover and mutation operators defined in the literature. Therefore, we introduce new operators which extend those for precedence feasible activity lists (cf. Subsection 5.2.2) by additionally considering mode assignments.

Crossover

For applying the crossover operator, we select two parent individuals for crossover, a mother $I^M = (\lambda^M, \mu^M)$ and a father $I^F = (\lambda^F, \mu^F)$ with

$$I^M = \begin{pmatrix} j_1^M & \cdots & j_J^M \\ \mu^M(j_1^M) & \cdots & \mu^M(j_J^M) \end{pmatrix}$$

and

$$I^F = \begin{pmatrix} j_1^F & \cdots & j_J^F \\ \mu^F(j_1^F) & \cdots & \mu^F(j_J^F) \end{pmatrix}.$$

Then we draw two random integers q_1 and q_2 with $1 \leq q_1, q_2 \leq J$. Now two new individuals, a daughter $I^D = (\lambda^D, \mu^D)$ and a son $I^S = (\lambda^S, \mu^S)$, are produced from the parents. We first consider I^D which is defined as follows: In the activity list λ^D of I^D, the positions $i = 1, \ldots, q_1$ are defined by the mother, that is, we set

$$j_i^D := j_i^M.$$

The partial activity list of positions $i = q_1 + 1, \ldots, J$ in λ^D is derived from the father, but the activities that have already been taken from the mother may not be considered again, that is,

$$j_i^D := j_k^F \text{ where } k \text{ is the lowest index such that } j_k^F \notin \{j_1^D, \ldots, j_{i-1}^D\}.$$

As for the single-mode case, this definition ensures that the relative positions in the parents' activity sequences are preserved. From Theorem 5.1, we know that the resulting job sequence is precedence feasible.

The modes of the activities on the positions $i = 1, \ldots, q_2$ in daughter I^D are defined by the mother's mode assignment μ^M, that is, we have

$$\mu^D(j_i^D) := \mu^M(j_i^D).$$

The modes of the remaining jobs on the positions $i = q_2 + 1, \ldots, J$ in I^D are derived from the father's mode assignment μ^F:

$$\mu^D(j_i^D) := \mu^F(j_i^D).$$

The son I^S of the parent individuals I^M and I^F is computed accordingly. However, the positions $1, \ldots, q_1$ of the son's activity list λ^S are taken from the father and the remaining positions are determined by the mother. Analogously, the first part up to position q_2 of the mode assignment μ^S of I^S is taken from μ^F while the second part is derived from μ^M.

These definitions are illustrated by the following example. We use again the project instance of Figure 7.1 and the example parents of (7.1). Setting $q_1 = 3$ and $q_2 = 4$, we obtain

$$I^D = \begin{pmatrix} 2 & 4 & 1 & 3 & 5 & 6 \\ 2 & 2 & 1 & 1 & 1 & 2 \end{pmatrix}, \quad I^S = \begin{pmatrix} 1 & 3 & 2 & 4 & 6 & 5 \\ 1 & 2 & 1 & 2 & 1 & 1 \end{pmatrix}. \tag{7.2}$$

Consider the daughter I^D. The first three positions of the activity list are equal to those of the mother's activity list. The order of the remaining activities is taken from I^F. According to the value of q_2, the modes of the first four activities in the activity list of I^D are determined by the mother's mode assignment while the last two activities get their modes from the father's mode assignment. Observe that, as we have $q_1 < q_2$ in this example, the fourth activity of the daughter's job sequence, activity 3, is determined by the father's job sequence. The mode of activity 3, however, is taken from the mother.

Mutation

The representation-specific mutation operator included in our GA is applied to each newly generated child individual. It is defined as follows. Given an individual $I = (\lambda, \mu)$ of the current population, the mutation operator first modifies the related activity list λ: For all positions $i = 1, \ldots, J-1$, activities j_i and j_{i+1} are exchanged with a probability of p_{mutation}, if the result is an activity list which fulfills the precedence assumption. Note that this does not affect the mode assignment, that is, all activities keep their modes even if their positions within the activity list are changed. Next, the mutation operator modifies the mode assignment μ: With probability p_{mutation}, we reselect $\mu(j_i)$ by randomly drawing a mode out of $\mathcal{M}_{j_i}$ for all positions $i = 1, \ldots, J$.

While the first step may create partial activity sequences (i.e., gene combinations) that could not have been procuced by the crossover operator, the second step may introduce a mode (i.e., gene) that did not occur in the current population.

7.2 Improving Schedules by Local Search

Motivated by the good results of the local search approach in the extended GA of Section 5.6, we will now discuss a local search method for the multi-mode problem to improve the schedule related to an individual. The approach is based on the definition of a multi-mode left shift which was originally defined for a bounding rule in an exact algorithm (cf. Subsection 3.2.3). Recall that a multi-mode left shift of an activity j is an operation on a given schedule which reduces the finish time of activitity j without changing the modes or finish times of the other activities and without violating the constraints. Thereby, the mode of activity j may be changed. Two characteristics make the multi-mode left shift a promising way to improve feasible schedules within our GA: First, multi-mode left shifts consider start times and modes simultaneously. Second, they cannot deteriorate the current schedule, that is, the schedule remains feasible and its makespan cannot be increased. In what follows, we discuss three approaches to incorporate multi-mode left shift improvement into our GA.

7.2.1 Single Pass Improvement

We employ the local search procedure after transforming an individual $I = (\lambda, \mu)$ into a schedule. If the schedule is feasible w.r.t. the nonrenewable resources, we try to improve it as follows: For each activity $j_1, \ldots, j_J$, we check whether a multi-mode left shift can be performed. Thereby, the modes of an activity j_i are tested w.r.t. non-decreasing duration, that is, the mode with the shortest duration is checked first. For each activity, the first feasible multi-mode left shift found (if any) is applied to the schedule. Then we skip to the next activity in the activity list. The result is a feasible schedule with a makespan equal to or lower than the makespan of the original schedule. Now the fitness $f(I)$ of individual I is set to be equal to the new makespan. This improvement procedure is applied to all individuals of the current population for which we have to compute the fitness. We call it a single pass procedure because each activity is considered only once for a multi-mode left shift.

For illustration, we consider again the project instance given in Figure 7.1. As already mentioned, example individual I^M of (7.1) is related to the schedule shown in Figure 7.2. This schedule is improved by the procedure described above as follows: While activities 2 and 4 cannot be left shifted, we can perform a multi-mode left shift on activity 1. Leaving activity 6 unchanged, we can now apply a multi-mode left shift to activity 3. Finally, left shifting activity 5 yields a new makespan of 13 periods which is 2 periods shorter than the makespan of the original schedule. The resulting schedule is displayed in Figure 7.3.

It should be emphasized that there is an important difference between the local search component of the extended GA for the single-mode case (cf. Section 5.6) and the multi-mode local search method outlined above. The single-mode local search phase starts after it was decided to stop the GA and tries to improve the individuals of the last population. Here, however, we perform GA and local search simultaneously. That is, whenever we have obtained a

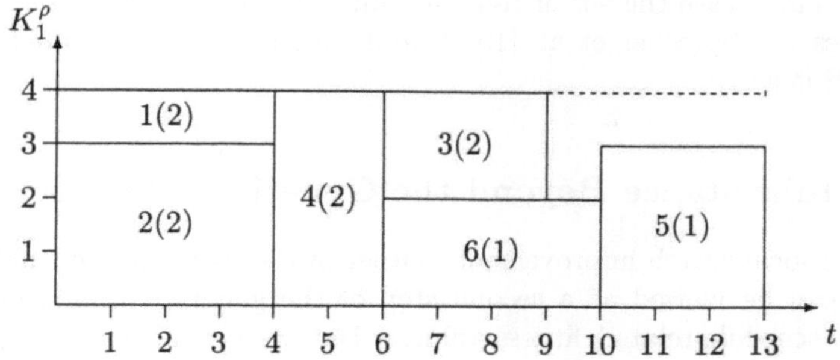

Figure 7.3: Improved schedule of example individual I^M

new individual (either for the initial population or by crossover and mutation) we compute its fitness in two steps: After computing the fitness by the standard serial SGS, we try to improve it by the local search method given above. Afterwards, the GA itself proceeds with the next generation. The main reason to do so is that the multi-mode local search method cannot deteriorate the current schedule whereas the single-mode local search procedure also deals with worse neighbors. In other words, the multi-mode approach given above only considers one neighbor of the current schedule which cannot be worse.

7.2.2 Multi Pass Improvement

As each activity is considered only once for a multi-mode left shift, a schedule derived by the above single pass local search algorithm is not necessarily tight (recall that a tight schedule is a schedule to which no multi-mode left shift can be applied, cf. Subsection 3.2.3). This is because a multi-mode left shift of some activity j_i might allow a multi-mode left shift of some activity j_k with $k < i$ that had not been possible before. In the improved schedule of Figure 7.3, for example, a multi-mode left shift of activity 2 is possible because the total consumption of the nonrenewable resource decreased due to the multi-mode left shift of activity 1.

Consequently, we have tested a second variant of our local search extension which we call multi pass procedure: We repeatedly apply the above single pass improvement algorithm until we have obtained a tight schedule. In contrast to the single pass algorithm, the multi pass approach always leads to a local optimum as the resulting schedule cannot be further improved using multi-mode left shifts.

Note that neither the single pass nor the multi pass approach can improve schedules for the single-mode RCPSP found by the GA. This is because in the single-mode case the set of tight schedules coincides with the set of the active ones (cf. Sprecher et al. [193]), and each schedule computed by the serial SGS is active.

7.2.3 Inheritance Beyond the Genetic Metaphor

So far, our local search improvement—either in the single pass or multi pass variant—can be viewed as a second step of the genotype evaluation as it computes schedule-related fitness values. But we can do more: Applying the local search approach to a schedule S related to an individual I, we obtain an improved schedule S'. Now we can transform the new schedule S' into an individual I', that is, we can find an individual I' (genotype) which corresponds to the improved schedule S' (phenotype). Subsequently, we can replace individual I with the improved individual I' in the current population. Clearly, the activity list of individual I' is given by the sequence of activities ordered w.r.t. non-decreasing start times of schedule S'; the mode assignment is straightforward. For illustration, we consider again the project instance of Figure 7.1 and example individual I^M which is, after application of the single-pass improvement, related to the schedule of Figure 7.3. This improved schedule leads to genotype

$$I^{M'} = \begin{pmatrix} 1 & 2 & 4 & 6 & 3 & 5 \\ 2 & 2 & 2 & 1 & 2 & 1 \end{pmatrix}.$$

Considering evolution in biology, the improvement procedure which only affects the phenotype (schedule) can be compared to individual or ontogenetic learning. The transformation of its results into a new genotype, i.e., into hereditary information, corresponds to the possibility to inherit the results of ontogenetic learning as proposed by Lamarck (cf. Subsection 5.1.1). In nature, however, changes in the phenotype of an individual usually do not affect its genotype.

7.3 Computational Results

In this section we present the results of the computational study for the multi-mode genetic algorithm. Again, the experiments have been performed on a Pentium-based IBM-compatible personal computer with 133 MHz clock-pulse and 32 MB RAM running under the Linux operating system. The GA has been coded in ANSI C and compiled with the GNU C compiler. As test instances, we used the standard ProGen sets for the multi-mode case which are described in Appendix A.2.2.

7.3.1 Configuration of the Algorithm

In the numerical investigation reported in this subsection we determined the best configuration of our GA. We summarize the results only for the instance set with 20 non-dummy activities per project as the results for the smaller projects are similar.

We start with the examination of the preprocessing procedure (cf. Bounding Rule 3.3). It eliminated 4.4 % of the modes. Moreover, it was able to show that for 29 % of the project instances both nonrenewable resources are redundant. Given the low computational effort for the preprocessing procedure, we include it into our GA.

Next, we test the performance of the methodology to generate the initial population. Considering the instances with at least one nonrenewable resource left after preprocessing, only 53 % of the mode assignments in the initial population are feasible if generated randomly. Adding the local search procedure to modify the mode assignment, already 99 % of the mode assignments in the initial population are feasible. Moreover, the computation time of this approach is neglectable. This shows that our simple local search procedure is well suited to contribute to a good initial population for the GA and should therefore be incorporated.

So far, we have shown that the preprocessing procedure and the local search procedure for modifying the initial mode assignments are part of the best configuration of the GA. We now turn to the GA itself. Computational tests confirmed that the mutation probability of $p_{\text{mutation}} = 0.05$ that was chosen for the single-mode GAs of Chapter 5 also yields the best results for the multi-mode case.

Finally, we determine the best GA variant concerning the local search schedule improvement. We have five possible variants: The plain GA without schedule improvement, the GA with single pass schedule improvement, the GA with single pass improvement including additional inheritance of the local search results, the GA with multi-pass local search, and the GA with multi-pass improvement including additional inheritance of the local search results.

As the local search types require a different computational effort for each individual, we chose a time limit instead of a limited number of individuals as basis for the tests. Given a time limit, only a restricted number of individuals can be computed. Therefore, the population size *POP* is another important parameter to be determined: A large population size will lead to an evolution over only a few generations and, as we will see, the relationship between population size and number of generations has an impact on the solution quality (cf. also the results for the single-mode case given in Subsection 5.5.1). As we will also observe, there are interdependencies between the choice of the GA variant and the population size. Consequently, the following experiment simultaneously takes into account both the GA variant and the population size. Given a time limit of one second, Table 7.1 summarizes the average percentage deviation from the optimal makespan for the three GA variants and four population size settings.

Improvement	*inheritance*	$POP =$	30	60	90	120
—	—		3.00 %	1.83 %	1.51 %	1.79 %
single-pass	no		1.77 %	1.21 %	1.38 %	1.66 %
single-pass	yes		2.42 %	1.81 %	1.69 %	1.85 %
multi-pass	no		1.51 %	1.32 %	1.53 %	1.71 %
multi-pass	yes		2.13 %	1.66 %	1.71 %	1.75 %

Table 7.1: Impact of local search improvement — 1 second, $J = 20$

There are several observations to be made: First and most important, the best configuration makes use of the local search without additional inheritance and, with respect to the time limit of one second, a population size of $POP = 60$.[2]

Second, the GA with single pass improvement, but without inheritance is, independently from the population size, always better than the plain GA. This confirms that the GA benefits from the local search improvement. This approach, however, cannot be improved by using the multi pass procedure or by additionally allowing inheritance of the local search results. The disappointing results of the multi pass procedure are due to the fact that multiple application only leads to minor improvements compared to the single pass application while it increases the computation time needed to compute the schedule for one individual. Hence, within some time limit, less individuals can be computed, and the minor effect of obtaining tight schedules is thus over-consumed. On the other hand, the observation that the inheritance mechanism consistently worsens the results of the GA with local search improvement is rather a surprise as one may have assumed that inheriting improved genes should be advantageous. The computational effort of the inheritance mechanism cannot be the reason as it is neglectable when compared to that of the local search procedure itself. In fact, we need to examine the behavior of the GA variants more carefully to provide an explanation, as will be done in the next subsection.

Finally, all variants perform best for a medium population size. If the population size is too large, only a few generations can be computed within the time limit, and the procedure cannot fully exploit the advantages of

[2]Within the time limit of one second, on the average 2350 individuals were computed, corresponding to approximately $GEN = 40$ generations. Thus, the relationship $GEN \approx \frac{2}{3} \cdot POP$ provides a good rule of thumb for the parameter selection. This is in line with the findings of Subsection 5.5.1.

genetic optimization. Otherwise, if it is too small, the gene pool is too small. Observe also that the best population size for the plain GA is larger than that for the GA with single pass improvement but without inheritance. This is due to the additional computational effort needed for the local search improvement. That is, within the same time limit less individuals can be computed, leading to a smaller favorable population size (and also a smaller number of generations).

7.3.2 Population Analysis

Up to this point, we know that it pays to incorporate our single pass local search component for schedule improvement into the GA. This subsection proceeds with an analysis of the generations produced by the GA in order to answer a question that has been arising in the previous subsection: Why is it disadvantageous to inherit the local search results? To obtain comparable results, we fix the population size to $POP = 60$ individuals within the GA variants with and without inheritance. Again, we employ only the set with 20 activities for each project.

Our first experiment takes a closer look at the intermediate results of the artificial evolution. Table 7.2 gives the average percentage deviations after 0.2, 0.4, 0.8, and 1.6 CPU seconds for both GA variants. Shortly after the beginning of the evolution, i.e., after only a few generations have been computed, the GA variant with inheritance leads to better intermediate results than its counterpart without. Then, however, the GA without inheritance becomes superior. This result indicates that the inheritance mechanism should be used together with a larger population size and thus, within some time limit, a smaller number of generations. This explains that, according to Table 7.1, the best POP value for the improvement with inheritance is larger than that for the variant without. However, Table 7.1 also shows that, given the best population size for both variants, the GA without inheritance is superior.

Improvement	*inheritance*	*0.20 sec*	*0.40 sec*	*0.80 sec*	*1.60 sec*
single-pass	no	4.70 %	2.69 %	1.42 %	0.98 %
single-pass	yes	4.12 %	2.45 %	1.89 %	1.64 %

Table 7.2: Impact of local search improvement — intermediate results, $J = 20$

So far, we have seen that inheriting the local search results has some positive effect in the first few generations. Now we want to find out why there is a negative effect in the long term. We need some definitions for an analysis of the population.

First, we define a measure for the similarity of two individuals $I = (\lambda, \mu)$ and $I' = (\lambda', \mu')$. We start with a definition of the similarity of the related activity lists. Our goal is to check if two activities have the same relative positions in the activity lists λ and λ'. Since it is sufficient to consider only those activities that are not precedence related, we define

$$\mathcal{Q} = \{\{i, j\} \mid i, j = 1, \ldots, J;\ i \neq j;\ i \notin \overline{\mathcal{P}}_j;\ j \notin \overline{\mathcal{P}}_i\}.$$

Given two activities i and j that are not precedence related, i.e., $\{i, j\} \in \mathcal{Q}$, we reflect their relative positions within the activity lists of I and I' by

$$\alpha^{I,I'}_{\{i,j\}} = \begin{cases} 1, & \text{if } i \text{ is before } j \text{ in } \lambda \text{ and } \lambda', \text{ or if } j \text{ is before } i \text{ in } \lambda \text{ and } \lambda', \\ 0, & \text{otherwise.} \end{cases}$$

Now we are ready to define the following measure for the similarity of the activity lists of I and I': If there are activities that are not precedence related, i.e., $\mathcal{Q} \neq \emptyset$, we set

$$\alpha^{I,I'} = \frac{1}{|\mathcal{Q}|} \sum_{\{i,j\} \in \mathcal{Q}} \alpha^{I,I'}_{\{i,j\}}.$$

Otherwise, if $\mathcal{Q} = \emptyset$, we have a serial network structure which implies that there is only one precedence feasible activity sequence. In this case, we define $\alpha^{I,I'} = 1$, reflecting that the activity sequences of individuals I and I' are equal.

The next definition reflects whether an activity j is assigned the same mode by the mode assignments μ and μ' of two individuals I and I':

$$\beta^{I,I'}_j = \begin{cases} 1, & \text{if } \mu^I(j) = \mu^{I'}(j), \\ 0, & \text{otherwise.} \end{cases}$$

This enables us to define the following measure for the similarity of the mode assignments of I and I':

$$\beta^{I,I'} = \frac{1}{J} \sum_{j=1}^{J} \beta^{I,I'}_j.$$

Combining the above definitions, we obtain a measure $\sigma^{I,I'}$ for the similarity of individuals I and I' in which both the activity lists and the mode assignments are considered:

$$\sigma^{I,I'} = \frac{\alpha^{I,I'} + \beta^{I,I'}}{2}.$$

Clearly, the higher $\sigma^{I,I'}$, the more identical information is contained in the genotypes of individuals I and I'. Observe that we have $\sigma^{I,I'} \in [0,1]$. Especially, we have $\sigma^{I,I'} = 0$ if I and I' do not have any genetic information in common, and $\sigma^{I,I'} = 1$ if they are identical, that is, if we have $I = I'$.

Now we use this similarity measure for analyzing the different generations produced by our GA. More precisely, we want to partition each generation into sets of similar individuals. In order to obtain these partitions, we have implemented a cluster analysis algorithm.[3] Given a generation with POP individuals, we first compute the similarity value for each pair of individuals. Then the cluster analysis algorithm starts with the trivial partition in which each individual forms a cluster, that is, we have POP clusters. After that we unite clusters as follows: Consider two clusters C and C'. C and C' are united if we have $\sigma^{I,I'} \geq 0.8$ for all individuals $I \in C$ and $I' \in C'$. This is repeated until there are no clusters left that can be united w.r.t. this similarity criterion. Each resulting cluster contains highly similar individuals.

We have analyzed the populations generated by the GAs with and without inheritance of the single pass local search results. Table 7.3 lists the average number of clusters that have been obtained by both variants for every fifth generation. As the first generation is randomly determined, there are no similarities of more than 0.8, inducing 60 clusters with one individual each. With an increasing number of generations, the number of clusters in a generation decreases, that is, more similar individuals occur in the population. Clearly, this is due to the crossover and selection operators which tend to copy "fit" and remove "unfit" information. Table 7.3, however, shows that the inheritance mechanism accelerates the reduction of clusters: While the GA without inheritance leads to 25 different clusters after 15 generations, the GA with inheritance results in only 12 clusters at the same time.

Improvement	*inherit.*	*1*	*5*	*10*	*15*	*20*	*25*	*30*	*35*	*40*	*45*	*50*
single-pass	no	60	38	32	25	17	14	10	9	8	8	7
single-pass	yes	60	31	20	12	9	7	5	4	3	2	2

Table 7.3: Average number of clusters w.r.t. generation number

These results explain why including the inheritance mechanism into the GA deteriorates the quality of the solutions in a long term evolution: As

[3]For a general introduction into cluster analysis the reader is referred to, e.g., Backhaus et al. [10].

already outlined, the basic strategy of any GA is to gather information about promising regions of the search space. Each of our clusters can be viewed as such a promising region. At the same time, however, information that is not considered as promising is removed. Clearly, this leads to a loss of genetic variety. If the number of clusters decreases too fast—in other words, if too much information is lost too fast—the GA gets stuck in some promising regions of the search space. As each cluster contains similar information, the GA is likely to fail to construct individuals from previously unsearched regions of the (usually huge) search space if only few clusters are left. Consequently, many regions remain unexplored, and better solutions may be left undetected. On the other hand, the focus on a few promising clusters is advantageous if the evolution is restricted to a small number of generations, see again Table 7.2. However, a short term evolution does not fully exploit the power of genetic optimization.

Basically, one encounters the following difficulty when designing a GA: An evolution proceeding too fast leads to a loss of genetic variety and is thus disadvantageous. On the other hand, an evolution proceeding too slowly may be unable to identify promising regions of the search space. Therefore, the variants and parameters have to be chosen carefully.

The results obtained here are in line with the findings of Whitley et al. [210]. They state that a Larmarckian evolution (like that induced by our inheritance approach) leads to a faster search with a tendency to converge to a local optimum whereas a genetic algorithm enhanced by learning, but without inheritance rather converges to a global optimum.

7.3.3 Comparison with other Heuristics

In this subsection we summarize the results obtained from a comparison of our GA with other heuristics for solving the MRCPSP that have recently been proposed in the literature. We use the best variant of our GA, that is, with single-pass improvement, but without inheritance of the local search results.

Kolisch and Drexl [125] suggested a local search procedure which successively constructs a neighbor mode assigment based on slack calculations of the current schedule and, after fixing the modes accordingly, computes a schedule for the resulting single-mode RCPSP using a single pass priority rule method. After a given number of moves, the procedure tries to improve the schedule for the best current mode assignment by the adaptive sampling approach of Kolisch and Drexl [124] (cf. Subsection 4.2.2). The experimental investigation of Kolisch and Drexl [125] shows that their approach outperforms the algorithms of Boctor [21] and of Drexl and Grünewald [61].

Özdamar [154] developed a GA based on an encoding which is made up by the priority rule representation (cf. Section 5.4) and a mode assignment.

As decoding procedure, the parallel SGS is used (cf. Subsection 4.1.1). For each individual, two schedules are computed by forward-backward scheduling (cf. Subsection 4.2.2).

As a basis for the comparison of our GA with the two heuristics described above, we use the result reported by Özdamar [154] obtained from computing 3000 individuals (which corresponds to 6000 schedules) for each instance of the ProGen multi-mode set with 10 non-dummy activities in a project. We recompiled the original PASCAL code of Kolisch and Drexl [125] and limited the number of schedules to 6000 for each ProGen instance with $J = 10$. Finally, we tested our GA with 3000 individuals (which corresponds to 6000 schedules due to the single pass improvement for each individual) for each project instance of the same set without imposing a time limit. We may assume that the effort to compute one schedule is similar in the three procedures. Hence, this should yield a fair comparison (in fact, as our GA does not require to compute eligible activities or priority values, it is probably the fastest). We obtained the results that are displayed in Table 7.4. They show that our GA clearly outperforms the other two heuristics. The results confirm our findings for the single-mode case (cf. Chapters 5 and 6) because again two genetic algorithms show a different behavior. That is, the problem representation has a much higher influence on the performance than the metaheuristic strategy.

Heuristic	*av. dev.*	*feasible*	*optimal*
new GA	0.10 %	100.0 %	98.1 %
Kolisch, Drexl [125]	0.50 %	100.0 %	91.8 %
Özdamar [154]	0.86 %	100.0 %	88.1 %

Table 7.4: New GA vs. two other heuristics — 6000 schedules, $J = 10$

Next, we compare the new GA with a truncated version of the branch-and-bound (B&B) procedure of Sprecher and Drexl [192]. We do so for two reasons: First, the authors have suggested to employ their exact algorithm as a heuristic by imposing a time limit. Second, as shown in Chapter 3, their approach is the currently most efficient exact method for solving the MRCPSP. We have used the best variant of this branch-and-bound method as described in Chapter 3, that is, we have extended the original approach of Sprecher and Drexl [192] by the new Order Swap Rule and the new formulation of the Precedence Tree Rule. For the comparison, we have employed our reimplementation of that algorithm that has also been used for the study of Chapter 3. We used the activity selection rule suggested by Sprecher [190], that is, the next eligible activity to be selected for branching is the one with the lowest number. The modes are selected w.r.t. non-decreasing processing time. A time limit is added as basis for the comparison with the GA. We have used the ProGen instance sets with up to 20 activities in a project.

Table 7.5 summarizes the results obtained from both algorithms for a time limit of one second. For each project size, it lists the average and the maximal deviation from the optimum, the percentage of instances for which an feasible solution was found, and the percentage of instances for which an optimal solution was found. While the truncated exact procedure solves all instances with 10 activities to optimality within one second, its average deviation for the instances with 20 activities is more than nine times higher than that obtained by the GA. In contrast to the GA which results in moderate maximal deviations of at most 15 %, the maximal deviation of the truncated branch-and-bound algorithm is almost 80 % for $J = 20$. While our GA finds a feasible solution for every instance, the truncated exact procedure fails to do so for instances with more than 12 activities.

Heuristic	J	*av. dev.*	*max. dev.*	*feasible*	*optimal*
new GA	10	0.06 %	6.3 %	100.0 %	98.7 %
	12	0.14 %	9.1 %	100.0 %	97.3 %
	14	0.44 %	10.3 %	100.0 %	89.8 %
	16	0.59 %	10.5 %	100.0 %	87.8 %
	18	0.99 %	13.3 %	100.0 %	78.3 %
	20	1.21 %	14.2 %	100.0 %	73.3 %
truncated B&B	10	0.00 %	0.0 %	100.0 %	100.0 %
	12	0.12 %	17.9 %	100.0 %	98.2 %
	14	1.46 %	33.3 %	99.6 %	85.7 %
	16	3.81 %	52.4 %	99.5 %	69.5 %
	18	7.48 %	77.4 %	98.0 %	57.4 %
	20	11.51 %	78.6 %	96.4 %	47.3 %

Table 7.5: New GA vs. truncated B&B w.r.t. project size — 1 sec

Table 7.6 gives the results for four different time limits between 1 and 125 seconds and the projects with 20 activities. We observe that both approaches benefit from increasing the computation time. The GA is clearly superior for all time limits and reaches near-optimal solutions within 125 seconds. The truncated branch-and-bound approach still fails to find a feasible schedule for some projects within this time.

Finally, we examine the impact of the renewable resource strength RS^ρ on the solution quality of the GA and the truncated branch-and-bound procedure. We know that a low renewable resource strength makes a project instance harder to solve as it increases computation times of exact algorithms (cf. Chapter 3) as well as deviations from the optimal makespan for heuristics

Heuristic	*CPU-sec*	*av. dev.*	*max. dev.*	*feasible*	*optimal*
new GA	1	1.21 %	14.2 %	100.0 %	73.3 %
	5	0.49 %	10.7 %	100.0 %	87.9 %
	25	0.22 %	10.5 %	100.0 %	94.4 %
	125	0.11 %	7.1 %	100.0 %	96.8 %
truncated B&B	1	11.51 %	78.6 %	96.4 %	47.3 %
	5	6.24 %	89.4 %	98.6 %	63.7 %
	25	2.88 %	53.6 %	99.5 %	76.4 %
	125	1.04 %	34.2 %	99.6 %	87.9 %

Table 7.6: New GA vs. truncated B&B w.r.t. time limit — $J = 20$

(cf. Chapter 6). Table 7.7 shows that the average percentage deviations from the optimal makespan increase with decreasing resource strength for both procedures tested here, given the instance set with $J = 20$ and a time limit of one second. For all RS^ρ values, the deviation of the GA is approximately nine times lower than that of the truncated branch-and-bound algorithm. It is interesting to note that the truncated branch-and-bound procedure dominates on the sets of small instances, that is, those instances are very easy with respect to the project size (see again Table 7.5), but not on those that are easy with respect to the resource strength. This indicates that the GA is much better suited for scheduling medium or large sized real-world projects, independently from the level of the resource strength.

Heuristic	$RS^\rho = 0.25$	$RS^\rho = 0.50$	$RS^\rho = 0.75$	$RS^\rho = 1.00$
new GA	2.02 %	1.26 %	1.06 %	0.69 %
truncated B&B	18.27 %	10.61 %	9.93 %	6.55 %

Table 7.7: New GA vs. truncated B&B w.r.t. resource strength — 1 sec, $J = 20$

Chapter 8

Case Studies

In this chapter, we study two real-world applications of resource-constrained project scheduling. First, we deal with scheduling the experiments of a medical research project. Here, various constraints have to be observed, especially scarce laboratory equipment and the arrangement of different experiment types. Then we consider the task of scheduling the interviews of a market research study which can be viewed as a project. This includes the selection of interviewers with respect to several constraints such as regional distribution of the interviews, qualification, and available working time of the interviewers.

These two real-world projects are used to show how the various project scheduling models of Chapter 2 can be applied to capture situations of practical relevance formally. Moreover, as we were able to obtain the original data of the medical research project, we will demonstrate the applicability of a genetic algorithm of Chapter 5 to a real-world project.

8.1 Scheduling Medical Research Experiments

In this section, we deal with a medical research project that consists of a number of different experiments which have to be replicated several times. Scheduling such a project involves the temporal arrangement of the experiments with respect to several constraints. Constructing good schedules for such projects is crucial because this allows to utilize as much of the capacity of the laboratory equipment as possible.

We consider a medical research project that was performed in 1994 at the University of Kiel (Germany) according to a hand-made schedule. Our goal is to show that the models and methods discussed in this work are applicable to this project. Furthermore, we point out that scheduling this project using an algorithmic tool would not only have made the scheduling process more convenient, but would also have resulted in a much better schedule than the hand-made one.

This section is organized as follows: After the description of the medical research project and the original data, we formally model it using project scheduling concepts. We then report on computational experiments, where the focus is on a comparison of the schedule obtained from a GA with the original hand-made schedule. Subsequently, we consider some optimality issues of the GA and the computed schedule in particular. The section is closed with a discussion of the possibilities to obtain alternative schedules and some concluding remarks on modeling aspects.[1]

8.1.1 Problem Description

We consider a medical research project that took place in 1994 at the medical faculty of the University of Kiel (Germany). A detailed description of this project as well as the results can be found in Fitting [77], see also Löser et al. [137]. The research deals with the relationship between polyamine synthesis and cancer. While it has been shown by, e.g., Löser et al. [138] that polyamines cannot be used for cancer diagnosis, the inhibition of polyamine synthesis provides a successful approach to tumor growth inhibition, cf., e.g., Marton and Pegg [140]. The objective of the research project considered here is to examine the impact of certain medicaments and a special diet on the polyamine synthesis and on the stimulated pancreas growth of rats. The medicaments are given to (male) rats. After a prespecified number of days, a rat is sacrificed. Immediately afterwards, several organs (pancreas, liver, prostate, and small gut) are examined.

In the following, we give a description of those details of the medical research project that are relevant for scheduling the project. As our intention is to compute a schedule for the original project, we will describe it using the original data. Nevertheless, the general structure of this project is typical for many medical, biological, and pharmacological research projects which can be modeled analogously.

Experiments

We have 6 medicaments, which will simply be denoted as $a, \dots, f$, that are tested in 7 specific combinations $A, \dots, G$. Each medicament combination is tested over several specific durations on rats which are given a normal diet as well as on rats which are given a special diet. If special food is given, the test duration is 7 days. Otherwise, for the normal diet, we have test durations of 2, 3, and 6 days. Any medicament except for a and b

[1] With the exception of Subsection 8.1.6, the contents of this section can also be found in Hartmann [91].

requires an additional preparation time of 2 days when tested in accordance with the normal food, resulting in total durations of 4, 5, and 8 days for a corresponding combination. Testing a medicament combination with a given diet type over a given duration is called an experiment. Once an experiment has been started, it may not be interrupted.

Repetitions

Each experiment is repeated several times in order to allow a statistical evaluation. The number of repetitions varies from experiment to experiment due to the following reasons: First, some of the experiments have already been performed in a similar way, therefore only a few repetitions are sufficient for obtaining reliable results (clearly, the number of rats to be sacrificed must be kept as small as possible). Second, some of the medicaments are scarce and expensive. In fact, three of the experiments are not performed at all, i.e., we have 0 repetitions. Table 8.1 displays the number of repetitions with respect to medicament combination, duration, and diet type of the experiments of the original project.

Temporal Arrangement

Several repetitions should be carried out in parallel, that is, they should start and finish at the same day. This keeps the schedule easier to survey. Moreover, it allows the researcher to dose the medicaments more exactly. However, performing too many repetitions of an experiment in a parallel block may cause systematical errors. Especially the last day of an experiment (i.e., the day on which the organs are examined) is assumed to be critical in this sense. Therefore, the repetitions of one experiment should finish on 2 different days if up to 4 repetitions have to be carried out, and on 3 different days otherwise. Moreover, the repetitions of an experiment should be evenly distributed on the repetition blocks. That is, the distribution of repetitions should be arranged in a way that the number of repetitions finishing on different days should not differ by more than one. For example, 4 repetitions of the same experiment lead to 2 finish days, and on both of them 2 repetitions must finish (instead 3 repetitions on one finish day and 1 on the other).

Examination Days

Due to limited laboratory capacities, the organs of a rat can only be examined on Wednesday, Thursday, and Friday, which will thereafter be called examination days throughout this section. As examinations must take place on the last day of an experiment, an experiment must finish on an examination day. In addition, the capacity of some equipment in the laboratory is limited: On each examination day, the organs of at most 6 rats can be examined. The calendar showing the examination days is given in Table 8.2. The days are consecutively numbered, up to the planning horizon of 84 days.

Working Days

The researcher is allowed to specify some days for vacation and for evaluation of some preliminary results. On the remaining days which are called working days the researcher is in the laboratory. The first working day of the project was June 6, 1994. The original working days are entered into the calendar of Table 8.2. The tasks of the researcher are examining on the last day of an experiment as well as feeding and giving the medicaments. During the duration of an experiment based on normal food, the researcher must be in the laboratory on each day. However, an experiment related to special food (which always takes 7 days) requires his presence only on days 1, 5, 6, and 7, while on the other days, feeding and giving medicaments are not necessary. Due to the high effort of feeding, giving medicaments, and examining, the researcher can handle only 20 rats at the same time. That is, on each working day at most 20 experiment repetitions requiring his presence in the laboratory can be processed.

Objective

The researcher is responsible for determining a project schedule which observes the restrictions given above. His objective is an early project completion. This also leads to free laboratory capacities for further research projects.

8.1.2 Modeling Approach

We now show how this medical research project can be modeled. We will employ the basic RCPSP and resource parameters varying with time, i.e., the RCPSP/τ (cf. Chapter 2). As already mentioned, the underlying structure of the medical research project considered here occurs in many natural science projects. Especially the concepts of laboratory equipment with limited capacity, a researcher, and experiments with different durations, several repetitions, and restricted temporal arrangement can be viewed as typical. The following approach to capture this structure with project scheduling concepts uses again original data, but the modeling approach can be easily generalized to many similar research projects.

Resources

We start the transformation by defining the set of renewable resources which will be given by $\mathcal{K}^\rho = \{1, \ldots, 27\}$. The capacities of the first two resources

Medicament	*diet:*			*normal*				*special*
combination	*duration:*	*2*	*3*	*4*	*5*	*6*	*8*	*7*
$A = \{a\}$		4	2			2		2
$B = \{b\}$		4	4			4		2
$C = \{b, c\}$				6	9		5	3
$D = \{b, d\}$				5	7		5	3
$E = \{b, c, e, f\}$				5	6		0	5
$F = \{b, d, e, f\}$				6	5		0	5
$G = \{c\}$				4	3		3	0

Table 8.1: Experiments and repetitions

Mo	*Tu*	*We*	*Th*	*Fr*	*Sa*	*Su*	*Mo*	*Tu*	*We*	*Th*	*Fr*	*Sa*	*Su*
1	2	3	4	5	6	7	8	9	10	11	12	13	14
W	W	W	W	W			W	W	W	W	W		
		E	E	E					E	E	E		
15	16	17	18	19	20	21	22	23	24	25	26	27	28
							W	W	W	W	W	W	W
		E	E	E					E	E	E		
29	30	31	32	33	34	35	36	37	38	39	40	41	42
W	W	W	W	W									
		E	E	E					E	E	E		
43	44	45	46	47	48	49	50	51	52	53	54	55	56
W	W	W	W	W									
		E	E	E					E	E	E		
57	58	59	60	61	62	63	64	65	66	67	68	69	70
W	W	W	W	W	W	W	W	W	W	W	W	W	W
		E	E	E					E	E	E		
71	72	73	74	75	76	77	78	79	80	81	82	83	84
W	W	W	W	W			W	W	W	W	W		
		E	E	E					E	E	E		

Table 8.2: Calendar — working (W) and examination (E) days

are varying with time. Therefore, we have to specify the set of periods first. Each period corresponds to one day, and we have a planning horizon of $T = 84$ days (see Table 8.2). This leads us to a set of periods $\mathcal{T}' = \{1, \ldots, 84\}$. Now we are ready to define resource $k = 1$ which reflects the laboratory equipment. On day $t \in \mathcal{T}'$, its capacity is given by

$$R_1^\rho(t) = \begin{cases} 6, & \text{if } t \text{ is an examination day} \\ 0, & \text{otherwise.} \end{cases}$$

The second resource corresponds to the researcher. His capacity on day $t \in \mathcal{T}'$ is defined as

$$R_2^\rho(t) = \begin{cases} 20, & \text{if } t \text{ is a working day} \\ 0, & \text{otherwise.} \end{cases}$$

Finally, we introduce one resource for each experiment in order to control its temporal arrangement. According to Table 8.1, we have 25 experiments with a number of repetitions greater than zero. Hence, we obtain 25 resources $k = 3, \ldots, 27$ of this type with a constant availability of

$$R_k^\rho(t) = 1 \text{ for all } t \in \mathcal{T}'.$$

The idea behind these latter resources will become clear when we define the activities.

Activities

The basic idea of the definition of the activities of the project is to comprise those repetitions of an experiment that should be processed in parallel into one activity. Consequently, as the repetitions of an experiment should finish on 2 or 3 different days, each experiment will consist of 2 or 3 activities. An experiment related to 4 repetitions then corresponds to 2 activities, each of which consists of 2 repetitions. An experiment related to 5 repetitions corresponds to 3 activities, two of which consist of 2 repetitions while the third one consists of the remaining repetition. Table 8.3 defines the transformation of experiment repetitions into activities. For each number of repetitions of one experiment in the first row, the number of activities corresponding to that experiment is shown in the second row. The third row then displays the number of repetitions of each of the resulting activities. In accordance with the number of repetitions stated in Table 8.1, we obtain $J = 62$ activities. The processing time p_j of activity $j \in \{1, \ldots, 62\}$ is given by the duration of the related experiment. There are no precedence relations between the activities. Clearly, a dummy source and a dummy sink activity can be added.

Now we have to define the resource requirements of the activities. We consider an activity j which corresponds to ϱ repetitions of the related experiment. The first resource which reflects the laboratory equipment is requested

Repetitions	2	3	4	5	6	7	9
activities	2	2	2	3	3	3	3
repetition jobs	1,1	2,1	2,2	2,2,1	2,2,2	3,2,2	3,3,3

Table 8.3: Transforming experiment repetitions into activities

only on the last day of an activity:

$$r_{j1}(t) = \begin{cases} \varrho, & \text{if } t = p_j \\ 0, & \text{otherwise.} \end{cases}$$

The second resource is related to the researcher. If the experiment related to activity j is based on normal food, the researcher must be in the laboratory on each day, that is, we obtain a constant request of

$$r_{j2}(t) = \varrho \text{ for all } t \in \{1, \dots, p_j\}.$$

Otherwise, if the special diet has to be considered, we have a resource requirement varying with time (recall, the duration of such an activity is always 7 days):

$$r_{j2}(t) = \begin{cases} \varrho, & \text{if } t \in \{1,5,6,7\} \\ 0, & \text{otherwise.} \end{cases}$$

As already mentioned, the remaining resources are responsible for the temporal arrangement of the experiments. Each of these resources is related to a unique experiment and vice versa. First, we consider the resource $k > 2$ that is related to the experiment of activity j. We define the time-varying resource requirement by

$$r_{jk}(t) = \begin{cases} 1, & \text{if } t = p_j \\ 0, & \text{otherwise.} \end{cases}$$

That is, the activities of one experiment request their experiment-specific resource in their last period. As the capacity of this resource is one unit per period, this ensures that two activities of an experiment cannot finish on the same day. Finally, activity j does not request any resource $k > 2$ that is related to another experiment:

$$r_{jk}(t) = 0 \text{ for all } t \in \{1, \dots, p_j\}.$$

Note that abstract resources in project scheduling models do not necessarily reflect traditional physical resources such as manpower or machines. They can also be employed to impose desired properties of a schedule. Actually, the use of resources 3,... ,27 is an example for this technique.

Objective

The objective to complete the experiments of the medical research project as early as possible is achieved by minimizing the project's makespan.

8.1.3 Computational Results for Original Data

We now apply a heuristic algorithm to the medical research project with the original data. For this we have selected the activity list based GA of Section 5.2. It should be noted that the extended GA of Section 5.6 (which performed even better in the investigation of Chapter 6) could not be used: The extended representation which includes both SGS is not suitable because the parallel SGS is not applicable to time-dependent resource parameters without modification (in contrast, the plain activity list based GA with the serial SGS can be used).

Like the previous computational experiments discussed in this work, also the following tests have been performed on a Pentium-based computer with 133 MHz clock-pulse and 32 MB RAM running under Linux. We have adapted the implementation of the GA in order to include the time-dependent resource parameters of the RCPSP/τ. Again, the GA was compiled with the GNU C compiler.

In order to gain computational experience, we have applied the GA to the original project data and varied the maximal number of schedules to be computed. Table 8.4 summarizes the results. Limiting the number of schedules to 1000, we obtain a makespan of 68 days. The best schedule with a makespan of 67 days is found within a moderate computation time of less than 12 seconds after 2000 schedules have been evaluated. Further increasing the number of schedules does not lead to a shorter project duration. In fact, we will show in the next subsection that a makespan of 67 days is already optimal.

Schedules	*makespan*	*CPU-sec*
1000	68	5.6
2000	67	11.8
5000	67	29.5
10000	67	58.8
100000	67	581.8
hand-made	75	—

Table 8.4: Makespan w.r.t. computation time

Before the medical research project was carried out, the researcher made a schedule by hand, i.e., without any computer based support. As listed in

Table 8.4, the resulting makespan of the project as performed in 1994 was 75 days. Thus, a heuristic like our GA would not only have made the scheduling process much easier and more convenient, it would also have determined a schedule with a makespan 10.7 % shorter than that of the hand-made schedule. Moreover, the GA would have decreased the number of working days the researcher had to spend in the laboratory by 17.4 %.

8.1.4 Optimality Issues

Before we examine the schedule computed by the GA for the original project data, we study the general capability of the GA to solve instances of the RCPSP/τ. We show that the search space of the GA does not necessarily contain an optimal or even feasible solution when applied to this problem class. This is because the activity list based GA employs the serial SGS which schedules each activity as early as possible.

Theorem 8.1 *There are instances of the RCPSP/τ for which the GA cannot find an (existing) optimal solution.*

Proof. We consider the following counterexample which consists of $J = 2$ non-dummy activities without precedence relations among them. Both activities have a processing time of $p_1 = p_2 = 2$ periods. The set of periods is $\mathcal{T}' = \{1,2,3,4\}$. We have one resource, that is, $\mathcal{K}^\rho = \{1\}$, with time-varying capacity

$$R_1^\rho(t) = \begin{cases} 2, & \text{if } t \in \{1,2,4\} \\ 4, & \text{if } t = 3. \end{cases}$$

The time-varying resource requirements of the activities are given by

$$r_{11}(t) = r_{21}(t) = \begin{cases} 1, & \text{if } t = 1 \\ 2, & \text{if } t = 2. \end{cases}$$

Now consider the schedules shown in Figure 8.1. Schedule (a) is optimal with a makespan of 3 periods. The search space of the GA consists of two individuals with activity sequences 1,2 and 2,1, respectively. The related schedules are those of Figure 8.1 (b) and (c), respectively. As the first activity in the sequence is always started as early as possible, i.e., at time 0, the GA can only find these suboptimal schedules with a makespan of 4 periods. □

Theorem 8.2 *There are instances of the RCPSP/τ for which the GA cannot find an (existing) feasible solution.*

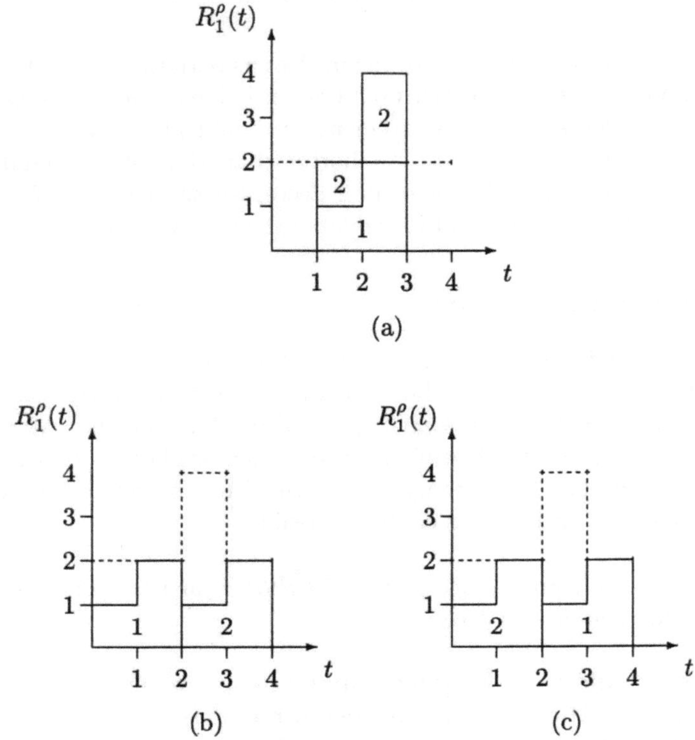

Figure 8.1: Schedules for the RCPSP/τ example instance

Proof. We consider again the counterexample defined in the proof of Theorem 8.1. Setting $R_1^\rho(4) := 1$ instead of 2 induces that none of the two activity sequences of the search space of the GA is related to a feasible schedule as the first job in the sequence is always started at time 0. The feasible (and optimal) solution for this modified instance still is obtained from starting both activities at time 1, cf. Figure 8.1 (a). □

The above results state that the serial SGS is not sufficient when dealing with resource requirements that vary with time which have to be considered for the research project at hand. Similar findings for exact methods have been reported by Sprecher [190] who states that the precedence tree based branch-and-bound algorithm (which also uses a serial scheduling approach) does not necessarily find optimal or feasible solutions if time-varying resource requests are given. That is, resource requirements varying with time make the problem harder to solve because the search space that has to be considered increases.

Nevertheless, the GA (or any other heuristic based on the serial SGS which successively schedules an activity at its earliest feasible start time) may be an appropriate approach to the RCPSP/τ. Consider as an example the parallel SGS which is widely applied to the classical RCPSP although it cannot always find an optimal schedule for this problem class (cf. Section 4.1). In some cases, searching only a restricted solution space may be an advantageous heuristic strategy.

In fact, we can prove that the schedule found by the GA for the original data of the medical research project is optimal:

Theorem 8.3 *The optimal duration of the medical research project considered here is 67 days.*

Proof. From Table 8.1 we know that 109 experiment repetitions have to be scheduled. Given that only 6 rats may be examined per examination day, we need at least 19 examination days which are also working days. Considering the calendar of Table 8.2, the earliest project completion is on day 66 by the above arguments.

We now show that there is no feasible schedule with a makespan of 66 days. The number of experiment repetitions with a duration of more than 3 days is 95 (cf. again Table 8.1). These repetitions require at least 16 examination days which are also working days. As we consider durations of more than 3 days, however, these repetitions cannot finish on any of the days 3, 24, 45, and 59 (cf. the calendar of Table 8.2). Consequently, the 16th examination and working day for finishing repetitions with a duration of more than 3 days is day 67. That is, 67 days is a lower bound on the project duration. As the upper bound found by the GA is also 67 days, the related schedule is optimal. □

8.1.5 Impact of Data Variations

Applying a computer-based scheduling system to a real-world project makes it easier to find a good schedule which fulfills all the restrictions. In addition, such a system offers the possibility of varying some of the data and rerun the scheduling procedure in order to find alternative schedules with a low effort. In particular, this allows to answer the following questions: Can we find a schedule of equal length if we tighten one of the constraints? Can we find a schedule with a shorter makespan if we loosen some of the restrictions?

The first approach to finding alternative schedules is by varying the number of repetitions that can be handled by the researcher at the same time (i.e., the capacity of the researcher resource). The resulting project durations can be found in Table 8.5. Probably the researcher would accept a higher number of simultaneously processed repetitions if this could shorten the project.

The results, however, show that this is not the case. In fact, this is not a surprise as the proof of Theorem 8.3 indicates that a makespan shorter than 67 days can only be achieved when changing the examination or working day contraints. Moreover, the researcher would prefer a schedule with less than 20 repetitions at the same time if this would not lead to a longer project duration. Table 8.5 shows that a schedule with equal makespan can be found for only 18 simultaneous repetitions. Note that tightening this constraint makes it harder for the GA to find an optimal solution as it takes more than 10 seconds. Decreasing the maximum number of simultaneous repetitions to 16, however, increases the makespan by 6 days. Observe that the last day of the project must be an examination day, and that days 69, 70, 71, and 72 are no examination days.

Repetitions	*makespan after 10 sec*	*makespan after 60 sec*
22	67	67
20 (original)	67	67
18	68	67
16	73	73

Table 8.5: Varying the maximal number of repetitions in process each day

Next, we examine the impact of calendar changes concerning the working and examination days. Table 8.6 shows that additional vacations of the researcher result in a longer project duration. On the other hand, additionally working on one weekend does not shorten the makespan (this is again due to the fact that the examination constraints are critical). Finally, we have examined the impact of using the laboratory equipment on a Monday and/or Tuesday as well, e.g., if there is some flexibility concerning other research projects which use this laboratory. The last two rows of Table 8.6 indicate that this may result in a reduction of the makespan (as well as a reduction of the number of days the researcher has to be in the laboratory).

The last data variation to be tested affects the temporal arrangement of activities belonging to the same experiment. Up to this point, we have tried to exclude systematical errors by distributing the examinations related to one experiment on different days (as is common practice). One can argue, however, that other potential sources for errors (in addition to the examination process) occur during the total experiment duration. An example is the dosing of the medicaments. In order to avoid these errors, we have to ensure that different activities of one experiment do not overlap at all. This can easily be achieved by adapting the request of activity $j = 1, \ldots, J$ for the resource k that is related to its experiment as follows:

$$r_{jk}(t) = 1 \text{ for all } t \in \{1, \ldots, p_j\}.$$

Calendar change	*makespan*
none (original)	67
no work on day 57	68
no work on days 57, 58	73
no work on days 62, 63	73
additionally work on days 6, 7	67
additionally examine on day 30	67
additionally examine on day 65	66
additionally examine on days 64, 65	65

Table 8.6: Impact of calendar changes — time limit: 60 sec

This adaption allows further changes of the project data which improve the behaviour of the genetic algorithm. So far, we have enforced the activities of one experiment to be performed in sequence (i.e., they do not overlap). Now consider two activities of one experiment that correspond to the same number of repetitions. As these activities are equal, the order in which they are executed is irrelevant. Consequently, we may introduce a precedence relation between these two activities. Doing so, we reduce the search space of the GA, of course without excluding all optimal solutions. Notice that the GA exploits the added precedence relations when computing the initial population.

Finally, consider those experiments for which all (two or three) activities correspond to the same number of repetitions. As the order of these equal activities is irrelevant, we may impose an arbitrary order by adding precedence relations. In this case, we may omit the resource which is responsible for the temporal arrangement of the experiment. Reducing the number of resource constraints results in lower computation times for each schedule. Consequently, the GA can evaluate more schedules within the same time limit.

Table 8.7 shows that forcing the activities of one experiment to be performed in sequence (without overlapping) increases the project makespan by one week. This is still less than the duration of the project according to the original hand-made schedule, see again Table 8.4.

Repetition jobs of one experiment	*makespan*
overlapping allowed (original)	67
always in sequence	74

Table 8.7: Changing the temporal arrangement — time limit: 60 sec

8.1.6 Concluding Remarks

So far, we have expressed the real-world problem using modeling concepts that enabled us to employ a solution procedure for the basic RCPSP without having to modify the procedure. Nevertheless, there are possibilities to improve the modeling approach which allow for a more efficient solution procedure. Recall that partial temporal overlapping of the activities (or repetition blocks of one experiment) was allowed but equal finish times were not. This was maintained by the definition of renewable resources $k = 3, \ldots, 27$. Additionally, we could secure this property partially by introducing non-standard precedence relations (cf. Subsection 2.2.2). This approach is based on the observation that for two identical activities related to the same experiment (i.e., corresponding to the same number of repetitions) an arbitrary but fixed order can be assumed without excluding all optimal solutions from the search space. More precisely, considering two such activities i and j, we may assume that j always finishes at least one period after i. This can be done by introducing a start-start precedence relation between i and j or, equivalently, a negative minimal time lag in accordance with a finish-start precedence relation. An example for both cases is sketched out in Figure 8.2. If all activities related to one experiment are identical, a complete ordering can be imposed this way, and we may omit the related renewable resource.

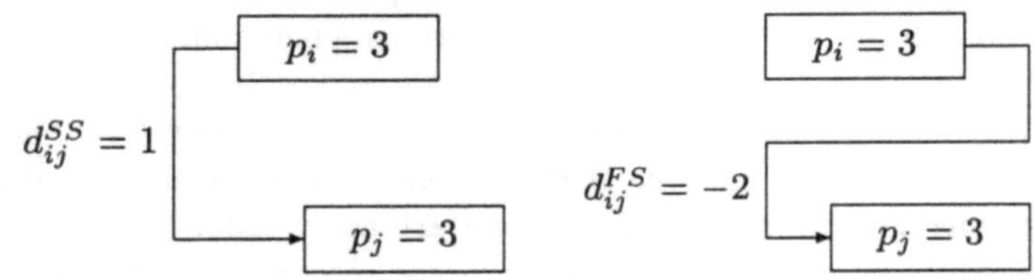

Figure 8.2: Modeling approach based on new precedence relations

Note that a similar approach of introducing precedence relations in order to narrow the search space has been discussed at the end of the previous subsection where, however, overlapping was not allowed. The benefit is the same in both cases: The search space becomes smaller (note again that for each excluded schedule there remains one with identical makespan in the search space), making both heuristic and exact search more efficient. Moreover, omitting some of the previously necessary renewable resources speeds up the computation time for a schedule. Hence, the number of schedules that can be evaluated in some time limit increases. Finally, additional precedence relations are exploited when computing the initial population of our GA, leading to better start solutions.

It is important, however, that introducing such non-standard precedence relations requires a (straightforward) modification of the solution procedure. In the GA, we must consider the new types of precedence relations when computing the earliest feasible start time of an activity as well as when deriving the latest finish times for the priority rule based start heuristic.

8.2 Selecting Market Research Interviewers

An important part of many market research studies (e.g., for testing a new product before launching it or for analyzing the effect of an advertising campaign) is to conduct interviews. In this section, we consider the problem to select interviewers as done at the market research company IVE Research International GmbH, Hamburg (Germany). When selecting interviewers for a study, numerous requirements have to be observed, such as the qualifications and working times of the interviewers, the time span in which the project has to be completed, an appropriate regional distribution of the respondents, and cost issues.

Currently, IVE Research International employs a database to support selection of the interviewers. This database contains information about the interviewers such as their addresses and qualifications, and also their available working time in each calendar week which is updated when they are commisioned to conduct interviews for a study. IVE Research International wants to use as much of the interviewer capacities as possible in order to be able to conduct as many studies as possible. However, the interviewer selection is done manually. It is not supported by any computer based optimization tool.

Our purpose is to show that the problem to select interviewers for a study can be expressed in terms of project scheduling concepts. Such a formalization could provide the basis for the development of project scheduling based software. Using such software, the interviewer selection could be done automatically which would be more convenient than manual planning. Moreover, we indicate that such a software would be able to explicitly consider the objective of using as much as possible of the interviewer capacities. Considering that there are approximately 2000 interviewers among which IVE Research International has to select, this is a selection problem which is not easy to survey when doing it manually. That is, using an optimization tool would probably lead to a more effective interviewer selection than manual selection.

After a detailed description of the interviewer selection problem, we show that we can capture the real-world situation formally by using the modeling concepts of Chapter 2. Finally, we briefly consider the process of scheduling interviews for several different market research studies within a rolling planning horizon.

8.2.1 Problem Description

This subsection describes the selection of interviewers within market research studies at IVE Research International. Generally, market research studies involve the collection of data, e.g., by means of personal interviews, interviews by telephone, or panels. Here, we consider studies with personal interviews. More precisely, we deal with those interviews for which the interviewer visits the respondent either at home (e.g., for studies on consumer goods) or at the place where the respondent works (e.g., when interviewing physicians for studies on medicaments). The field work department of IVE Research International is responsible for selecting the interviewers to conduct these personal interviews (the field work department does not deal with other than these personal interviews). Currently, approximately 2000 interviewers work for the field work department as free-lancers. Before we describe the interviewer selection problem itself, let us begin with a general discussion of the processing of a study involving personal interviews as it is done at IVE Research International.

First, a market researcher of IVE Research International negotiates with a customer on the study's methodology and the price. When a contract has been concluded, the design of the study is planned in detail, e.g., the questionnaire is set up.

As soon as possible, the field work department is informed about the number of interviews needed, the estimated duration of each interview, and further requirements such as the distribution of the respondents with respect to regional characteristics and urbanization. The earliest day for the interviews is the day on which the interviewers can receive the material they need to carry out the interviews (e.g., the questionnaire). The latest day typically results from the contractual delivery date, that is, the day on which the study's results must be presented to the customer. Occasionally, the earliest or latest day depends on other considerations such as advertising campaigns. On the basis of this information, the field work department selects interviewers to carry out the interviews for the study (our goal will be to apply project scheduling concepts to this interviewer selection).

When the material is completed, the selected interviewers are commissioned to conduct interviews for the study. Each selected interviewer receives the material along with information on the number of interviews he should carry out and the latest day on which he must send back the completed interviews. A selected interviewer who knows that he will be unable to conduct the requested number of interviews (e.g., due to sickness) must inform IVE Research International which then has to select another interviewer.

For the completed interviews that are sent back to IVE Research International, a quality check is made, e.g., by verifying whether the questionnaires are filled in correctly. If there are interviews that are not usable, additional interviews have to be carried out. Once the required number of interviews has been completed correctly, the data are analyzed, and the results are presented to the customer of IVE Research International.

The remainder of this subsection summarizes the requirements that must be observed when selecting the interviewers for a study.

Interviews

For a market research study which involves personal interviews, the number of interviews to be carried out is given. Each interview of a market research study consists of two or more parts. Typically, the interviewer who is selected to carry out an interview is responsible for recruiting a respondent who fulfills certain criteria (e.g., the respondent must be using some product frequently or have a specific minimum income). Therefore, the first part of an interview usually is recruitment. The second part is often the interviewing itself (e.g., visiting the respondent at home to fill in the questionnaire). Some studies involve more than two parts. This may occur within studies for testing a product before introducing it to the market. In this case, the first part is again the recruitment, the second part is to visit the respondent for bringing a test product, and the third part, typically after a minimum number of days reserved for testing, is the interviewing itself. Commonly, all parts of an interview must be carried out by the same interviewer. For each part, the duration is estimated in advance by the field work department, and the duration of a part is the same in all interviews.

In most studies, all interviews are equal, that is, they consist of an equal number of parts with equal durations. In some cases, however, different types of interviews may be necessary. Consider, e.g., a study concerning some medicament which may involve interviewing 200 physicians and 200 patients. Due to different questionnaires for both groups, interviewing a doctor may take longer than interviewing a patient. In such a case, a study consists of different interview types, and the interviews of one type are again assumed to have identical durations. The number of interviews of each type is fixed.

Working Times of Interviewers

Each interviewer communicates the maximum time per week he or she is available for IVE Research International (usually at least 15 hours per week). For scheduling, this available time has to be adjusted due to vacation or interviews for other studies already scheduled.

Quotas

Most studies require a sample that is representative for the entire population or for some target group with respect to socio-demographic characteristics,

At IVE Research International, this is assured by defining quotas. Quotas essentially consist of socio-demographic characteristics along with numbers of respondents in the sample to which the characteristics apply. For example, a quota could demand that 50 % of the persons to be interviewed must live in northern Germany and 50 % in the south, or that one third must live in large, medium-sized, and small towns, respectively. Also quotas for income or age ranges could be defined.

At IVE Research International, quotas for characteristics related to regions and urbanization are treated differently from other quotas. Let us first consider quotas on regions and urbanization. The desired distribution within the sample is maintained as follows: Each interviewer is associated with his so-called domicile which is usually the place he or she lives. A domicile is characterized by the size of the city or town and the part of Germany it is situated (e.g., state or eastern and western Germany). Generally, an interviewer carries out all of his or her interviews in the region of his or her domicile. Consequently, the required distribution w.r.t. regions and urbanization is achieved by appropriately selecting the interviewers w.r.t. their domicile characteristics.

Other quotas (e.g., on income or age distribution), on the other hand, do not influence the selection of the interviewers. Generally, a selected interviewer is commissioned to carry out a specific number of interviews. As mentioned above, the interviewer is responsible to recruit the respondents. The remaining quotas are taken into account by the field work department telling each selected interviewer which socio-demographic characteristics (e.g., age or income level) the respondents he recruits must fulfill to meet the overall quotas.

Some studies have a regional focus. That is, all persons to be interviewed must live in a specific region in Germany. This may occur, e.g., in studies for local radio stations. In case of a regional focus, the number of interviewers having their domicile in that region may not be sufficient. Then interviewers from other regions are asked to carry out some interviews in the focus region, which may cause travel times and costs. Selecting interviewers for traveling is, however, typically only done after personal communication with the interviewers. Therefore, interviewer selection for traveling would probably be done manually even if an automatic selection software was available. We thus do not consider studies with regional focus here in more detail.

Interview Distribution

In addition to the regional distribution and urbanization characteristics, further requirements influence the distribution of interviews among the interviewers. First, certain considerations decide whether an interviewer may generally be selected for a study. For example, some studies require a certain equipment such as a laptop for computer aided interviews or a freezer to store deep-frozen test products. In some cases, time considerations may exclude an interviewer from a study, e.g., if the interviewer can only work in the evenings but the interviews must be carried out during the day time (which often occurs if the respondents are to be interviewed at their place of work). In addition, interviewers may refuse to participate in certain studies, e.g., a non-smoker might not be willing to carry out interviews for the cigarette industry. In what follows, we will only consider eligible interviewers, that is, interviewers who can be selected for a study.

Second, there is a maximal number of interviewers who can be selected for a study which is ususally lower than the number of interviews. This is mainly due to cost considerations, because sending material such as questionnaires or test products as well as supporting the interviewers if they have questions causes costs. Clearly, these costs depend on the number of interviewers participating in a study, which is therefore limited. Some studies further reduce the maximal number of interviewers, e.g., if each participating interviewer has to be equipped with a product model such as a mobile telephone of which only a small number is available.

Third, each interviewer can only carry out a limited number of interviews of one study. The reason for this is the purpose to keep systematical errors low.

Costs

Most of the field work costs cannot be influenced by decisions on interviewer selection. The main portion of the costs arise from paying the interviewers. The interviewers are free-lancers and are only paid for the interviews they carry out. The resulting payments depend on the estimated interview duration (including estimated recruitment time) only and are independent of the selection of the interviewers as all interviewers get the same amount of money for an interview.

As discussed above, further costs arise from sending interview material to the interviewers and from supporting them. These latter costs depend on the number of selected interviewers and can therefore be influenced by interviewer selection decisions. However, they are low compared to the entire costs of the study. Hence, limiting the number of selected interviewers should normally be sufficient to bound the assessable costs.

For studies with a regional focus, travel costs may require additional attention. As mentioned above, however, travel would be planned manually rather than automatically.

Objective

The most appropriate objective is to finish the interviews for the current study as early as possible because an early end of the current study makes interviewers available for future studies as soon as possible. This leads to a good utilization of the capacities and allows to carry out as many studies as possible. Moreover, it helps to complete the study on time even if unpredictable delays occur, e.g., due to sickness of a selected interviewer.

Another possible objective would be a fair distribution of the interviews among the interviewers. Currently, this is considered by preferring interviewers that were commisioned with only a few interviews in the recent weeks.

8.2.2 Modeling Approach

This subsection sketches out how the problem to select interviewers for market research interviews can be expressed in terms of project scheduling concepts. We have to assign an interviewer to each interview. This will be reflected by using the multi-mode extension of the RCPSP. In order to fully map the requirements, we will additionnally employ the mode identity concept, partially renewable resources, and generalized minimal time lags (cf. Chapter 2). The description of the modeling approach will be rather informal and points out to the general proceeding and the modeling concepts needed. In order to keep the description simple, we consider interviews of a single type only. If more than one type has to be taken into account, each type can be treated separately.

Activities

We consider a study which requires $\mathcal{I}$ interviews of the same type. Each interview consists of one or several parts, e.g., the first part can be the recruitment of a respondent and the second one the interviewing itself. For each of these parts, we define an activity. Each activity can be performed in different modes (cf. Subsection 2.2.1). A mode corresponds to an interviewer that can carry out the related interview. We only have to define modes for those interviewers who have the required equipment and qualifications, who have enough time capacity left in the planning horizon to conduct at least one interview, and who can be selected w.r.t. their domiciles, considering the quotas on regions and urbanization.

The different parts of an interview must be carried out by the same interviewer. This is reflected by the mode identity concept (cf. Subsection 2.2.1): We demand that the activities related to the same interview must be performed in the same mode. The processing times of all modes of all activities are equal to one period (although possibly surprising at first glance, the durations of the interview parts are not reflected by the activities' processing times but by resources which are discussed below).

The activities defined above are interrelated by precedence constraints. Before we can establish them, we have to define the interpretation of a period. Each period corresponds to one day. With this interpretation, we can now introduce precedence relations. We first consider the standard case of two activities related to an interview, one corresponding to the recruitment part and one to the interviewing part. The recruitment part of an interview must not be performed on a later day than the interviewing part. Consequently, we introduce a precedence relation associated with a minimal time lag of zero periods between the start of the recruitment activity and the start of the interviewing activity (cf. Subsection 2.2.2). Note that this allows recruitment and interviewing to be performed on the same day. Next, we consider the case of more than two interview parts. We assume the typical case of recruitment as first part, bringing test products as second part, and the interviewing itself as third part. The precedence relation between the activities corresponding to the first and the second part is defined as above. Here, this allows recruitment and bringing test products to be carried out on the same day. Now we discuss the relationship between the activities corresponding to the second and third part. We introduce a precedence relation between the completion of the activity corresponding to bringing the test products and the start of the interviewing activity. This minimal time lag corresponds to the minimal number of days that the respondent should be given to test the product. There are no precedence relations between activities belonging to different interviews. Of course, a dummy source and a dummy sink activity can be added to complete the network.

Note that determining the modes of the activities corresponds to selecting the interviewers. The transformation of a project of personal market research interviews into an activity network is visualized in Figure 8.3. As example, we have used interviews consisting of three parts, where the first part is the recruitment, the second one is reserved for bringing test products to the respondent, and the third one is the interviewing itself. The interviews are depicted as dashed boxes, containing the activities related to the parts of the same interview. From $\mathcal{I}$ interviews with three parts each, we obtain $3 \cdot \mathcal{I}$ non-dummy activities corresponding to interviews. As displayed in Figure 8.3, the network is further extended by so-called blocking activities which will be explained below in connection with resource restrictions.

Resources for Working Time of the Interviewers

For scheduling, we consider only those interviewers that are eligible for the study at hand, e.g., interviewers that have the required equipment. Each such interviewer is associated with a partially renewable resource (cf. Subsection

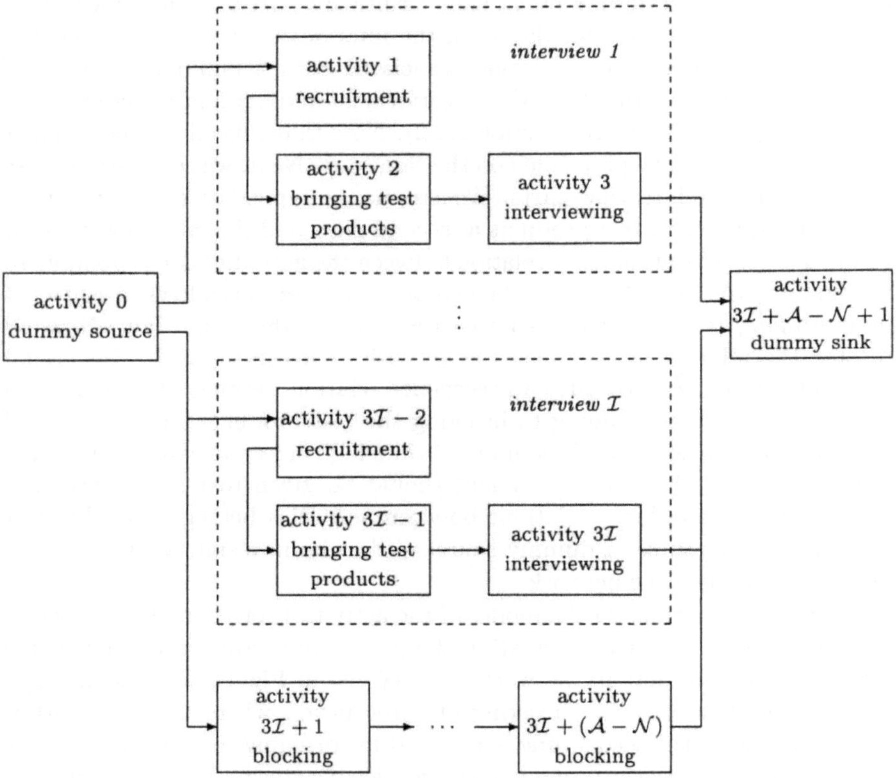

Figure 8.3: Activity network of the interview project

2.2.3). This resource reflects his maximal workload for each calendar week within the planning horizon (which is induced by the deadline). More precisely, given an interviewer, we define a period subset for each calendar week within the planning horizon. For each period subset, the related resource availability is given by the time capacity of the interviewer in that week.

Having set up the interviewer resources along with their availablities, the activities' requests for these resources are defined as follows: Each mode of an activity corresponds to an eligible interviewer, along with a request for that interviewer's resource determined by the duration of the interview part of that activity.

Recall that we have employed the mode identity concept to make sure that all parts of an interview are carried out by the same interviewer (and thus consume the same interviewer resource). That is, assigning a mode to the activities of an interview corresponds to selecting an interviewer for this interview.

Resources for Quotas

Next, we show how the quotas are maintained. Recall that only the quotas for regional distribution and urbanization are relevant for selecting the interviewers. Let us assume that we are given a list of regional and urban characteristics, each with a related number of interviews to be performed. For example, it may be required to perform 200 interviews with respondents from northern Germany and 200 with respondents from southern Germany.

We introduce a nonrenewable resource for each relevant regional characteristic. The availability of this resource is given by the number of interviews that are to be carried out for the related regional characteristic. Consider the first activity of an interview. The request of a mode for a regional distribution resource is defined as 1 if this regional characteristic applies to the domicile of the interviewer associated with that mode, and 0 otherwise. The requests of the modes of the remaining activities for these resources are set to 0.

For illustration, we consider the example quotas given above: We obtain two nonrenewable resources, both the "northern" and the "southern" resource with a capacity of 200 units. A mode which is associated with an interviewer having his domicile in the north consumes one unit of the "northern" resource and has a request of zero units for the "southern" resource. Clearly, modes related to interviewers from the south are treated accordingly. As each interview activity is assigned a mode related to an interviewer either living in the north or south, the regional distribution is observed. Other characteristics such as size of town are captured analogously.

Resources for Interview Distribution

We now consider the distribution of interviews among the interviewers that can be selected for the study. The number of interviewers that are eligible for the study is given by $\mathcal{A}$. There are two kinds of limitations to be observed: The maximal number of interviews that may be carried out by one interviewer is given by $\mathcal{D}$. Moreover, the maximal number of interviewers that may be selected for the study is denoted as $\mathcal{N}$.

We introduce a nonrenewable resource for each of the $\mathcal{A}$ available interviewers. The capacity of each of these resources is defined as $\mathcal{D}$, that is, the maximal number of interviews per interviewer. For setting up the request for these resources, we first consider an activity corresponding to the first part of an interview. A mode of such an activity has a request of one unit for the nonrenewable resource related to the interviewer that is associated with this mode. Moreover, this mode does not request the respective resources related to the other interviewers. The modes of the activities corresponding to the remaining parts of an interview do not request these resources at all. Clearly, these nonrenewable resources prevent the selection of an interviewer for more than $\mathcal{D}$ interviews.

Next, we have to assure that at most $\mathcal{N}$ interviewers are selected for the study. To do so, we use the nonrenewable resources introduced above for each interviewer. There is, however, no standard constraint type in project scheduling models that would allow to limit the number of resources used (whereas the capacity of each resource is, of course, limited). As a consequence, we introduce additional activities (which we can be viewed as "dummy" activities as they do not correspond to performing an interview). Obviously, selecting more interviewers than permitted can only occur if we have $\mathcal{A} > \mathcal{N}$. If this is the case, we define $\mathcal{A} - \mathcal{N}$ new activities. Roughly speaking, they will be used for "blocking" the nonrenewable capacities of $\mathcal{A} - \mathcal{N}$ interviewers. Each of the new blocking activities has $\mathcal{A}$ modes. Each mode $a \in \{1, \ldots, \mathcal{A}\}$ consumes the entire capacity of the interviewer associated with mode a, that is, it has a request of $\mathcal{D}$ units for the nonrenewable resource associated with that interviewer. It does not request any other resources and has a duration of zero periods. The mechanism of these blocking activities is as follows: When scheduling the project, we have to assign a mode to them. Any mode selection will leave only $\mathcal{N}$ interviewers with a nonzero capacity that allows to carry out the first activity related to an interview. Via mode identity, only these $\mathcal{N}$ interviewers can be selected for the entire interviews. For these blocking activities, the resulting start times and hence also the position within the network are irrelevant. Thus, we can impose an arbitrary order by precedence relations, with the first of the blocking activities being a successor of the network's source activity and the last one being a predecessor of the sink activity. For illustration, see again Figure 8.3.

Objective

The objective to finish the interviews of the study as early as possible is achieved by the common project scheduling objective function to minimize the makespan.

It should be noted that scheduling a project as described here leads to start times and modes for the activities. The selected modes corresponds to the selected interviewers while the activity start times refer to the start times of the interview parts. However, the interviewers may perform the interviews whenever they want to as long as the are finished by the deadline. Therefore, the start times are not relevant for the processing of the interviews. Nevertheless, they are needed to check whether an interviewer has enough available time before the deadline to finish some interviews, eventually observing minimal time lags. Moreover, the day-wise scheduling allows the precise computation of a makespan. If the makespan is substantially lower than the deadline, this implies that there is enough interviewer capacity to finish the interviews of the study under consideration much earlier than the deadline. In this case, the interviewers could be told a deadline earlier than the original one. This would force them to complete the interviews sooner which in turn allows the field work department to assure that the interviewer capacities are in fact available for future studies as early as possible.

Another goal can be a fair distribution of interviews among the interviewers. This would lead to an objective of the resource leveling type.

8.2.3 Dynamic Planning Environment

In this subsection, we will briefly examine the scheduling of market research interviews under a rolling planning horizon.

As we have seen in the general description of Subsection 8.2.1, certain situations may imply the need to reschedule some interviews of a study. A selected interviewer may refuse to carry out all or some of the interviews he has been selected for, or he may be sick and thus unable to carry them out. If this happens, the interviewer must inform IVE Research International immediately, and another interviewer must be found. Furthermore, if the quality checks show that additional interviews have to be carried out, rescheduling is indispensable as well.

The interviews for different studies cannot be scheduled independently because the interviewers may perform interviews for several studies that are carried out simultaneously. Clearly, while the interviews of one study are still in process, the interviews for the next study may already have to be scheduled. This leads, of course, to an adaptation of the available working time of the interviewers when scheduling the interviews for the next study. Note, however, that a precise (day-wise) adaptation of the interviewers' working time is not possible because the interviewers can carry out the interviews whenever they want to as long as they complete it before the deadline. Consequently, the field work department uses the following rule of thumb to assess the remaining working time of an interviewer: It is assumed that the interviewer distributes the working time for each study evenly over the weeks until the respective deadline. Considering the resources, this means that we would reduce the weekly working time capacities of a participating interviewer accordingly. We emphasize again that the capacities are not reduced according to the start times given by the computed schedule, as the experience of the field work department has shown that the interviewers do not conduct the interviews as early as possible.

Furthermore, it often happens that the interviews of several studies are scheduled on the same day. This results in a multi-project scheduling environment, where each project is associated with a release date and a deadline.

Finally, there is a possibility to reserve field work capacity. This may happen if a market researcher of IVE Research International assumes that it is very probable that a contract will be concluded for a study which is still in the negotiation phase. Given that this study would be very urgent, the market researcher can reserve interviewer capacities for the expected field work time span. Moreover, certain studies are repeated periodically. This is the case for so-called tracking studies which take place on a regular basis, typically each month, e.g., for investigating the impact of advertising campaigns. As the interviewer capacity requirements for such tracking studies are known in advance, they can be reserved. Reserving field work capacity assures that the reserved capacities cannot be used when scheduling interviews for other studies. Currently, the field work department only considers the expected number of interviews and the estimated interview durations for reservations.

Reserving field work capacity can also be done with a scheduling tool, which would additionally allow to consider other requirements such as the expected regional distribution and the qualifications of the interviewers. It should be emphasized, however, that the interviewer selection made for reservation can be changed (as long as sufficient capacities remain reserved), because the decisions are fixed only when the selected interviewers are commissioned. Consider, e.g., the following situation: We have reserved the full capacity of an interviewer living in Berlin for a study based on questionnaires. Assume that this interviewer is qualified to carry out computer aided interviews. Now the next study requires several interviewers for computer aided interviews in Berlin. If there are not enough interviewers with that qualification available in Berlin, we can change the reservation and select this interviewer for the computer-aided study. Then we would reschedule the reservation and reserve capacity of another interviewer living in Berlin that cannot conduct computer aided interviews. That is, using a computer based scheduling tool would allow a flexible and more accurate field work reservation mechanism than manual planning.

Chapter 9

Conclusions

In this work, we have considered models, solution methods, and applications for project scheduling under scarce resources. We finish with a summary of the main results and some comments on opportunities in future research.

After an introduction to project scheduling in Chapter 1, Chapter 2 described the classical resource-constrained project scheduling problem (RCPSP). Then an overview of several model extensions was given, including the multi-mode extension of the RCPSP, the MRCPSP. Finally, we showed that another important class of combinatorial optimization problems, the packing and cutting problems, can be viewed as a special case of project scheduling models.

Chapter 3 provided a comparison of exact algorithms for optimally solving the MRCPSP. We compared two procedures from the literature and a newly proposed branch-and-bound approach both theoretically and in computational experiments. For this study, we considered all bounding rules available from the literature and suggested two new ones. According to our results, the best performing exact algorithm for the MRCPSP is the so-called precedence tree procedure from the literature, which was further improved by the new bounding concepts. Like for many other combinatorial optimization problems, however, we can currently not expect to determine optimal solutions for projects of real-world size. The use of the exact methods therefore lies in the possibility to determine optimal benchmark solutions for test problems that are used to evaluate heuristics.

With Chapter 4, we turned to heuristic procedures for project scheduling. Here, we provided a literature survey of heuristics for the single-mode RCPSP. The approaches were classified with respect to methodical characteristics. For all procedures, the underlying schedule generation scheme was described. Priority rule based methods were further distinguished with respect to the employed priority rules and with respect to sampling concepts. Metaheuristic approaches were characterized in terms of problem representation and related operators. This classification provides a basis for the development of new heuristic algorithms.

In Chapter 5, we tested three different problem representations within genetic algorithms for the RCPSP. Observing a high impact of the representation on the solution quality in our experiments, we noticed that the activity list based encoding consistently yields the best results. Proceeding from the activity list representation, we developed new concepts leading to a so-called extended genetic algorithm. Among the most noteworthy features is the consideration of the decoding procedure to be used by the genetic algorithm in the representation. This allows the genetic algorithm to adapt itself by selecting the appropriate schedule generation scheme while solving some specific instance. Moreover, we added a local search phase which starts after stopping the genetic algorithm. The local search neighborhood is based on an analysis of the information contained in the current schedule. Whereas these ideas substantially improved the solution quality, extending the basic genetic algorithm paradigm by introducing several isolated subpopulations on different islands and by allowing migration did not have a positive effect. We pointed out that the concept of self-adaptation introduced here is a general metaheuristic strategy applicable to a wide range of optimization problems, leading to genetic algorithm structures which are subject to genetic optimization.

Chapter 6 was devoted to an in-depth computational evaluation of the new genetic algorithms introduced in this work and other single-mode heuristics from the literature. The experiments on a large set of standard RCPSP instances revealed that the new extended genetic algorithm is currently the most promising heuristic for the RCPSP. Furthermore, we observed that the best metaheuristics clearly outperformed the best priority rule methods which is due to the fact that only the former have the inherent capability of learning. Among the metaheuristics, the procedures which make use of the activity list representation performed best. The underlying metaheuristic strategy (such as genetic algorithm, simulated annealing and tabu search) does not seem to have the same impact as the representation; two genetic algorithms and a simulated annealing approach share the top ranks in our analysis.

In Chapter 7, we developed a genetic algorithm heuristic for the MRCPSP by employing many of the ideas used in the extended genetic algorithm for the single-mode case. The representation enhances the activity list concept by a mode assignment function. We integrated a multi-mode specific local search procedure into the genetic algorithm which improves schedules by successively applying multi-mode left shifts. Using this approach to compute better fitness values substantially improved the results. It is noteworthy, however, that additionally inheriting the schedule information obtained from the local search component by adapting the genotype was not beneficial. In our computational experiments, the genetic algorithm clearly outperformed all other heuristics for the multi-mode case including a truncated branch-and-bound method.

Finally, Chapter 8 described two real-world applications of the project scheduling concepts discussed here. We considered a medical research project which consists of several experiments and a market research project which is made up by a number of personal interviews to be assigned to interviewers. We showed that these real-world situations can be captured formally using general project scheduling models. In addition to the concepts already contained in the basic RCPSP, also extensions by multiple modes, mode identity, time-dependent resource availabilities and requests, partially renewable resources, release dates, deadlines, and generalized precedence relations with time lags appeared to be of high practical relevance. Applying our activity list based genetic algorithm to the original data of the medical research project, we obtained a far better schedule than the original hand-made one. This demonstrated the advantage of using computer based project scheduling tools, and the applicability of our genetic algorithm in particular.

With these results in mind, we will now point out to some perspectives in future research. Clearly, the development of new exact and heuristic algorithms for standard project scheduling models such as the RCPSP and the MRCPSP will remain an important area. According to our experience with heuristics, metaheuristic strategies are far more promising than other approaches such as priority rule methods or truncated branch-and-bound. Considering metaheuristics, the choice of an appropriate problem representation with related operators should be given more attention than the selection of the underlying metaheuristic strategy itself (such as genetic algorithm, simulated annealing and tabu search). We can also recommend to incorporate as much problem specific knowledge as possible, e.g., by using schedule information when designing a local search neighborhood. Moreover, developing a flexible heuristic which is capable of learning and self-adaptation appears to be a promising approach.

Another point of interest is the development of solution algorithms for more general project scheduling problems which are of special interest for project managers. Considering the experience gained in this work, it seems to be a good idea to use successful methods for standard models as starting points and extend them in order to cover more realistic problem classes. We have seen, for example, that the activity list representation together with the serial schedule generation scheme may exclude all optimal (or even all feasible) schedules from the search space if resource capacities and requests vary with time. The same holds if partially renewable resources have to be taken into account. These drawbacks can be overcome by extending the

MRCPSP-representation of an activity list λ and a mode assignment μ. We could simply add a delay vector $\Delta = (\Delta_1, \dots, \Delta_J)$ to (λ, μ) and obtain a new representation of type (λ, μ, Δ). Now we define a decoding procedure by adapting the serial schedule generation scheme as follows: We successively schedule the next activity j_i of activity list λ in mode $\mu(j_i)$ at the earliest precedence and resource feasible start time that is not smaller than the earliest precedence feasible start time plus a delay of Δ_{j_i} periods. Note that this approach is different from the shift vector representation (cf. Subsection 4.3.2) which does not consider an underlying activity list and may lead to resource infeasible schedules even if the RCPSP with constant resource availability is considered. This way, we have constructed a representation which fully covers the search space of the MRCPSP with time-dependent resource parameters and partially renewable resources (which would be the MRCPSP/$\tau\pi$). Still, however, we would have to adapt this new approach to obtain an efficient heuristic because some activities might be delayed by too many periods which would deteriorate the makespan. This could be prevented partly by computing tight upper bounds for the delays Δ_j and, moreover, by improving the schedules by multi-mode left shift based local search.

Summarizing, recent years have brought a considerable progress in designing new modeling concepts and solution algorithms for resource-constrained project scheduling. But there are still many open questions, and there is still a high potential for further improvements. Therefore we believe that this will remain a fruitful field of research in the future.

Appendix A

Test Instances

For testing the algorithms developed in this work, we have employed several standard project instance sets which have been used in many studies reported in the literature. Section A.1 describes the classical Patterson set of single-mode project instances. Subsequently, Section A.2 summarizes the so-called ProGen instance sets, which contain both single-mode and multi-mode instances.

A.1 Patterson Instance Set

For a comparison of algorithms for the RCPSP in 1984, Patterson [162] collected several project instances that had been used for testing procedures before. This benchmark test set then became known as the Patterson instance set. It contains 110 single-mode instances with up to 51 activities and up to 3 resources. For all of these test problems, the optimal solutions are known, see, e.g., Demeulemeester and Herroelen [48].

As it was subsequently used by many researchers in their studies, the Patterson set became a standard for testing both heuristic and exact algorithms for the RCPSP (cf., e.g., Bell and Han [15], Cho and Kim [30], Demeulemeester and Herroelen [48, 51], Hartmann [92], Lee and Kim [133], Leon and Ramamoorthy [134], Klein [115], Kolisch [120, 121], Mingozzi et al. [145], Özdamar and Ulusoy [156, 157], Sampson and Weiss [173], and Thomas and Salhi [201]).

The Patterson instances are available from the internet based project scheduling problem library PSPLIB at the University of Kiel (Germany). For further information, we refer to Kolisch and Sprecher [129] and Kolisch et al. [131].

A.2 Instance Sets Generated by ProGen

The Patterson instance set described in the previous section was among the first of widely used standard test sets to evaluate exact and heuristic algorithms for resource-constrained project scheduling. There were, however, several points of attack: First, as a collection of instances, the Patterson set was not systematically generated in terms of adjustable problem parameters. Hence, it does not allow a detailed investigation of the impact of project characteristics on the behavior of solution procedures. Second, with continuous progress in project scheduling research as well as in the development of faster computers, the Patterson instances became too easy to solve for modern algorithms in the early nineties. Therefore, appropriate computational tests required more challenging problem instances. Third, the Patterson set considers only the single-mode RCPSP but not any of its extensions.

To overcome some or all of these shortcomings, several researchers developed project instance generators which allowed to generate instances on the basis of controllable problem parameters (cf. Agrawal et al. [1], Demeulemeester et al. [47], and Kolisch et al. [130]). In this work, we consider the project instance generator ProGen introduced by Kolisch et al. [130]. We have selected ProGen because it allows to generate both single- and multi-mode instances on the basis of parameters which have been shown to have a high impact on the behavior of solution procedures. Moreover, several sets of instances have already been generated and used in many previous studies such that we were able to use existing standard instance sets instead of generating new ones.

In order to allow a convenient access to ProGen and the standard ProGen instance sets, the internet based project scheduling problem library PSPLIB has been set up at the University of Kiel (Germany). For further information on the instance sets and on recent developments of the project scheduling problem library PSPLIB, the reader is referred to Kolisch and Sprecher [129] and Kolisch et al. [131].

Motivated by the broad acceptance of ProGen and the related instance sets in the project scheduling community, several researchers have extended ProGen in order to cover further general project scheduling models. A ProGen based generator for networks with minimal and maximal time-lags (cf. Subsection 2.2.2) called ProGen/max has been developed by Schwindt [180]. Drexl et al. [64] introduced ProGen/πx which extends ProGen by partially renewable resources (cf. Subsection 2.2.3), the mode identity concept (cf. Subsection 2.2.1), and some other new modeling features.

The remainder of this section summarizes the main characteristics of those ProGen instance sets that have been used throughout this work. Subsection A.2.1 describes the single-mode instances while Subsection A.2.2 reports on the multi-mode instances.

A.2.1 Single-Mode Instance Sets

We use three standard ProGen instance sets which have been introduced in Kolisch et al. [130], Kolisch and Sprecher [129], and Kolisch et al. [131], respectively. Each set is characterized by the number of activities within a project. In the three sets, we have $J = 30$, $J = 60$, and $J = 120$ non-dummy activities, respectively. As displayed in Table A.1, all instances were generated with certain fixed parameter ranges, leading to activity durations between one and ten periods and four renewable resources for each project.

Parameter	*min*	*max*
p_j	1	10
$\vert\mathcal{K}^\rho\vert$	4	4

Table A.1: ProGen single-mode instances: Fixed parameter levels

Kolisch et al. [130] identified three parameters which have a strong impact on the performance of solution procedures, namely the network complexity, the resource factor, and the resource strength. The network complexity NC reflects the average number of immediate successors of an activity. The renewable resource factor RF^ρ is a measure of the average number of resources requested per job. The renewable resource strength RS^ρ describes the scarceness of the resource capacities. If the latter is high (i.e., close to 1), the availability is high, which leads to a smaller solution space and hence easier problems. On the other hand, a low resource strength (i.e., close to 0) implies scarce resources and more difficult instances.

The instance sets with $J = 30$ and $J = 60$ were generated by a full factorial design obtained from three network complexity levels, four resource factor levels, and four resource strength levels. For each of the resulting $3 \cdot 4 \cdot 4 = 48$ parameter combinations, 10 instance were randomly generated, leading to 480 instances in each of the two sets. The instance set with $J = 120$ was generated similarly, with the exception that five levels for the resource strength were chosen. Again, 10 instances for each parameter combination were randomly constructed, yielding 600 instances. An overview of the systematically varied parameter settings within the three sets is given in Table A.2.

The set with 30 non-dummy activities currently is the hardest standard set of RCPSP-instances for which all optimal objective function values are known (cf. Demeulemeester and Herroelen [51]). For the other two sets, lower bounds on the project's makespan can be easily derived using forward recursion (cf. Subsection 2.1.2). Clearly, the earliest precedence feasible start time ES_{J+1} of the dummy sink activity is a lower bound on the makespan, the so-called critical path based lower bound (cf. also Stinson et al. [195]). Further lower bounds have been developed by, e.g., Baar et al. [8], Brucker and Knust

J		parameter	levels				
30	60	RF^{ρ}	0.25	0.50	0.75	1.00	
		RS^{ρ}	0.20	0.50	0.70	1.00	
		NC	1.50	1.80	2.10		
120		RF^{ρ}	0.25	0.50	0.75	1.00	
		RS^{ρ}	0.10	0.20	0.30	0.40	0.50
		NC	1.50	1.80	2.10		

Table A.2: ProGen single-mode instances: Variable parameter levels

[27], Heilmann and Schwindt [99], Klein and Scholl [117], Mingozzi et al. [145], and Stinson et al. [195]. The library PSPLIB which is frequently updated contains the currently best lower and upper bounds for these instances.

Some or all of the three instance sets considered here have been widely used by researchers, making them a standard for evaluating and comparing solution algorithms. We refer to the studies of Baar et al. [8], Bouleimen and Lecocq [25], Brucker et al. [29], Demeulemeester and Herroelen [51], Hartmann [92], Hartmann and Kolisch [95], Klein [115], Klein and Scholl [116], Kohlmorgen et al. [118], Kolisch [120, 121, 122], Kolisch and Hartmann [126], Mingozzi et al. [145], Schirmer [174], Schirmer and Riesenberg [176, 177], and Sprecher [191].

A.2.2 Multi-Mode Instance Sets

We consider six standard ProGen instance sets for the MRCPSP. As for the single-mode case, each set is characterized by the number of activities within a project. We have $J = 10$, $J = 12$, $J = 14$, $J = 16$, $J = 18$, and $J = 20$. Table A.3 shows the fixed parameter ranges which were used to generate all of these multi-mode instances. We have three modes for each non-dummy activity and two renewable as well as two nonrenewable resources. Observe that, for the multi-mode case, the network complexity NC (cf. Subsection A.2.1) has been fixed to 1.8 arcs per activity.

Parameter	min	max
p_j	1	10
M_j	3	3
NC	1.8	1.8
$\|\mathcal{K}^{\rho}\|$	2	2
$\|\mathcal{K}^{\nu}\|$	2	2

Table A.3: ProGen multi-mode instances: Fixed parameter levels

In order to obtain the multi-mode instance sets including nonrenewable resources, the following four ProGen parameters were systematically varied: The resource strengths for the renewable and nonrenewable resources, RS^{ρ} and RS^{ν}, were treated separately, as well as the resource factors for the renewable and nonrenewable resources, RF^{ρ} and RF^{ν}. With the two resource factor levels and the four resource strength levels listed in Table A.4, a full factorial design with 10 instances for each parameter level resulted in 640 instance for each project size.[1] Those instances for which no feasible solution exists due to nonrenewable resource restrictions were determined using the branch-and-bound algorithm of Sprecher and Drexl [192] and removed from the instance sets. Hence, we have 536 feasible instances with $J = 10$ activities, 547 feasible instances with $J = 12$ activities, 551 feasible instances with $J = 14$ activities, 550 feasible instances with $J = 16$ activities, 552 feasible instances with $J = 18$ activities, and 554 feasible instances with $J = 20$ activities in the library PSPLIB.

J					parameter	levels			
10					RF^{ρ}	0.50	1.00		
					RS^{ρ}	0.20	0.50	0.70	1.00
					RF^{ν}	0.50	1.00		
					RS^{ν}	0.20	0.50	0.70	1.00
12	14	16	18	20	RF^{ρ}	0.50	1.00		
					RS^{ρ}	0.25	0.50	0.75	1.00
					RF^{ν}	0.50	1.00		
					RS^{ν}	0.25	0.50	0.75	1.00

Table A.4: ProGen multi-mode instances: Variable parameter levels

For all of the multi-mode ProGen instances described above, the optimal objective function values are known (cf. Sprecher and Drexl [192]). These sets (or at least some of them) have been used in several studies, cf. Hartmann [90], Hartmann and Drexl [93], Kolisch [120], Kolisch and Drexl [125], Özdamar [154], Sprecher [190], Sprecher and Drexl [192], and Sprecher et al. [193].

[1] Due to the history of the project scheduling problem library, the resource strength levels used to generate the instances with 10 non-dummy activities slightly differ from those that have been used to generate the other problems.

Appendix B

Solving the MRCPSP using AMPL

In what follows we show how the multi-mode resource-constrained project scheduling problem (MRCPSP) can be solved using standard software. The approach described here makes use of the modeling language AMPL (cf. Fourer et al. [78]). The mathematical programming formulation of the MRCPSP as given by (2.7)–(2.12) can be easily expressed in AMPL. Subsequently, AMPL employs a mathematical problem solver such as CPLEX (cf. Bixby and Boyd [18]) to solve a problem instance. The advantage of such an approach based on standard methods is that one only has to formulate the problem at hand by means of AMPL but needs no knowledge about the solution methodology. Recall, however, that we have mentioned in Chapter 3 that this mathematical programming approach is not capable of finding optimal solutions even for very small test problems in reasonable computation times.

The AMPL model code for the MRCPSP is given in Section B.1. Section B.2 then introduces the AMPL data format for an example instance of the MRCPSP.

B.1 AMPL-Formulation of the MRCPSP

This section provides a formulation of the MRCPSP in AMPL. The AMPL code should be self-explanatory; for AMPL keywords we refer to Fourer et al. [78]. The names of some of the parameters and variables had to be adapted; an overview of the symbols is given in Table B.1.

The option at the beginning of the AMPL code selects CPLEX for solving the problem. After the definition of the parameters, variables, objective function, and constraints, a reference to the data file containing the project instance is made. Then the problem is defined and solved. Finally, the decision variables and the objective function value are displayed.

The makespan minimization objective is that of (2.7). The constraints correspond to (2.8)–(2.11) while the variable declaration equals (2.12). Observe that we have used the time window based approach of (2.6) for the renewable resource constraints in order to save variables and obtain the most efficient formulation.

MRCPSP symbol	*symbol in AMPL*
T	T
J	J
M_j	M[j]
p_{jm}	p[j,m]
$\mathcal{P}_j$	P[j]
$\mathcal{K}^\rho$	KR
$\mathcal{K}^\nu$	KN
r_{jmk}	r[j,m,k]
R_k^ρ	RR[k]
R_k^ν	RN[k]
EF_j	EF[j]
LF_j	LF[j]
x_{jmt}	x[j,m,t]

Table B.1: MRCPSP symbols in AMPL formulation

```
# OPTIONS

option solver cplex;


# PARAMETERS

param T  integer;
param J  integer;
param M  {0..J+1} integer;
param p  {j in 0..J+1, 1..M[j]} integer;
set   P  {0..J+1} within {0..J};

set   KR ;
set   KN ;
param r  {j in 0..J+1, 1..M[j], KR union KN} integer;
```

```
param RR {KR} integer;
param RN {KN} integer;

param EF {0..J+1} integer;
param LF {0..J+1} integer;



# VARIABLES

var x {j in 0..J+1, 1..M[j], EF[j]..LF[j]} binary;



# MODEL

minimize Makespan:
  sum {t in EF[J+1]..LF[J+1]} t * x[J+1,1,t];

subject to JobModeCompletion {j in 0..J+1}:
  sum {m in 1..M[j]} sum {t in EF[j]..LF[j]} x[j,m,t] = 1;

subject to PrecedenceRelations {j in 1..J+1, h in P[j]}:
  sum {m in 1..M[h]} sum {t in EF[h]..LF[h]} t * x[h,m,t] <=
  sum {m in 1..M[j]} sum {t in EF[j]..LF[j]} (t-p[j,m]) * x[j,m,t];

subject to RenewableResources {k in KR, t in 1..T}:
  sum {j in 1..J} sum {m in 1..M[j]} r[j,m,k] *
  sum {q in max(t,EF[j])..min(t+p[j,m]-1, LF[j]) } x[j,m,q]
  <= RR[k];

subject to NonrenewableResources {k in KN}:
  sum {j in 1..J} sum {m in 1..M[j]} r[j,m,k] *
  sum {t in EF[j]..LF[j]} x[j,m,t] <= RN[k];



# READ DATA FROM FILE

data instance.dat;



# SOLVE PROBLEM

problem MRCPSP:
  x,
```

```
  Makespan,
  JobModeCompletion,
  PrecedenceRelations,
  RenewableResources,
  NonrenewableResources;

solve MRCPSP;

display x;
display Makespan;
```

B.2 AMPL-Data File for the MRCPSP

This section describes the data file that is read by the AMPL-file of the previous section. As example, we have used the project instance of Figure 7.1. Note that Bounding Rule 3.3 has been executed before setting up the data file. Clearly, the preprocessing steps may reduce the number of constraints and variables. In our case, the second mode of activity 5 could be deleted because it is non-executable with respect to the nonrenewable resource.

```
param T := 22;
param J := 6;

param M :=
   [0]  1
   [1]  2
   [2]  2
   [3]  2
   [4]  2
   [5]  1
   [6]  2
   [7]  1;

param p :=
   [0,1]  0
   [1,1]  3   [1,2]  4
   [2,1]  2   [2,2]  4
   [3,1]  2   [3,2]  3
   [4,1]  2   [4,2]  2
   [5,1]  3
   [6,1]  4   [6,2]  6
   [7,1]  0 ;

set P [0] :=  ;
set P [1] :=  0;
```

```
set P [2] :=  0;
set P [3] :=  1;
set P [4] :=  2;
set P [5] :=  3;
set P [6] :=  4;
set P [7] :=  5  6;

set KR :=  1;
set KN :=  2;

param r :=
  [0,1,1]  0   [0,1,2]  0
  [1,1,1]  2   [1,1,2]  5   [1,2,1]  1   [1,2,2]  1
  [2,1,1]  3   [2,1,2]  6   [2,2,1]  3   [2,2,2]  2
  [3,1,1]  4   [3,1,2]  2   [3,2,1]  2   [3,2,2]  2
  [4,1,1]  3   [4,1,2]  6   [4,2,1]  4   [4,2,2]  4
  [5,1,1]  3   [5,1,2]  1
  [6,1,1]  2   [6,1,2]  1   [6,2,1]  1   [6,2,2]  1
  [7,1,1]  0   [7,1,2]  0 ;

param RR :=
  [1]  4;

param RN :=
  [2]  15;

param EF :=
  [0]  0
  [1]  3
  [2]  2
  [3]  5
  [4]  4
  [5]  8
  [6]  8
  [7]  8 ;

param LF :=
  [0]  14
  [1]  17
  [2]  16
  [3]  19
  [4]  18
  [5]  22
  [6]  22
  [7]  22 ;
```

Bibliography

[1] M. K. Agrawal, S. E. Elmaghraby, and W. S. Herroelen. DAGEN: A generator of testsets for project activity nets. *European Journal of Operational Research*, 90:376–382, 1996.

[2] T. Ahn and S. S. Erenguc. The resource-constrained project scheduling problem with multiple crashable modes – An exact solution method. Technical Report #95-101, University of Florida, Gainesville, 1995.

[3] T. Ahn and S. S. Erenguc. The resource-constrained project scheduling problem with multiple crashable modes – A heuristic procedure. *European Journal of Operational Research*, 107:250–259, 1998.

[4] C. Akkan. Two heuristics based on a graph induction method for the discrete time-cost tradeoff problem. Technical report, Koc University, Istanbul, Turkey, 1997.

[5] R. Alvarez-Valdés and J. M. Tamarit. Algoritmos heurísticos deterministas y aleatorios en secuenciacón de proyectos con recursos limitados. *Qüestiió*, 13:173–191, 1989.

[6] R. Alvarez-Valdés and J. M. Tamarit. Heuristic algorithms for resource–constrained project scheduling: A review and an empirical analysis. In Slowinski and Weglarz [187], pages 113–134.

[7] J. M. Anthonisse, K. M. van Hee, and J. K. Lenstra. Resource–constrained project scheduling: An international exercise in DSS development. *Decision Support Systems*, pages 249–254, 1988.

[8] T. Baar, P. Brucker, and S. Knust. Tabu-search algorithms and lower bounds for the resource-constrained project scheduling problem. In S. Voss, S. Martello, I. Osman, and C. Roucairol, editors, *Meta-heuristics: Advances and trends in local search paradigms for optimization*, pages 1–8. Kluwer, Boston, Massachusetts, 1998.

[9] A. J. G. Babu and N. Suresh. Project management with time, cost, and quality considerations. *European Journal of Operational Research*, 88:320–327, 1996.

[10] K. Backhaus, B. Erichson, W. Plinke, and R. Weiber. *Multivariate Analysemethoden: Eine anwendungsorientierte Einführung*. Springer, Berlin, Germany, 1996.

[11] A. B. Badiru. *Project Management in Manufacturing and High Technology Operations*. Wiley, New York, 1988.

[12] M. Bartusch, R. H. Möhring, and F. J. Radermacher. Scheduling project networks with resource constraints and time windows. *Annals of Operations Research*, 16:201–240, 1988.

[13] J. C. Bean. Genetic algorithms and random keys for sequencing and optimization. *ORSA Journal on Computing*, 6:154–160, 1994.

[14] U. Belhe and A. Kusiak. Resource-constrained scheduling of hierarchically structured design activity networks. *IEEE Transactions on Engineering Management*, 52:150–158, 1995.

[15] C. E. Bell and J. Han. A new heuristic solution method in resource-constrained project scheduling. *Naval Research Logistics*, 38:315–331, 1991.

[16] R. B. Bey, R. H. Doersch, and J. H. Patterson. The net present value criterion: Its impact on project scheduling. *Project Management Quarterly*, 12:35–45, 1981.

[17] L. Bianco, P. Dell'Olmo, and M. G. Speranza. Heuristics for multimode scheduling problems with dedicated resources. *European Journal of Operational Research*, 107:260–271, 1998.

[18] N. Bixby and E. Boyd. *Using the CPLEX callable library*. CPLEX Optimization Inc., Houston, Texas, 1996.

[19] J. Blazewicz, J. K. Lenstra, and A. H. G. Rinnooy Kan. Scheduling subject to resource constraints: Classification and complexity. *Discrete Applied Mathematics*, 5:11–24, 1983.

[20] F. F. Boctor. Some efficient multi–heuristic procedures for resource–constrained project scheduling. *European Journal of Operational Research*, 49:3–13, 1990.

[21] F. F. Boctor. Heuristics for scheduling projects with resource restrictions and several resource-duration modes. *International Journal of Production Research*, 31:2547–2558, 1993.

[22] F. F. Boctor. An adaptation of the simulated annealing algorithm for solving resource-constrained project scheduling problems. *International Journal of Production Research*, 34:2335–2351, 1996.

[23] F. F. Boctor. A new and efficient heuristic for scheduling projects with resource restrictions and multiple execution modes. *European Journal of Operational Research*, 90:349–361, 1996.

[24] J. Böttcher, A. Drexl, R. Kolisch, and F. Salewski. Project scheduling under partially renewable resource constraints. *Management Science*, 45:543–559, 1999.

[25] K. Bouleimen and H. Lecocq. A new efficient simulated annealing algorithm for the resource-constrained project scheduling problem. Technical report, Université de Liège, Belgium, 1998.

[26] P. Brucker, A. Drexl, R. Möhring, K. Neumann, and E. Pesch. Resource-constrained project scheduling: Notation, classification, models, and methods. *European Journal of Operational Research*, 112:3–41, 1999.

[27] P. Brucker and S. Knust. A linear programming and constraint propagation-based lower bound for the RCPSP. Technical report, Universität Osnabrück, Germany, 1998.

[28] P. Brucker and S. Knust. Solving large-sized resource-constrained project scheduling problems. In Weglarz [207], pages 27–51.

[29] P. Brucker, S. Knust, A. Schoo, and O. Thiele. A branch-and-bound algorithm for the resource-constrained project scheduling problem. *European Journal of Operational Research*, 107:272–288, 1998.

[30] J. H. Cho and Y. D. Kim. A simulated annealing algorithm for resource-constrained project scheduling problems. *Journal of the Operational Research Society*, 48:736–744, 1997.

[31] N. Christofides, R. Alvarez-Valdes, and J. M. Tamarit. Project scheduling with resource constraints: A branch and bound approach. *European Journal of Operational Research*, 29:262–273, 1987.

[32] P. C. Chu and J. E. Beasley. A genetic algorithm for the multidimensional knapsack problem. Technical report, The Management School, Imperial College, London, England, 1997.

[33] D. I. Cleland and W. R. King. *Systems analysis and project management*. McGraw-Hill, New York, 1983.

[34] R. W. Conway, W. L. Maxwell, and L. W. Miller. *Theory of scheduling*. Addison-Wesley, Reading, Massachusetts, 1967.

[35] D. F. Cooper. Heuristics for scheduling resource–constrained projects: An experimental investigation. *Management Science*, 22:1186–1194, 1976.

[36] D. F. Cooper. A note on serial and parallel heuristics for resource–constrained project scheduling. *Foundations of Control Engineering*, 2:131–133, 1977.

[37] E. M. Davies. An experimental investigation of resource allocation in mulitactivity projects. *Operations Research Quarterly*, 24:587–591, 1973.

[38] E. W. Davis and J. H. Patterson. A comparison of heuristic and optimum solutions in resource–constrained project scheduling. *Management Science*, 21:944–955, 1975.

[39] N. Dayanand and R. Padman. On modelling payments in projects. *Journal of the Operational Research Society*, 48:906–918, 1997.

[40] P. De, J. Dunne, J. B. Ghosh, and C. E. Wells. Complexity of the discrete time-cost tradeoff problem for project networks. *Operations Research*, 45:302–306, 1997.

[41] B. de Reyck, E. L. Demeulemeester, and W. S. Herroelen. Local search methods for the discrete time/resource trade-off problem in project networks. *Naval Research Logistics*, 45:533–578, 1998.

[42] B. de Reyck and W. S. Herroelen. Assembly line balancing by resource-constrained project scheduling – A critical appraisal. Technical Report 9505, Katholieke Universiteit Leuven, Belgium, 1995.

[43] B. de Reyck and W. S. Herroelen. A branch-and-bound procedure for the resource-constrained project scheduling problem with generalized precedence relations. *European Journal of Operational Research*, 111:157–174, 1998.

[44] F. Della Croce. Generalized pairwise interchanges and machine scheduling. *European Journal of Operational Research*, 83:310–319, 1995.

[45] E. L. Demeulemeester. Minimizing resource-availability costs in time-limited project networks. *Management Science*, 41:1590–1598, 1995.

[46] E. L. Demeulemeester, B. de Reyck, and W. S. Herroelen. The discrete time/resource trade-off problem in project networks – a branch-and-bound approach. Technical Report 9717, Katholieke Universiteit Leuven, Belgium, 1997.

[47] E. L. Demeulemeester, B. Dodin, and W. S. Herroelen. A random network activity generator. *Operations Research*, 41:972–980, 1993.

[48] E. L. Demeulemeester and W. S. Herroelen. A branch-and-bound procedure for the multiple resource-constrained project scheduling problem. *Management Science*, 38:1803–1818, 1992.

[49] E. L. Demeulemeester and W. S. Herroelen. Modelling setup times, process batches and transfer batches using activity network logic. *European Journal of Operational Research*, 89:355–365, 1996.

[50] E. L. Demeulemeester and W. S. Herroelen. A branch-and-bound procedure for the generalized resource-constrained project scheduling problem. *Operations Research*, 45:201–212, 1997.

[51] E. L. Demeulemeester and W. S. Herroelen. New benchmark results for the resource-constrained project scheduling problem. *Management Science*, 43:1485–1492, 1997.

[52] E. L. Demeulemeester, W. S. Herroelen, and S. E. Elmaghraby. Optimal procedures for the discrete time/cost trade-off problem in project networks. *European Journal of Operational Research*, 88:50–68, 1996.

[53] E. L. Demeulemeester, W. S. Herroelen, W. P. Simpson, S. Baroum, J. H. Patterson, and K.-K. Yang. On a paper by Christofides et al. for solving the multiple-resource constrained single project scheduling problem. *European Journal of Operational Research*, 76:218–228, 1994.

[54] R. H. Doersch and J. H. Patterson. Scheduling a project to maximize its present value: A zero-one programming approach. *Management Science*, 23:882–889, 1977.

[55] W. Domschke and A. Drexl. *Einführung in Operations Research*. Springer, Berlin, Germany, 1990.

[56] M. Dorigo, V. Maniezzo, and A. Colorni. The ant system: Optimization by a colony of cooperating agents. *IEEE Transactions on Systems, Man, and Cybernetics*, 26:1–13, 1996.

[57] U. Dorndorf and E. Pesch. Evolution based learning in a job shop scheduling environment. *Computers & Operations Research*, 22:25–40, 1995.

[58] U. Dorndorf, E. Pesch, and T. Phan Huy. A time-oriented branch-and-bound algorithm for resource-constrained project scheduling with generalized precedence constraints. Technical report, Universität Bonn, Germany, 1998.

[59] A. Drexl. Scheduling of project networks by job assignment. *Management Science*, 37:1590–1602, 1991.

[60] A. Drexl, W. Eversheim, R. Grempe, and H. Esser. CIM im Werkzeugmaschinenbau: Der PRISMA-Montageleitstand. *Zeitschrift für betriebswirtschaftliche Forschung*, 46:279–295, 1994.

[61] A. Drexl and J. Grünewald. Nonpreemptive multi-mode resource-constrained project scheduling. *IIE Transactions*, 25:74–81, 1993.

[62] A. Drexl, J. Juretzka, F. Salewski, and A. Schirmer. New modelling concepts and their impact on resource-constrained project scheduling. In Weglarz [207], pages 413–432.

[63] A. Drexl and R. Kolisch. Assembly management in machine tool manufacturing and the PRISMA-Leitstand. *Production and Inventory Management Journal*, 37(4):55–57, 1996.

[64] A. Drexl, R. Nissen, J. H. Patterson, and F. Salewski. ProGen/πx — An instance generator for resource-constrained project scheduling problems with partially renewable resources and further extensions. Technical report, Universität Kiel, Germany, 1997.

[65] A. Drexl and F. Salewski. Distribution requirements and compactness constraints in school timetabling. *European Journal of Operational Research*, 102:193–214, 1997.

[66] G. Dueck. New optimization heuristics: The great deluge algorithm and the record-to-record travel. *Journal of Computational Physics*, 104:86–92, 1993.

[67] G. Dueck and T. Scheuer. Threshold accepting: A general purpose optimization algorithm appearing superior to simulated annealing. *Journal of Computational Physics*, 90:161–175, 1990.

[68] H. Dyckhoff. A typology of cutting and packing problems. *European Journal of Operational Research*, 44:145–159, 1990.

[69] H. Dyckhoff and U. Finke. *Cutting and packing in production and distribution.* Physica, Heidelberg, Germany, 1992.

[70] A. E. Eiben, E. H. L. Aarts, and K. M. van Hee. Global convergence of genetic algorithms: A markov chain analysis. *Lecture Notes in Computer Science*, 496:4–12, 1990.

[71] S. E. Elmaghraby. An algebra for the analysis of generalized networks. *Management Science*, 10:419–514, 1964.

[72] S. E. Elmaghraby. *Activity networks: Project planning and control by network models.* Wiley, New York, 1977.

[73] S. E. Elmaghraby. Resource allocation via dynamic programming in activity networks. *European Journal of Operational Research*, 64:199–215, 1993.

[74] E. A. Elsayed. Algorithms for project scheduling with resource constraints. *International Journal of Production Research*, 20:95–103, 1982.

[75] H. Exeler. *Das homogene Packproblem in der betriebswirtschaftlichen Logistik*. Physica, Heidelberg, Germany, 1988.

[76] F. Farid and S. Manoharan. Comparative analysis of resource allocation capabilities of project management software packages. *Project Management Journal*, 24:35–44, 1996.

[77] T. Fitting. Bedeutung der intrazellulären S-Adenosylmethionindecarboxylase-Aktivität für die Regulation des Polyaminstoffwechsels während des Camostat-stimulierten Pankreaswachstums von Ratten. MD Dissertation, 1998. Universität Kiel, Germany.

[78] R. Fourer, D. M. Gay, and B. W. Kernighan. *AMPL — A modeling language for mathematical programming*. Boyd & Fraser Publishing Company, Danvers, Massachusetts, 1993.

[79] B. Franck and K. Neumann. Resource-constrained project scheduling with time windows: Structural questions and priority rule methods. Technical Report WIOR-492, Universität Karlsruhe, Germany, 1997.

[80] B. Franck and C. Schwindt. Different resource-constrained project scheduling models with minimal and maximal time-lags. Technical Report WIOR-450, Universität Karlsruhe, Germany, 1995.

[81] B. Franck and J. Zimmermann. Meta-Heuristiken. Technical Report WIOR-496, Universität Karlsruhe, Germany, 1997.

[82] S. French. *Sequencing and scheduling: An introduction to the mathematics of the job-shop*. Wiley, New York, 1982.

[83] M. R. Garey, R. L. Graham, D. S. Johnson, and A. C.-C. Yao. Resource constrained scheduling as generalized bin packing. *Journal of Combinatorial Theory*, 21:257–298, 1976.

[84] M. R. Garey and D. S. Johnson. *Computers and intractability: A guide to the theory of NP-completeness*. Freeman, San Francisco, California, 1979.

[85] F. Glover. Tabu search - Part I. *ORSA Journal on Computing*, 1:190–206, 1989.

[86] F. Glover. Tabu search – Part II. *ORSA Journal on Computing*, 2:4–32, 1989.

[87] F. Glover and H. J. Greenberg. New approaches for heuristic search: A bilateral linkage with artificial intelligence. *European Journal of Operational Research*, 39:119–130, 1989.

[88] D. E. Goldberg. *Genetic algorithms in search, optimization, and machine learning*. Addison-Wesley, Reading, Massachusetts, 1989.

[89] M. Hapke, A. Jaszkiewicz, and R. Slowinski. Interactive analysis of multiple-criteria project scheduling problems. *European Journal of Operational Research*, 107:315–324, 1998.

[90] S. Hartmann. Project scheduling with multiple modes: A genetic algorithm. Manuskripte aus den Instituten für Betriebswirtschaftslehre 435, Universität Kiel, Germany, 1997.

[91] S. Hartmann. Scheduling medical research experiments — An application of project scheduling methods. Manuskripte aus den Instituten für Betriebswirtschaftslehre 452, Universität Kiel, Germany, 1997.

[92] S. Hartmann. A competitive genetic algorithm for resource-constrained project scheduling. *Naval Research Logistics*, 45:733–750, 1998.

[93] S. Hartmann and A. Drexl. Project scheduling with multiple modes: A comparison of exact algorithms. *Networks*, 32:283–297, 1998.

[94] S. Hartmann, J. Frahm, and F. Salewski. Planning attractive travel routes — Model, methods, and applications. Technical report, Universität Kiel, Germany. In preparation.

[95] S. Hartmann and R. Kolisch. Experimental investigation of state-of-the-art heuristics for the resource-constrained project scheduling problem. *European Journal of Operational Research*. Forthcoming.

[96] S. Hartmann and A. Sprecher. A note on "Hierarchical models for multi-project planning and scheduling". *European Journal of Operational Research*, 94:377–383, 1996.

[97] A. C. Hax and D. Candea. *Production and inventory management*. Prentice-Hall, New Jersey, 1984.

[98] R. Heilmann. A branch-and-bound procedure for MRCPSP/max. Technical Report WIOR-512, Universität Karlsruhe, Germany, 1998.

[99] R. Heilmann and C. Schwindt. Lower bounds for RCPSP/max. Technical Report WIOR-511, Universität Karlsruhe, Germany, 1997.

[100] J. W. Herrmann, C.-Y. Lee, and J. Hinchman. Global job shop scheduling with a genetic algorithm. *Production and Operations Management*, 4:30–45, 1995.

[101] W. S. Herroelen, E. L. Demeulemeester, and B. de Reyck. A classification scheme for project scheduling. In Weglarz [207], pages 1–26.

[102] W. S. Herroelen, P. van Dommelen, and E. L. Demeulemeester. Project network models with discounted cash flows: A guided tour through recent developments. *European Journal of Operational Research*, 100:97–121, 1997.

[103] H. J. Holland. *Adaptation in natural and artificial systems*. University of Michigan Press, Ann Arbor, 1975.

[104] J. J. Hopfield and D. W. Tank. Neural computation of decisions in optimization problems. *Biological Cybernetics*, 52:141–152, 1985.

[105] O. Icmeli and S. S. Erenguc. A branch and bound procedure for the resource constrained project scheduling problem with discounted cash-flows. *Management Science*, 42:1395–1408, 1996.

[106] O. Icmeli, S. S. Erenguc, and C. J. Zappe. Project scheduling problems: A survey. *International Journal of Operations & Production Management*, 13:80–91, 1993.

[107] O. Icmeli-Tukel and W. O. Rom. Ensuring quality in resource constrained project scheduling. *European Journal of Operational Research*, 103:483–496, 1997.

[108] C. Jordan. *Batching and scheduling – Models and methods for several problem classes.* Number 437 in Lecture Notes in Economics and Mathematical Systems. Springer, Berlin, Germany, 1996.

[109] T. T. Kapuscinska, T. E. Morton, and P. Ramnath. High-intensity heuristics to minimize weighted tardiness in resource-constrained multiple dependent project scheduling. Technical report, Carnegie Mellon University, Pittsburgh, Pennsylvania, 1998.

[110] J. E. Kelley, Jr. Critical-path planning and scheduling: Mathematical basis. *Operations Research*, 9:296–320, 1961.

[111] J. E. Kelley, Jr. The critical path method: Resources planning and scheduling. In J. F. Muth and G. L. Thompson, editors, *Industrial scheduling*, pages 347–365. Prentice-Hall, New Jersey, 1963.

[112] Y.-D. Kim. A backward approach in list scheduling algorithms for multi-machine tardiness problems. *Computers & Operations Research*, 22:307–319, 1995.

[113] A. Kimms. Optimization guided lower and upper bounds for the resource investment problem. Manuskripte aus den Instituten für Betriebswirtschaftslehre 481, Universität Kiel, Germany, 1998.

[114] S. Kirkpatrick, C. D. Gelatt, Jr., and M. P. Vecchi. Optimization by simulated annealing. *Science*, 220:671–680, 1983.

[115] R. Klein. Bidirectional planning — Improving priority rule based heuristics for scheduling resource-constrained projects. Schriften zur Quantitativen Betriebswirtschaftslehre 10/98, Technische Universität Darmstadt, Germany, 1998.

[116] R. Klein and A. Scholl. Scattered branch and bound — An adaptive search strategy applied to resource-constrained project scheduling. Schriften zur Quantitativen Betriebswirtschaftslehre 6/98, Technische Universität Darmstadt, Germany, 1998.

[117] R. Klein and A. Scholl. Computing lower bounds by destructive improvement — An application to resource-constrained project scheduling. *European Journal of Operational Research*, 112:322–346, 1999.

[118] U. Kohlmorgen, H. Schmeck, and K. Haase. Experiences with fine-grained parallel genetic algorithms. *Annals of Operations Research*. Forthcoming.

[119] R. Kolisch. Resource allocation capabilities of commercial project management systems — Resource management boosts up the German stock exchange. *Interfaces*. Forthcoming.

[120] R. Kolisch. *Project scheduling under resource constraints – Efficient heuristics for several problem classes.* Physica, Heidelberg, Germany, 1995.

[121] R. Kolisch. Efficient priority rules for the resource-constrained project scheduling problem. *Journal of Operations Management*, 14:179–192, 1996.

[122] R. Kolisch. Serial and parallel resource-constrained project scheduling methods revisited: Theory and computation. *European Journal of Operational Research*, 90:320–333, 1996.

[123] R. Kolisch. Planungsfunktionen von Projektmanagementsystemen. *Marktforschung & Management*, 41:234–239, 1997.

[124] R. Kolisch and A. Drexl. Adaptive search for solving hard project scheduling problems. *Naval Research Logistics*, 43:23–40, 1996.

[125] R. Kolisch and A. Drexl. Local search for nonpreemptive multi-mode resource-constrained project scheduling. *IIE Transactions*, 29:987–999, 1997.

[126] R. Kolisch and S. Hartmann. Heuristic algorithms for solving the resource-constrained project scheduling problem: Classification and computational analysis. In Weglarz [207], pages 147–178.

[127] R. Kolisch and K. Hempel. Entscheidungstheoretisch fundierte Bewertung von Standardsoftware für das Projektmanagement. *Wirtschaftsinformatik*, 38:399–410, 1996.

[128] R. Kolisch and R. Padman. An integrated survey of project scheduling. Manuskripte aus den Instituten für Betriebswirtschaftslehre 463, Universität Kiel, Germany, 1997.

[129] R. Kolisch and A. Sprecher. PSPLIB – a project scheduling problem library. *European Journal of Operational Research*, 96:205–216, 1996.

[130] R. Kolisch, A. Sprecher, and A. Drexl. Characterization and generation of a general class of resource-constrained project scheduling problems. *Management Science*, 41:1693–1703, 1995.

[131] R. Kolisch, A. Sprecher, and C. Schwindt. Benchmark instances for project scheduling problems. In Weglarz [207], pages 197–212.

[132] S. R. Lawrence. Resource constrained project scheduling – A computational comparison of heuristic scheduling techniques. Technical report, Carnegie Mellon University, Pittsburgh, Pennsylvania, 1985.

[133] J.-K. Lee and Y.-D. Kim. Search heuristics for resource-constrained project scheduling. *Journal of the Operational Research Society*, 47:678–689, 1996.

[134] V. J. Leon and B. Ramamoorthy. Strength and adaptability of problem-space based neighborhoods for resource-constrained scheduling. *OR Spektrum*, 17:173–182, 1995.

[135] K. Y. Li and R. J. Willis. An iterative scheduling technique for resource-constrained project scheduling. *European Journal of Operational Research*, 56:370–379, 1992.

[136] F.-H. F. Liu and C.-J. Hsiao. A three-dimensional pallet loading method for single-size boxes. *Journal of the Operational Research Society*, 48:726–735, 1997.

[137] C. Löser, T. Fitting, and U. R. Fölsch. Importance of intracellular s-adenosylmethionine decarboxylase activity for the regulation of camostate-induced pancreatic polyamine metabolism and growth: In vivo effect of two novel s-adenosylmethionine decarboxylase inhibitors. *Digestion*, 58:258–265, 1997.

[138] C. Löser, U. R. Fölsch, C. Paprotny, and W. Creutzfeld. Polyamines in colorectal cancer: Evaluation of polyamine concentrations in colon tissue, serum, and urine of 50 patients with colorectal cancer. *Cancer*, 65:958–966, 1990.

[139] D. G. Malcolm, J. H. Roseboom, C. E. Clark, and W. Fazar. Applications of a technique for research and development program evaluation. *Operations Research*, 7:646–669, 1959.

[140] L. J. Marton and A. E. Pegg. Polyamines as targets for therapeutic intervention. *Annual Review of Pharmacology and Toxicology*, 35:55–91, 1995.

[141] D. C. Mattfeld. *Evolutionary search and the job shop*. Physica, Heidelberg, Germany, 1996.

[142] H. E. Mausser and S. R. Lawrence. Exploiting block structure to improve resource–constrained project schedules. Technical report, Graduate School of Business Administration, University of Colorado, 1995.

[143] W. S. McCulloch and W. Pitts. A logical calculus of the ideas immanent in nervous activity. *Bulletin of Mathematical Biophysics*, 5:115–133, 1943.

[144] Z. Michalewicz. Heuristic methods for evolutionary computation techniques. *Journal of Heuristics*, 1:177–206, 1995.

[145] A. Mingozzi, V. Maniezzo, S. Ricciardelli, and L. Bianco. An exact algorithm for the resource-constrained project scheduling problem based on a new mathematical formulation. *Management Science*, 44:714–729, 1998.

[146] J. J. Moder, C. R. Phillips, and E. W. Davis. *Project Management with CPM, PERT and precedence diagramming*. Van Nostrand Reinhold, New York, 1983.

[147] R. H. Möhring, F. Stork, and M. Uetz. Resource–constrained project scheduling with time windows: A branching scheme based on dynamic release dates. Technical Report 596, Fachbereich Mathematik, Technische Universität Berlin, Germany, 1998.

[148] R. Morabito and S. Morales. A simple and effective recursive procedure for the manufacturer's pallet loading problem. *Journal of the Operational Research Society*, 49:819–828, 1998.

[149] M. Mori and C. C. Tseng. A genetic algorithm for the multi-mode resource-constrained project scheduling problem. *European Journal of Operational Research*, 100:134–141, 1997.

[150] K. S. Naphade, S. D. Wu, and R. H. Storer. Problem space search algorithms for resource-constrained project scheduling. *Annals of Operations Research*, 70:307–326, 1997.

[151] K. Neumann. *Stochastic project networks: Temporal analysis, scheduling and cost minimization.* Number 344 in Lecture Notes in Economics and Mathematical Systems. Springer, Berlin, Germany, 1990.

[152] M. J. Norusis. *The SPSS guide to data analysis.* SPSS Inc., Chicago, Illinois, 1990.

[153] O. Oguz and H. Bala. A comparative study of computational procedures for the resource constrained project scheduling problem. *European Journal of Operational Research*, 72:406–416, 1994.

[154] L. Özdamar. A genetic algorithm approach to a general category project scheduling problem. *IEEE Transactions on Systems, Man, and Cybernetics.* Forthcoming.

[155] L. Özdamar and G. Ulusoy. A local constraint based analysis approach to project scheduling under general resource constraints. *European Journal of Operational Research*, 79:287–298, 1994.

[156] L. Özdamar and G. Ulusoy. A survey on the resource-constrained project scheduling problem. *IIE Transactions*, 27:574–586, 1995.

[157] L. Özdamar and G. Ulusoy. An iterative local constraint based analysis for solving the resource-constrained project scheduling problem. *Journal of Operations Management*, 14:193–208, 1996.

[158] L. Özdamar and G. Ulusoy. A note on an iterative forward/backward scheduling technique with reference to a procedure by Li and Willis. *European Journal of Operational Research*, 89:400–407, 1996.

[159] R. Padman, D. E. Smith-Daniels, and V. L. Smith-Daniels. Heuristic scheduling of resource-constrained projects with cash flows. *Naval Research Logistics*, 44:364–381, 1997.

[160] J. H. Patterson. Alternate methods of project scheduling with limited resources. *Naval Research Logistics Quarterly*, 20:767–784, 1973.

[161] J. H. Patterson. Project scheduling: The effects of problem structure on heuristic performance. *Naval Research Logistics Quarterly*, 23:95–123, 1976.

[162] J. H. Patterson. A comparison of exact approaches for solving the multiple constrained resource, project scheduling problem. *Management Science*, 30:854–867, 1984.

[163] J. H. Patterson, R. Slowinski, F. B. Talbot, and J. Weglarz. An algorithm for a general class of precedence and resource constrained scheduling problems. In Slowinski and Weglarz [187], pages 3–28.

[164] S. Philips, Jr. Project management duration/resource tradeoff analysis: An application of the cut search approach. *Journal of the Operational Research Society*, 47:697–701, 1996.

[165] E. Pinson, C. Prins, and F. Rullier. Using tabu search for solving the resource-constrained project scheduling problem. In *Proceedings of the fourth international workshop on project management and scheduling*, pages 102–106. Leuven, Belgium, 1994.

[166] M. Pirlot. General local search methods. *European Journal of Operational Research*, 92:493–511, 1996.

[167] B. Pollack-Johnson. Hybrid structures and improving forecasting and scheduling in project management. *Journal of Operations Management*, 12:101–117, 1995.

[168] A. A. B. Pritsker and W. W. Happ. GERT: Graphical evaluation and review technique — Part I: Fundamentals. *Journal of Industrial Engineering*, 17:267–274, 1966.

[169] A. A. B. Pritsker, L. J. Watters, and P. M. Wolfe. Multiproject scheduling with limited resources: A zero-one programming approach. *Management Science*, 16:93–107, 1969.

[170] F. J. Radermacher. Scheduling of project networks. *Annals of Operations Research*, 4:227–252, 1985.

[171] C. R. Reeves. Genetic algorithms and combinatorial optimization. In V. J. Rayward-Smith, editor, *Applications of modern heuristic methods*, pages 111–125. Alfred Waller Ltd., Henley-on-Thames, 1995.

[172] F. Salewski, A. Schirmer, and A. Drexl. Project scheduling under resource and mode identity constraints: Model, complexity, methods, and application. *European Journal of Operational Research*, 102:88–110, 1997.

[173] S. E. Sampson and E. N. Weiss. Local search techniques for the generalized resource-constrained project scheduling problem. *Naval Research Logistics*, 40:665–675, 1993.

[174] A. Schirmer. Case-based reasoning and improved adaptive search for project scheduling. Manuskripte aus den Instituten für Betriebswirtschaftslehre 472, Universität Kiel, Germany, 1998.

[175] A. Schirmer and A. Drexl. Allocation of partially renewable resources — Concepts, models, and applications. Manuskripte aus den Instituten für Betriebswirtschaftslehre 455, Universität Kiel, Germany, 1997.

[176] A. Schirmer and S. Riesenberg. Parameterized heuristics for project scheduling — Biased random sampling methods. Manuskripte aus den Instituten für Betriebswirtschaftslehre 456, Universität Kiel, Germany, 1997.

[177] A. Schirmer and S. Riesenberg. Class-based control schemes for parameterized project scheduling heuristics. Manuskripte aus den Instituten für Betriebswirtschaftslehre 471, Universität Kiel, Germany, 1998.

[178] L. Schrage. Solving resource-constrained network problems by implicit enumeration - Nonpreemptive case. *Operations Research*, 18:263–278, 1970.

[179] J. M. J. Schutten. List scheduling revisited. *Operations Research Letters*, 18:167–170, 1996.

[180] C. Schwindt. ProGen/max: A new problem generator for different resource-constrained project scheduling problems with minimal and maximal time lags. Technical Report WIOR-449, Universität Karlsruhe, Germany, 1995.

[181] C. Schwindt. *Verfahren zur Lösung des ressourcenbeschränkten Projektdauerminimierungsproblems mit planungsabhängigen Zeitfenstern.* Shaker, Aachen, Germany, 1998.

[182] L. R. Shaffer, J. B. Ritter, and W. L. Meyer. *The critical-path method.* McGraw-Hill, New York, 1965.

[183] A. Shtub, L. J. LeBlanc, and Z. Cai. Scheduling programs with repetitive projects: A comparison of a simulated annealing, a genetic and a pair-wise swap algorithm. *European Journal of Operational Research*, 88:124–138, 1996.

[184] R. Slowinski. Two approaches to problems of resource allocation among project activities: A comparative study. *Journal of the Operational Research Society*, 31:711–723, 1980.

[185] R. Slowinski. Multiobjective network scheduling with efficient use of renewable and nonrenewable resources. *European Journal of Operational Research*, 7:265–273, 1981.

[186] R. Slowinski, B. Soniewicki, and J. Weglarz. DSS for multiobjective project scheduling subject to multiple-category resource constraints. *European Journal of Operational Research*, 79:220–229, 1994.

[187] R. Slowinski and J. Weglarz, editors. *Advances in project scheduling.* Elsevier, Amsterdam, the Netherlands, 1989.

[188] M. G. Speranza and C. Vercellis. Hierarchical models for multi-project planning and scheduling. *European Journal of Operational Research*, 64:312–325, 1993.

[189] A. Sprecher. A competitive exact algorithm for assembly line balancing. *International Journal of Production Research.* Forthcoming.

[190] A. Sprecher. *Resource-constrained project scheduling: Exact methods for the multi-mode case.* Number 409 in Lecture Notes in Economics and Mathematical Systems. Springer, Berlin, Germany, 1994.

[191] A. Sprecher. Solving the RCPSP efficiently at modest memory requirements. Manuskripte aus den Instituten für Betriebswirtschaftslehre 425, Universität Kiel, Germany, 1996.

[192] A. Sprecher and A. Drexl. Multi-mode resource-constrained project scheduling by a simple, general and powerful sequencing algorithm. *European Journal of Operational Research*, 107:431–450, 1998.

[193] A. Sprecher, S. Hartmann, and A. Drexl. An exact algorithm for project scheduling with multiple modes. *OR Spektrum*, 19:195–203, 1997.

[194] A. Sprecher, R. Kolisch, and A. Drexl. Semi-active, active and non-delay schedules for the resource-constrained project scheduling problem. *European Journal of Operational Research*, 80:94–102, 1995.

[195] J. P. Stinson, E. W. Davis, and B. M. Khumawala. Multiple resource-constrained scheduling using branch and bound. *AIIE Transactions*, 10:252–259, 1978.

[196] R. H. Storer, S. D. Wu, and V. Vaccari. New search spaces for sequencing problems with application to job shop scheduling. *Management Science*, 38:1495–1509, 1992.

[197] F. B. Talbot. Resource-constrained project scheduling with time-resource tradeoffs: The nonpreemptive case. *Management Science*, 28:1197–1210, 1982.

[198] F. B. Talbot and J. H. Patterson. An efficient integer programming algorithm with network cuts for solving resource-constrained project scheduling problems. *Management Science*, 24:1163–1174, 1978.

[199] A. Thesen. Heuristic scheduling of activities under resource and precedence restrictions. *Management Science*, 23:412–422, 1976.

[200] P. R. Thomas and S. Salhi. An investigation into the relationship of heuristic performance with network–resource characteristics. *Journal of the Operational Research Society*, 48:34–43, 1997.

[201] P. R. Thomas and S. Salhi. A tabu search approach for the resource constrained project scheduling problem. *Journal of Heuristics*, 4:123–139, 1998.

[202] G. Ulusoy and L. Özdamar. Heuristic performance and network/resource characteristics in resource-constrained project scheduling. *Journal of the Operational Research Society*, 40:1145–1152, 1989.

[203] G. Ulusoy and L. Özdamar. A constraint–based perspective in resource-constrained project scheduling. *International Journal of Production Research*, 32:693–705, 1994.

[204] V. Valls, M. A. Pérez, and M. S. Quintanilla. Heuristic performance in large resource-constrained projects. Technical Report 92-2, Departament D'Estadistica I Invecigacio Operativa, Universitat de Valencia, Spain, 1992.

[205] J. Weglarz. On certain models of resource allocation problems. *Kybernetics*, 9:61–66, 1981.

[206] J. Weglarz. Project scheduling with continuously divisible, doubly-constrained resources. *Management Science*, 27:1040–1057, 1981.

[207] J. Weglarz, editor. *Project scheduling: Recent models, algorithms and applications.* Kluwer, Amsterdam, the Netherlands, 1999.

[208] J. Weglarz, J. Blazewicz, W. Cellary, and R. Slowinski. Algorithm 520: An automatic revised simplex method for constrained resource network scheduling. *ACM Transactions on Mathematical Software*, 3:295–300, 1977.

[209] G. E. Whitehouse and J. R. Brown. GENRES: An extension of Brooks algorithm for project scheduling with resource constraints. *Computers & Industrial Engineering*, 3:261–268, 1979.

[210] D. Whitley, V. S. Gordon, and K. Mathias. Lamarckian evolution, the Baldwin effect and function optimization. In *Proceedings of the parallel problem solving from nature*, pages 6–15. Springer, Berlin, Germany, 1994.

[211] T. Williams. A classified bibliography of recent research relating to project risk management. *European Journal of Operational Research*, 85:18–38, 1995.

[212] M. Wottawa. PACKLIB: Ein ASCII-Datenformat für Packungsprobleme. Technical Report 96-216, Universität Köln, Germany, 1996.

[213] J. Zimmermann. Heuristics for resource-levelling problems in project scheduling with minimum and maximum time lags. Technical Report WIOR-491, Universität Karlsruhe, Germany, 1997.

List of Abbreviations

B&B	branch-and-bound
BFS	best fit strategy
BRS	biased random sampling
cf.	confer
CPU	central processing unit
e.g.	for example
FFS	first fit strategy
GA	genetic algorithm
GRPW	greatest rank positional weight (priority rule)
i.e.	that is
LCBA	local constraint based analysis (priority rule)
LFT	latest finish time (priority rule)
LST	latest start time (priority rule)
MIRCPSP	mode identity resource-constrained project scheduling problem
MRBRS	modified regret based biased random sampling
MRCPSP	multi-mode resource-constrained project scheduling problem
MSLK	minimum slack (priority rule)
MTS	most total successors (priority rule)
NBRS	normalized biased random sampling
NPV	net present value
RAND	random (priority rule)
RBRS	regret based biased random sampling

RCPSP	resource-constrained project scheduling problem
RCPSP/π	resource-constrained project scheduling problem with partially renewable resources
RCPSP/τ	resource-constrained project scheduling problem with time-dependent resource parameters
RS	random sampling
SA	simulated annealing
sec	seconds
SGS	schedule generation scheme
TS	tabu search
vs.	versus
WCS	worst case slack (priority rule)
w.l.o.g.	without loss of generality
w.r.t.	with respect to
WRUP	weighted resource utilization and precedence (priority rule)

List of Basic Notation

$\mathcal{CHI}$	children produced in a genetic algorithm
d_{ij}^{FS}	minimal time lag between the finish time of activity i and the start time of activity j
d_{ij}^{SS}	minimal time lag between the start time of activity i and the start time of activity j
$\mathcal{DA}_g$	delay alternative at level g
$\underline{\delta}_j$	release date of activity j
$\overline{\delta}_j$	deadline of activity j
$\mathcal{EA}_g$	extension alternative at level g
EF_j	precedence based earliest finish time of activity j
EJ_g	set of eligible activities at level g
ES_j	precedence based earliest start time of activity j
$f(\cdot)$	fitness function
f_j	finish time of activity j
FJ_g	set of activities finished at or before the decision point at level g
g	level in branch-and-bound algorithm or schedule generation scheme
G	generation in genetic algorithm
GEN	number of generations in a genetic algorithm
I	individual in genetic algorithm
ISL	number of islands in extended genetic algorithm paradigm
J	number of non-dummy activities
$j = 0$	dummy source activity
$j = J + 1$	dummy sink activity
$\mathcal{J}$	set of non-dummy activities

$\mathcal{J}^+$	set of activities including summy source and sink
JIP_g	set of activities in process at level g
$\mathcal{K}^\rho$	set of renewable resources
$\mathcal{K}^\nu$	set of nonrenewable resources
$\mathcal{K}^\pi$	set of partially renewable resources
$L^\nu(\mu)$	nonrenewable resource units exceeding the capacities in mode assignment μ
$L_k^\nu(\mu)$	leftover capacity of nonrenewable resource k in mode assignment μ
LF_j	precedence based latest finish time of activity j
LS_j	precedence based latest start time of activity j
λ	activity list
M_j	number of modes of activity j
$\mathcal{M}_j$	set of modes of activity j
$\mathcal{MA}_g$	mode alternative at level g
$\mu(\cdot)$	mode assignment function
p_j	processing time of activity j
p_{jm}	processing time of activity j if performed in mode m
$p(j)$	selection probability of activity j in sampling methods
$p_{\text{death}}(\lambda)$	probability to die for individual λ
$p_{\text{migration}}$	migration probability for island model
p_{mutation}	mutation probability
$\mathcal{P}_j$	set of immediate predecessors of activity j
POP	number of individuals in the population of a genetic algorithm
$\mathcal{POP}$	population of genetic algorithm (list of individuals)
PS	partial schedule
π	priority rule list (representation)
π_i	priority rule for the i-th scheduling decision
q	position in one-point crossover
q_1, q_2	positions in two-point crossover
r_{jk}	constant per-period-request of activity j for resource k
$r_{jk}(t)$	request of activity j for resource k in the t-th period of its duration
r_{jmk}	request of activity j performed in mode m for resource k
R_k^ρ	constant per-period-availability of renewable resource k
$R_k^\rho(t)$	availability of renewable resource k in period t

R_k^ν	availability of nonrenewable resource k
$R_k^\nu(PS)$	leftover capacity of nonrenewable resource k in partial schedule PS
RF^ρ	resource factor of the renewable resources
RF^ν	resource factor of the nonrenewable resources
RS^ρ	resource strength of the renewable resources
RS^ν	resource strength of the nonrenewable resources
ρ	random key array
ρ_j	random key of activity j
s_j	start time of activity j
s_j^{prec}	earliest precedence feasible start time of activity j
S	schedule
$\mathcal{S}_j$	set of immediate successors of activity j
$\overline{\mathcal{S}}_j$	set of all successors of activity j
SJ_g	set of scheduled activities at level g
SGS_{serial}	gene in extended genetic representation indicating the decoding procedure to be used
$\mathcal{SOEA}_g$	set of extension alternatives at level g
$\mathcal{SODA}_g$	set of delay alternatives at level g
$\mathcal{SOMA}_g$	set of mode alternatives at level g
σ	shift vector
σ_j	shift of activity j for shift vector representation
t_g	decision point at level g (time instant)
T	planning horizon (number of periods)
$\mathcal{T}$	set of time instants
$\mathcal{T}'$	set of periods
$v(j)$	priority value of activity j, computed by a priority rule
x_{jt}	binary decision variable which indicates whether activity j finishes at time t or not
x_{jmt}	binary decision variable which indicates whether activity j is performed in mode m and finishes at time t or not
ξ_i	i-th random number in sequence for uniform crossover
Z	makespan (objective function value)

List of Tables

2.1	Time windows for example instance	9
2.2	Packing problems as special cases of project scheduling	31
3.1	Accelerated variants of the algorithms to be tested	56
3.2	Average computation times	58
3.3	Maximal computation times	58
3.4	Average computation times for resource classes	58
3.5	Distribution of the computation times	58
4.1	Example for serial SGS	63
4.2	Example for parallel SGS	65
4.3	Priority Rules	67
4.4	Selection probabilities for different sampling methods	70
4.5	Survey of priority rule based heuristics for the RCPSP	71
4.6	Survey of metaheuristic approaches for the RCPSP	78
5.1	Alternative genetic operators — activity list GA	96
5.2	Impact of population size — activity list GA	96
5.3	Impact of initial population — activity list GA	97
5.4	Comparison of genetic algorithms	97
5.5	Average deviations w.r.t. time limit	98
5.6	Average deviations from lower bound	98
5.7	Average deviations from best upper bound	99
5.8	Impact of genetic operators	100
5.9	Average percentage of the serial SGS in the initial population	104
6.1	Average deviations from optimal solution — $J = 30$	119
6.2	Average deviations from best solution — $J = 60$	119
6.3	Average deviations from best solution — $J = 120$	120
6.4	Average deviations from critical path lower bound — $J = 60$	120
6.5	Average deviations from critical path lower bound — $J = 120$	121
6.6	Comparison of heuristics — Patterson instance set	121
6.7	Average deviations from optimal solution w.r.t. RS^ρ	125

6.8 Average deviations from optimal solution w.r.t. RF^{ρ} 125
6.9 Average computation times of GAs w.r.t. project size 126

7.1 Impact of local search improvement 140
7.2 Impact of local search improvement — intermediate results . 141
7.3 Average number of clusters w.r.t. generation number 143
7.4 New GA vs. two other heuristics 145
7.5 New GA vs. truncated B&B w.r.t. project size 146
7.6 New GA vs. truncated B&B w.r.t. time limit 147
7.7 New GA vs. truncated B&B w.r.t. resource strength 147

8.1 Experiments and repetitions 153
8.2 Calendar — working and examination days 153
8.3 Transforming experiment repetitions into activities 155
8.4 Makespan w.r.t. computation time 156
8.5 Varying the maximal number of repetitions in process 160
8.6 Impact of calendar changes 161
8.7 Changing the temporal arrangement 161

A.1 ProGen single-mode instances: Fixed parameter levels 183
A.2 ProGen single-mode instances: Variable parameter levels . . . 184
A.3 ProGen multi-mode instances: Fixed parameter levels 184
A.4 ProGen multi-mode instances: Variable parameter levels . . . 185

B.1 MRCPSP symbols in AMPL formulation 188

List of Figures

2.1 Project instance 7
2.2 Example schedule 7
2.3 Transforming the two-dimensional bin packing problem . . . 27
2.4 Two-dimensional bin packing problem — rotating boxes . . . 27

3.1 Project Instance 49
3.2 Schedules of the Project Instance 49

5.1 Illustration of conditions for equal neighbor schedules 109

7.1 Project instance 130
7.2 Schedule of example individual I^M 133
7.3 Improved schedule of example individual I^M 137

8.1 Schedules for the RCPSP/τ example instance 158
8.2 Modeling approach based on new precedence relations 162
8.3 Activity network of the interview project 170

Index

active schedule, 63, 102, 123, 138
activity, 5
activity list, 63, 73, 86, 126, 131
activity-on-arc, 17
activity-on-node, 6, 17
adaptive method, 69, 104, 116, 123
ant system, 72
aspiration criterion, 72
assembly line balancing, 24

backward recursion, 8, 41, 133
best fit strategy, 72
bin packing problem, 25
bounding rule, 41
branch-and-bound, 34, 80, 145

cash flow, 21
computational results, 55, 94, 115, 138
continuously divisible resource, 19
crashable modes, 15
crossover, 72, 85, 87, 92, 94, 105, 134
- one-point, 87
- two-point, 88
- uniform, 89

cutset, 45
cutting problem, 22

deadline, 16, 20, 22, 29, 174
decision point, 37, 39, 64
dedicated resource, 19
delay alternative, 38
disjunctive arcs, 80
doubly constrained resource, 12, 17, 19
due date, 17, 20, 22
duration, 6

extension alternative, 39, 65

field work, 164
first fit strategy, 71, 133
fitness, 85, 86, 132
forbidden set, 80
forward recursion, 8, 76
forward-backward scheduling, 68, 145

GA, *see* genetic algorithm
genetic algorithm, 72, 83, 118, 122, 126, 129
genotype, 84, 86, 138
global optimum, 71, 144
great deluge algorithm, 71

hill climbing, 106

immediate selection, 46
individual, 84, 85
integer programming, 9, 13, 34, 81
interview, 164
interviewer, 163
island, 100

job, 5
job shop problem, 24
just-in-time, 20

knapsack packing problem, 28

knapsack problem, 29

Lamarckian evolution, 84, 138, 144
latest finish time, 8, 66, 87, 133
learning effects, 22
local left shift, 43, 51
local optimum, 71, 144
local search, 72, 105, 122, 133, 135, 141
logical nodes, 17

makespan, 6, 11, 20, 156, 173
market research, 163
maximal time lag, 16
medical research project, 149
metaheuristics, 70, 118, 122
migration, 84, 101
minimal time lag, 15
mode, *see* multiple modes
mode alternative, 37, 39
mode identity, 14, 168
mode reduction, 44
mode-minimal schedule, 43
MRCPSP, *see* multiple modes
multi pass, 67, 137, 139
multi priority rule methods, 67
multi-mode left shift, 43, 136
multiple modes, 11, 33, 129, 168
multiple projects, 22
mutation, 72, 85, 90, 92, 94, 105, 135

neighborhood, 71, 72, 107
net present value, 21
network, 6, 169
network complexity, 183
neural network, 72
non-delay schedule, 65, 102, 123
nonrenewable resource, 12, 14, 17, 43, 131, 171, 172
NP-complete, 14, 131
NP-hard, 10, 14, 33
NPV, *see* net present value

objective, 6, 20, 152, 156, 168, 173
ontogenetic learning, 84, 138
order swap, 44
order-monotonous schedule, 44

packing problem, 22
pallet loading problem, 28
parallel schedule generation scheme, 64, 123
Pareto-optimal, 22
partially renewable resource, 18, 171
Patterson instances, 117, 118, 181, 182
phenotype, 84, 86, 138
phylogenetic learning, 84
population, 72, 85
precedence relation, 6, 15, 169
  start-start, 16, 162, 169
precedence tree, 35, 47, 59
predecessor, 6
preemption, 6, 11, 19
preprocessing, 42, 130
priority rule, 66, 87, 93, 103, 122
problem-space representation, 75, 116
processing time, 6
ProGen instances, 55, 95, 116, 138, 145, 146, 182

quality, 21

random key, 74, 91
random sampling, 68, 86, 116
ready time, 16
real-world application, 149
record-to-record travel, 71
regret based biased random sampling, 69
release date, 16, 174
renewable resource, 6, 19
representation, 73
resource factor, 57, 123, 124, 183

resource investment, 20
resource strength, 57, 123, 124, 146, 183
resource-resource tradeoff, 11

SA, *see* simulated annealing
sampling, 68, 99, 122
schedule generation scheme, 62, 102, 103, 123
schedule scheme representation, 77, 116
selection, 72, 84, 85, 90
  proportional, 90
  ranking, 90
  tournament, 90
self-adaptation, 102, 103, 122, 124
semi-active schedule, 43, 51
serial schedule generation scheme, 62, 86, 91, 93, 123, 131
SGS, *see* schedule generation scheme
shift vector, 76
simulated annealing, 70, 72, 116
single pass, 67, 122, 136, 139
steepest descent/mildest ascent, 72
stochastic networks, 17
strip packing problem, 30
successor, 6

tabu search, 72, 116
threshold accepting, 71
tight schedule, 43, 137
time window, 7, 10, 41, 112
time-cost tradeoff problem, 15
time-resource tradeoff, 11
time-resource tradeoff problem, 14
tracking study, 174
truncated branch-and-bound, 80, 145
TS, *see* tabu search

weighted tardiness, 20

Lecture Notes in Economics and Mathematical Systems

For information about Vols. 1–290
please contact your bookseller or Springer-Verlag

Vol. 291: N. Takahashi, Design of Adaptive Organizations. VI, 140 pages. 1987.

Vol. 292: I. Tchijov, L. Tomaszewicz (Eds.), Input-Output Modeling. Proceedings, 1985. VI, 195 pages. 1987.

Vol. 293: D. Batten, J. Casti, B. Johansson (Eds.), Economic Evolution and Structural Adjustment. Proceedings, 1985. VI, 382 pages.

Vol. 294: J. Jahn, W. Knabs (Eds.), Recent Advances and Historical Development of Vector Optimization. VII, 405 pages. 1987.

Vol. 295. H. Meister, The Purification Problem for Constrained Games with Incomplete Information. X, 127 pages. 1987.

Vol. 296: A. Börsch-Supan, Econometric Analysis of Discrete Choice. VIII, 211 pages. 1987.

Vol. 297: V. Fedorov, H. Läuter (Eds.), Model-Oriented Data Analysis. Proceedings, 1987. VI, 239 pages. 1988.

Vol. 298: S.H. Chew, Q. Zheng, Integral Global Optimization. VII, 179 pages. 1988.

Vol. 299: K. Marti, Descent Directions and Efficient Solutions in Discretely Distributed Stochastic Programs. XIV, 178 pages. 1988.

Vol. 300: U. Derigs, Programming in Networks and Graphs. XI, 315 pages. 1988.

Vol. 301: J. Kacprzyk, M. Roubens (Eds.), Non-Conventional Preference Relations in Decision Making. VII, 155 pages. 1988.

Vol. 302: H.A. Eiselt, G. Pederzoli (Eds.), Advances in Optimization and Control. Proceedings, 1986. VIII, 372 pages. 1988.

Vol. 303: F.X. Diebold, Empirical Modeling of Exchange Rate Dynamics. VII, 143 pages. 1988.

Vol. 304: A. Kurzhanski, K. Neumann, D. Pallaschke (Eds.), Optimization, Parallel Processing and Applications. Proceedings, 1987. VI, 292 pages. 1988.

Vol. 305: G.-J.C.Th. van Schijndel, Dynamic Firm and Investor Behaviour under Progressive Personal Taxation. X, 215 pages.1988.

Vol. 306: Ch. Klein, A Static Microeconomic Model of Pure Competition. VIII, 139 pages. 1988.

Vol. 307: T.K. Dijkstra (Ed.), On Model Uncertainty and its Statistical Implications. VII, 138 pages. 1988.

Vol. 308: J.R. Daduna, A. Wren (Eds.), Computer-Aided Transit Scheduling. VIII, 339 pages. 1988.

Vol. 309: G. Ricci, K. Velupillai (Eds.), Growth Cycles and Multisectoral Economics: The Goodwin Tradition. III, 126 pages. 1988.

Vol. 310: J. Kacprzyk, M. Fedrizzi (Eds.), Combining Fuzzy Imprecision with Probabilistic Uncertainty in Decision Making. IX, 399 pages. 1988.

Vol. 311: R. Färe, Fundamentals of Production Theory. IX, 163 pages. 1988.

Vol. 312: J. Krishnakumar, Estimation of Simultaneous Equation Models with Error Components Structure. X, 357 pages. 1988.

Vol. 313: W. Jammernegg, Sequential Binary Investment Decisions. VI, 156 pages. 1988.

Vol. 314: R. Tietz, W. Albers, R. Selten (Eds.), Bounded Rational Behavior in Experimental Games and Markets. VI, 368 pages. 1988.

Vol. 315: I. Orishimo, G.J.D. Hewings, P. Nijkamp (Eds), Information Technology: Social and Spatial Perspectives. Proceedings 1986. VI, 268 pages. 1988.

Vol. 316: R.L. Basmann, D.J. Slottje, K. Hayes, J.D. Johnson, D.J. Molina, The Generalized Fechner-Thurstone Direct Utility Function and Some of its Uses. VIII, 159 pages. 1988.

Vol. 317: L. Bianco, A. La Bella (Eds.), Freight Transport Planning and Logistics. Proceedings, 1987. X, 568 pages. 1988.

Vol. 318: T. Doup, Simplicial Algorithms on the Simplotope. VIII, 262 pages. 1988.

Vol. 319: D.T. Luc, Theory of Vector Optimization. VIII, 173 pages. 1989.

Vol. 320: D. van der Wijst, Financial Structure in Small Business. VII, 181 pages. 1989.

Vol. 321: M. Di Matteo, R.M. Goodwin, A. Vercelli (Eds.), Technological and Social Factors in Long Term Fluctuations. Proceedings. IX, 442 pages. 1989.

Vol. 322: T. Kollintzas (Ed.), The Rational Expectations Equilibrium Inventory Model. XI, 269 pages. 1989.

Vol. 323: M.B.M. de Koster, Capacity Oriented Analysis and Design of Production Systems. XII, 245 pages. 1989.

Vol. 324: I.M. Bomze, B.M. Pötscher, Game Theoretical Foundations of Evolutionary Stability. VI, 145 pages. 1989.

Vol. 325: P. Ferri, E. Greenberg, The Labor Market and Business Cycle Theories. X, 183 pages. 1989.

Vol. 326: Ch. Sauer, Alternative Theories of Output, Unemployment, and Inflation in Germany: 1960–1985. XIII, 206 pages. 1989.

Vol. 327: M. Tawada, Production Structure and International Trade. V, 132 pages. 1989.

Vol. 328: W. Güth, B. Kalkofen, Unique Solutions for Strategic Games. VII, 200 pages. 1989.

Vol. 329: G. Tillmann, Equity, Incentives, and Taxation. VI, 132 pages. 1989.

Vol. 330: P.M. Kort, Optimal Dynamic Investment Policies of a Value Maximizing Firm. VII, 185 pages. 1989.

Vol. 331: A. Lewandowski, A.P. Wierzbicki (Eds.), Aspiration Based Decision Support Systems. X, 400 pages. 1989.

Vol. 332: T.R. Gulledge, Jr., L.A. Litteral (Eds.), Cost Analysis Applications of Economics and Operations Research. Proceedings. VII, 422 pages. 1989.

Vol. 333: N. Dellaert, Production to Order. VII, 158 pages. 1989.

Vol. 334: H.-W. Lorenz, Nonlinear Dynamical Economics and Chaotic Motion. XI, 248 pages. 1989.

Vol. 335: A.G. Lockett, G. Islei (Eds.), Improving Decision Making in Organisations. Proceedings. IX, 606 pages. 1989.

Vol. 336: T. Puu, Nonlinear Economic Dynamics. VII, 119 pages. 1989.

Vol. 337: A. Lewandowski, I. Stanchev (Eds.), Methodology and Software for Interactive Decision Support. VIII, 309 pages. 1989.

Vol. 338: J.K. Ho, R.P. Sundarraj, DECOMP: An Implementation of Dantzig-Wolfe Decomposition for Linear Programming. VI, 206 pages.

Vol. 339: J. Terceiro Lomba, Estimation of Dynamic Econometric Models with Errors in Variables. VIII, 116 pages. 1990.

Vol. 340: T. Vasko, R. Ayres, L. Fontvieille (Eds.), Life Cycles and Long Waves. XIV, 293 pages. 1990.

Vol. 341: G.R. Uhlich, Descriptive Theories of Bargaining. IX, 165 pages. 1990.

Vol. 342: K. Okuguchi, F. Szidarovszky, The Theory of Oligopoly with Multi-Product Firms. V, 167 pages. 1990.

Vol. 343: C. Chiarella, The Elements of a Nonlinear Theory of Economic Dynamics. IX, 149 pages. 1990.

Vol. 344: K. Neumann, Stochastic Project Networks. XI, 237 pages. 1990.

Vol. 345: A. Cambini, E. Castagnoli, L. Martein, P Mazzoleni, S. Schaible (Eds.), Generalized Convexity and Fractional Programming with Economic Applications. Proceedings, 1988. VII, 361 pages. 1990.

Vol. 346: R. von Randow (Ed.), Integer Programming and Related Areas. A Classified Bibliography 1984–1987. XIII, 514 pages. 1990.

Vol. 347: D. Ríos Insua, Sensitivity Analysis in Multi-objective Decision Making. XI, 193 pages. 1990.

Vol. 348: H. Störmer, Binary Functions and their Applications. VIII, 151 pages. 1990.

Vol. 349: G.A. Pfann, Dynamic Modelling of Stochastic Demand for Manufacturing Employment. VI, 158 pages. 1990.

Vol. 350: W.-B. Zhang, Economic Dynamics. X, 232 pages. 1990.

Vol. 351: A. Lewandowski, V. Volkovich (Eds.), Multiobjective Problems of Mathematical Programming. Proceedings, 1988. VII, 315 pages. 1991.

Vol. 352: O. van Hilten, Optimal Firm Behaviour in the Context of Technological Progress and a Business Cycle. XII, 229 pages. 1991.

Vol. 353: G. Ricci (Ed.), Decision Processes in Economics. Proceedings, 1989. III, 209 pages 1991.

Vol. 354: M. Ivaldi, A Structural Analysis of Expectation Formation. XII, 230 pages. 1991.

Vol. 355: M. Salomon. Deterministic Lotsizing Models for Production Planning. VII, 158 pages. 1991.

Vol. 356: P. Korhonen, A. Lewandowski, J . Wallenius (Eds.), Multiple Criteria Decision Support. Proceedings, 1989. XII, 393 pages. 1991.

Vol. 357: P. Zörnig, Degeneracy Graphs and Simplex Cycling. XV, 194 pages. 1991.

Vol. 358: P. Knottnerus, Linear Models with Correlated Disturbances. VIII, 196 pages. 1991.

Vol. 359: E. de Jong, Exchange Rate Determination and Optimal Economic Policy Under Various Exchange Rate Regimes. VII, 270 pages. 1991.

Vol. 360: P. Stalder, Regime Translations, Spillovers and Buffer Stocks. VI, 193 pages . 1991.

Vol. 361: C. F. Daganzo, Logistics Systems Analysis. X, 321 pages. 1991.

Vol. 362: F. Gehrels, Essays in Macroeconomics of an Open Economy. VII, 183 pages. 1991.

Vol. 363: C. Puppe, Distorted Probabilities and Choice under Risk. VIII, 100 pages . 1991

Vol. 364: B. Horvath, Are Policy Variables Exogenous? XII, 162 pages. 1991.

Vol. 365: G. A. Heuer, U. Leopold-Wildburger. Balanced Silverman Games on General Discrete Sets. V, 140 pages. 1991.

Vol. 366: J. Gruber (Ed.), Econometric Decision Models. Proceedings, 1989. VIII, 636 pages. 1991.

Vol. 367: M. Grauer, D. B. Pressmar (Eds.), Parallel Computing and Mathematical Optimization. Proceedings. V, 208 pages. 1991.

Vol. 368: M. Fedrizzi, J. Kacprzyk, M. Roubens (Eds.), Interactive Fuzzy Optimization. VII, 216 pages. 1991.

Vol. 369: R. Koblo, The Visible Hand. VIII, 131 pages.1991.

Vol. 370: M. J. Beckmann, M. N. Gopalan, R. Subramanian (Eds.), Stochastic Processes and their Applications. Proceedings, 1990. XLI, 292 pages. 1991.

Vol. 371: A. Schmutzler, Flexibility and Adjustment to Information in Sequential Decision Problems. VIII, 198 pages. 1991.

Vol. 372: J. Esteban, The Social Viability of Money. X, 202 pages. 1991.

Vol. 373: A. Billot, Economic Theory of Fuzzy Equilibria. XIII, 164 pages. 1992.

Vol. 374: G. Pflug, U. Dieter (Eds.), Simulation and Optimization. Proceedings, 1990. X, 162 pages. 1992.

Vol. 375: S.-J. Chen, Ch.-L. Hwang, Fuzzy Multiple Attribute Decision Making. XII, 536 pages. 1992.

Vol. 376: K.-H. Jöckel, G. Rothe, W. Sendler (Eds.), Bootstrapping and Related Techniques. Proceedings, 1990. VIII, 247 pages. 1992.

Vol. 377: A. Villar, Operator Theorems with Applications to Distributive Problems and Equilibrium Models. XVI, 160 pages. 1992.

Vol. 378: W. Krabs, J. Zowe (Eds.), Modern Methods of Optimization. Proceedings, 1990. VIII, 348 pages. 1992.

Vol. 379: K. Marti (Ed.), Stochastic Optimization. Proceedings, 1990. VII, 182 pages. 1992.

Vol. 380: J. Odelstad, Invariance and Structural Dependence. XII, 245 pages. 1992.

Vol. 381: C. Giannini, Topics in Structural VAR Econometrics. XI, 131 pages. 1992.

Vol. 382: W. Oettli, D. Pallaschke (Eds.), Advances in Optimization. Proceedings, 1991. X, 527 pages. 1992.

Vol. 383: J. Vartiainen, Capital Accumulation in a Corporatist Economy. VII, 177 pages. 1992.

Vol. 384: A. Martina, Lectures on the Economic Theory of Taxation. XII, 313 pages. 1992.

Vol. 385: J. Gardeazabal, M. Regúlez, The Monetary Model of Exchange Rates and Cointegration. X, 194 pages. 1992.

Vol. 386: M. Desrochers, J.-M. Rousseau (Eds.), Computer-Aided Transit Scheduling. Proceedings, 1990. XIII, 432 pages. 1992.

Vol. 387: W. Gaertner, M. Klemisch-Ahlert, Social Choice and Bargaining Perspectives on Distributive Justice. VIII, 131 pages. 1992.

Vol. 388: D. Bartmann, M. J. Beckmann, Inventory Control. XV, 252 pages. 1992.

Vol. 389: B. Dutta, D. Mookherjee, T. Parthasarathy, T. Raghavan, D. Ray, S. Tijs (Eds.), Game Theory and Economic Applications. Proceedings, 1990. IX, 454 pages. 1992.

Vol. 390: G. Sorger, Minimum Impatience Theorem for Recursive Economic Models. X, 162 pages. 1992.

Vol. 391: C. Keser, Experimental Duopoly Markets with Demand Inertia. X, 150 pages. 1992.

Vol. 392: K. Frauendorfer, Stochastic Two-Stage Programming. VIII, 228 pages. 1992.

Vol. 393: B. Lucke, Price Stabilization on World Agricultural Markets. XI, 274 pages. 1992.

Vol. 394: Y.-J. Lai, C.-L. Hwang, Fuzzy Mathematical Programming. XIII, 301 pages. 1992.

Vol. 395: G. Haag, U. Mueller, K. G. Troitzsch (Eds.), Economic Evolution and Demographic Change. XVI, 409 pages. 1992.

Vol. 396: R. V. V. Vidal (Ed.), Applied Simulated Annealing. VIII, 358 pages. 1992.

Vol. 397: J. Wessels, A. P. Wierzbicki (Eds.), User-Oriented Methodology and Techniques of Decision Analysis and Support. Proceedings, 1991. XII, 295 pages. 1993.

Vol. 398: J.-P. Urbain, Exogeneity in Error Correction Models. XI, 189 pages. 1993.

Vol. 399: F. Gori, L. Geronazzo, M. Galeotti (Eds.), Nonlinear Dynamics in Economics and Social Sciences. Proceedings, 1991. VIII, 367 pages. 1993.

Vol. 400: H. Tanizaki, Nonlinear Filters. XII, 203 pages. 1993.

Vol. 401: K. Mosler, M. Scarsini, Stochastic Orders and Applications. V, 379 pages. 1993.

Vol. 402: A. van den Elzen, Adjustment Processes for Exchange Economies and Noncooperative Games. VII, 146 pages. 1993.

Vol. 403: G. Brennscheidt, Predictive Behavior. VI, 227 pages. 1993.

Vol. 404: Y.-J. Lai, Ch.-L. Hwang, Fuzzy Multiple Objective Decision Making. XIV, 475 pages. 1994.

Vol. 405: S. Komlósi, T. Rapcsák, S. Schaible (Eds.), Generalized Convexity. Proceedings, 1992. VIII, 404 pages. 1994.

Vol. 406: N. M. Hung, N. V. Quyen, Dynamic Timing Decisions Under Uncertainty. X, 194 pages. 1994.

Vol. 407: M. Ooms, Empirical Vector Autoregressive Modeling. XIII, 380 pages. 1994.

Vol. 408: K. Haase, Lotsizing and Scheduling for Production Planning. VIII, 118 pages. 1994.

Vol. 409: A. Sprecher, Resource-Constrained Project Scheduling. XII, 142 pages. 1994.

Vol. 410: R. Winkelmann, Count Data Models. XI, 213 pages. 1994.

Vol. 411: S. Dauzère-Péres, J.-B. Lasserre, An Integrated Approach in Production Planning and Scheduling. XVI, 137 pages. 1994.

Vol. 412: B. Kuon, Two-Person Bargaining Experiments with Incomplete Information. IX, 293 pages. 1994.

Vol. 413: R. Fiorito (Ed.), Inventory, Business Cycles and Monetary Transmission. VI, 287 pages. 1994.

Vol. 414: Y. Crama, A. Oerlemans, F. Spieksma, Production Planning in Automated Manufacturing. X, 210 pages. 1994.

Vol. 415: P. C. Nicola, Imperfect General Equilibrium. XI, 167 pages. 1994.

Vol. 416: H. S. J. Cesar, Control and Game Models of the Greenhouse Effect. XI, 225 pages. 1994.

Vol. 417: B. Ran, D. E. Boyce, Dynamic Urban Transportation Network Models. XV, 391 pages. 1994.

Vol. 418: P. Bogetoft, Non-Cooperative Planning Theory. XI, 309 pages. 1994.

Vol. 419: T. Maruyama, W. Takahashi (Eds.), Nonlinear and Convex Analysis in Economic Theory. VIII, 306 pages. 1995.

Vol. 420: M. Peeters, Time-To-Build. Interrelated Investment and Labour Demand Modelling. With Applications to Six OECD Countries. IX, 204 pages. 1995.

Vol. 421: C. Dang, Triangulations and Simplicial Methods. IX, 196 pages. 1995.

Vol. 422: D. S. Bridges, G. B. Mehta, Representations of Preference Orderings. X, 165 pages. 1995.

Vol. 423: K. Marti, P. Kall (Eds.), Stochastic Programming. Numerical Techniques and Engineering Applications. VIII, 351 pages. 1995.

Vol. 424: G. A. Heuer, U. Leopold-Wildburger, Silverman's Game. X, 283 pages. 1995.

Vol. 425: J. Kohlas, P.-A. Monney, A Mathematical Theory of Hints. XIII, 419 pages, 1995.

Vol. 426: B. Finkenstädt, Nonlinear Dynamics in Economics. IX, 156 pages. 1995.

Vol. 427: F. W. van Tongeren, Microsimulation Modelling of the Corporate Firm. XVII, 275 pages. 1995.

Vol. 428: A. A. Powell, Ch. W. Murphy, Inside a Modern Macroeconometric Model. XVIII, 424 pages. 1995.

Vol. 429: R. Durier, C. Michelot, Recent Developments in Optimization. VIII, 356 pages. 1995.

Vol. 430: J. R. Daduna, I. Branco, J. M. Pinto Paixão (Eds.), Computer-Aided Transit Scheduling. XIV, 374 pages. 1995.

Vol. 431: A. Aulin, Causal and Stochastic Elements in Business Cycles. XI, 116 pages. 1996.

Vol. 432: M. Tamiz (Ed.), Multi-Objective Programming and Goal Programming. VI, 359 pages. 1996.

Vol. 433: J. Menon, Exchange Rates and Prices. XIV, 313 pages. 1996.

Vol. 434: M. W. J. Blok, Dynamic Models of the Firm. VII, 193 pages. 1996.

Vol. 435: L. Chen, Interest Rate Dynamics, Derivatives Pricing, and Risk Management. XII, 149 pages. 1996.

Vol. 436: M. Klemisch-Ahlert, Bargaining in Economic and Ethical Environments. IX, 155 pages. 1996.

Vol. 437: C. Jordan, Batching and Scheduling. IX, 178 pages. 1996.

Vol. 438: A. Villar, General Equilibrium with Increasing Returns. XIII, 164 pages. 1996.

Vol. 439: M. Zenner, Learning to Become Rational. VII, 201 pages. 1996.

Vol. 440: W. Ryll, Litigation and Settlement in a Game with Incomplete Information. VIII, 174 pages. 1996.

Vol. 441: H. Dawid, Adaptive Learning by Genetic Algorithms. IX, 166 pages.1996.

Vol. 442: L. Corchón, Theories of Imperfectly Competitive Markets. XIII, 163 pages. 1996.

Vol. 443: G. Lang, On Overlapping Generations Models with Productive Capital. X, 98 pages. 1996.

Vol. 444: S. Jørgensen, G. Zaccour (Eds.), Dynamic Competitive Analysis in Marketing. X, 285 pages. 1996.

Vol. 445: A. H. Christer, S. Osaki, L. C. Thomas (Eds.), Stochastic Modelling in Innovative Manufactoring. X, 361 pages. 1997.

Vol. 446: G. Dhaene, Encompassing. X, 160 pages. 1997.

Vol. 447: A. Artale, Rings in Auctions. X, 172 pages. 1997.

Vol. 448: G. Fandel, T. Gal (Eds.), Multiple Criteria Decision Making. XII, 678 pages. 1997.

Vol. 449: F. Fang, M. Sanglier (Eds.), Complexity and Self-Organization in Social and Economic Systems. IX, 317 pages, 1997.

Vol. 450: P. M. Pardalos, D. W. Hearn, W. W. Hager, (Eds.), Network Optimization. VIII, 485 pages, 1997.

Vol. 451: M. Salge, Rational Bubbles. Theoretical Basis, Economic Relevance, and Empirical Evidence with a Special Emphasis on the German Stock Market.IX, 265 pages. 1997.

Vol. 452: P. Gritzmann, R. Horst, E. Sachs, R. Tichatschke (Eds.), Recent Advances in Optimization. VIII, 379 pages. 1997.

Vol. 453: A. S. Tangian, J. Gruber (Eds.), Constructing Scalar-Valued Objective Functions. VIII, 298 pages. 1997.

Vol. 454: H.-M. Krolzig, Markov-Switching Vector Autoregressions. XIV, 358 pages. 1997.

Vol. 455: R. Caballero, F. Ruiz, R. E. Steuer (Eds.), Advances in Multiple Objective and Goal Programming. VIII, 391 pages. 1997.

Vol. 456: R. Conte, R. Hegselmann, P. Terna (Eds.), Simulating Social Phenomena. VIII, 536 pages. 1997.

Vol. 457: C. Hsu, Volume and the Nonlinear Dynamics of Stock Returns. VIII, 133 pages. 1998.

Vol. 458: K. Marti, P. Kall (Eds.), Stochastic Programming Methods and Technical Applications. X, 437 pages. 1998.

Vol. 459: H. K. Ryu, D. J. Slottje, Measuring Trends in U.S. Income Inequality. XI, 195 pages. 1998.

Vol. 460: B. Fleischmann, J. A. E. E. van Nunen, M. G. Speranza, P. Stähly, Advances in Distribution Logistic. XI, 535 pages. 1998.

Vol. 461: U. Schmidt, Axiomatic Utility Theory under Risk. XV, 201 pages. 1998.

Vol. 462: L. von Auer, Dynamic Preferences, Choice Mechanisms, and Welfare. XII, 226 pages. 1998.

Vol. 463: G. Abraham-Frois (Ed.), Non-Linear Dynamics and Endogenous Cycles. VI, 204 pages. 1998.

Vol. 464: A. Aulin, The Impact of Science on Economic Growth and its Cycles. IX, 204 pages. 1998.

Vol. 465: T. J. Stewart, R. C. van den Honert (Eds.), Trends in Multicriteria Decision Making. X, 448 pages. 1998.

Vol. 466: A. Sadrieh, The Alternating Double Auction Market. VII, 350 pages. 1998.

Vol. 467: H. Hennig-Schmidt, Bargaining in a Video Experiment. Determinants of Boundedly Rational Behavior. XII, 221 pages. 1999.

Vol. 468: A. Ziegler, A Game Theory Analysis of Options. XIV, 145 pages. 1999.

Vol. 469: M. P. Vogel, Environmental Kuznets Curves. XIII, 197 pages. 1999.

Vol. 470: M. Ammann, Pricing Derivative Credit Risk. XII, 228 pages. 1999.

Vol. 471: N. H. M. Wilson (Ed.), Computer-Aided Transit Scheduling. XI, 444 pages. 1999.

Vol. 472: J.-R. Tyran, Money Illusion and Strategic Complementarity as Causes of Monetary Non-Neutrality. X, 228 pages. 1999.

Vol. 473: S. Helber, Performance Analysis of Flow Lines with Non-Linear Flow of Material. IX, 280 pages. 1999.

Vol. 474: U. Schwalbe, The Core of Economies with Asymmetric Information. IX, 141 pages. 1999.

Vol. 475: L. Kaas, Dynamic Macroelectronics with Imperfect Competition. XI, 155 pages. 1999.

Vol. 476: R. Demel, Fiscal Policy, Public Debt and the Term Structure of Interest Rates. X, 279 pages. 1999.

Vol. 477: M. Théra, R. Tichatschke (Eds.), Ill-posed Variational Problems and Regularization Techniques. VIII, 274 pages. 1999.

Vol. 478: S. Hartmann, Project Scheduling under Limited Resources. XII, 221 pages. 1999.

Vol. 479: L. v. Thadden, Money, Inflation, and Capital Formation. IX, 192 pages. 1999.

FSC
www.fsc.org
MIX
Papier aus verantwortungsvollen Quellen
Paper from responsible sources
FSC® C105338

If you have any concerns about our products, you can contact us on
ProductSafety@springernature.com

In case Publisher is established outside the EU, the EU authorized representative is:
Springer Nature Customer Service Center GmbH
Europaplatz 3, 69115 Heidelberg, Germany

Printed by Libri Plureos GmbH
in Hamburg, Germany